The Profundity and Bifurcation of Change

The Intelligent Social Change Journey

Part II: *Learning from the Past*

MQIPress (2020)
Frost, West Virginia
ISBN 978-0-9985147-6-5

The Consciousness Series

*The human experience is a neuronal dance with the Universe, with each of us
in the driver's seat selecting our partners and directing our dance steps.*

"Been reading non-stop!!! Can't put it down. These pages lead to endless possibilities in understanding our relevance in our world today and tomorrow—wonderfully informative." -Cindy Kraus, Business Owner

"We are in a world with global warming, not enough resources, too many people, and more. We are at a fork in the road and can choose to combine our efforts to make changes and care for one another, or continue the path we're already on to our demise. By grounding ourselves and opening our minds to new concepts and ideas, a new awakening of global thought is ready to take a creative leap towards an enlightened future. The time is here, and the choice is ours! Dr. Alex Bennet and renowned others have combined their efforts to aid the coming change in the way we humans think. I've been truly inspired by the unreleased portions of the books I was privileged to read. If we all do something, ever so small, we will find a brighter future for humanity as a family, and for our children! Excitingly, we are standing in the doorway of an Enlightened Creative Leap ... Awaiting Our Awakening." -Cindy Scott, Poet

"This work guides the reader to insights that bear enormous potential for positive societal change. Our younger generations, in particular, can give momentum to this change if individuals understand and put into practice the ideas these authors so expertly expound." –Royce Sherlock, Lawyer

"Wow! I loved it! The wealth of the ideas! The wise weaving of the multiple perspectives! This is a great guiding tool for anybody who wishes to lead change instead of being led by it! The authors did a great job in creating a very rich body of knowledge on change—how to understand it on all levels—micro and macro—how to deal with it, how to turn it into a journey full of opportunities. This is both inspiring and practical—sheer joy! Bravo!" -Edna Pasher, Founder and Chair of Pasher Associates and of ISCI (Israel Smart Cities Institute) and of Status - Management Magazine.

Original release (as eBook): 2017
Second printing (soft cover): 2020

MQIPress
Frost, West Virginia
303 Mountain Quest Lane
Marlinton, WV 24954
United States of America
Telephone: 304-799-7267

alex@mountainquestinstitute.com
www.mountainquestinstitute.com
www.mountainquestinn.com
www.MQIPress.com
www.Myst-art.com

ISBN 978-0-9985147-6-5

Man considering the Universe of which he is a unit, sees nothing but change in matter, forces and mental states. He sees that nothing really is, but that everything is becoming and changing. Nothing stands still. Everything is being born, growing, dying. At the very instant a thing reaches its height, it begins to decline. The law of rhythm is in constant operation. There is no fixed reality, enduring quality or substantiality in anything –nothing is permanent but Change. Man sees all things evolve from other things and resolve into other things; a constant action and reaction, inflow and outflow, building up and tearing down, creation and destruction, birth, growth and death. Nothing endures but Change. And if he is a thinking man, he realizes that all of these changing things must be outward appearances or manifestations of some underlying power, some Substantial Reality.

The Kybalion (1940, p. 53)

Part II*

Table of Contents

* This book is Part I of *The Profundity and Bifurcation of Change*, available from Amazon.com in hard copy and Kindle format, and in PDF format from MQIPress.net

Part II
Tables, Figures, and Tools

TABLES

FIGURES

TOOLS

In Appreciation

Hundreds of people, named and unnamed, have contributed thousands of ideas to this book in the context of conversations and dialogues, articles and books, and quotes and stories. We are all indeed one, sharing ideas in groups and communities, face-to-face and virtual, appearing and connecting where we will, in an ever-looping creative embrace and continuous expansion toward intelligent activity.

Our deep appreciation to our co-authors, who each bring a unique focus and value to this work. These are Arthur Shelley, Theresa Bullard, and John Lewis. It is our sincere hope that each of them—who now are co-creators with us—will share this work largely in their day-to-day lives. Also, our appreciation to Donna Panucci, Maik Fuellmann, Jackie Urbanovic and Barbara Wheeler for their contributing and expanding thoughts, and to Mark Boyes, who co-created the thought-provoking image in Chapter 10.

Across our consilience approach, there are a handful of authors whose work has both inspired our thinking and excited our creativity. *Life's Hidden Meaning* by Niles MacFlouer provides insights from Ageless Wisdom, just coming into our realms of understanding. Serving as an example of committed knowledge sharing, MacFlouer has hosted a weekly radio show on Ageless Wisdom since 2004! This massive and incredibly insightful body of work is available on the Internet at http://www.agelesswisdom.com/archives_of_radio_shows.htm Over the past year we have listened, reflected, associated and created connections to this work, such that it is nearly impossible to follow these connections. In this regard, we try to err on the side of over-referencing, and since there is not one specific reference, but, rather, a way of thinking, we have referenced this body of work as MacFlouer (2004-16). We encourage those who resonate with this material to explore it more fully.

In 1996, Ken Wilber wrote *A Brief History of Everything*, and his brilliance continues to emerge from that point. While we applaud his continuing search for a simple and elegant theory of everything, we would be reluctant to eliminate *any* of the rich truths and theories explored in his dozens of books. *Paths of Change* by Will McWhinney served as a baseline for exploring world views and combinations of reality in the change journey. *Spontaneous Evolution: Our Positive Future* by Bruce H. Lipton and Steve Bhaerman is inspirational and informative from the viewpoint of cell biology. Jean Houston's *Jump Time* was way ahead of its time, and is a must read for any decision-maker in today's environment, and that is all of us. And where would we be as a humanity without the brilliance and wisdom of Bohm, Cozolino, Csikszentmihalyi, Damasio, Edelman, Gardner, Goleman, Goswami, Handy, Hawkins, Kant, Kolb, Kurzweil, Laszlo, McTaggart, Polanyi, Stonier, Templeton, Tiller, Wilber, and so many others! Our appreciation to all of the contributors called out in our references, and to those who may not be in our references but whose thought has seeped into our minds and hearts in the course of living.

Our continued thanks to the professionals, colleagues and thought leaders who participated in the KMTL study and follow-on Sampler Call. These include: Dorothy E. Agger-Gupta, Verna Allee, Debra Amidon, Ramon Barquin, Surinder Kumar Batra, Juanita Brown, John Seely Brown, Frada Burstein, Francisco Javier Carrillo, Robert Cross, Tom Davenport, Ross Dawson, Steve Denning, Charles Dhewa, Nancy Dixon, Leif Edvinsson, Kent Greenes, Susan Hanley, Clyde Holsapple, Esko Kilpi, Dorothy Leonard, Geoff Malafsky, Martha Manning, Carla O'Dell, Edna Pasher, W. Barnett Pearce, Larry Prusak, Madanmohan Rao, Tomasz Rudolf, Melissie Rumizen, Hubert Saint-Onge, Judi Sandrock, Charles Seashore, Dave Snowden, Milton Sousa, Michael Stankosky, Tom Stewart, Michael J.D. Sutton, Karl-Erik Sveiby, Doug Weidner, Steve Weineke, Etienne Wenger-Trayner and Karl Wiig.

There are very special people who assisted in ensuring the quality of this work. Kathy Claypatch with Ageless Wisdom Publishers served as a conduit to assure consistency with that work; Ginny Ramos, a rehabilitation counselor and Alex's daughter, served in the role of editor; and four readers played instrumental roles in assuring consistent and understandable concepts. These are Joyce Avedisian, Susan Dreiband, Denise Sumner and Deb Tobiasson, all knowledgeable explorers in the journey of life.

A special thanks to our families who ground us: from David to Steve, Melanie, John, Cindy, Jackson, Rick, Chris and the grandchildren that help to keep us young; from Alex to Ginny, Bill and Andrew and her long-lost new family; from Arthur to Joy, Cath and Helen; from Theresa to Barbara and Jay, as well as to Dennis H. and Gudni G. and her MMS friends and family; and from John to Mary, Shannon and Jonathan. Thank you to all our friends who support this work in so many ways, and who have supported Mountain Quest since its 2001 beginnings. And our continuing thankfulness to Cindy Taylor and Theresa Halterman, part of our MQI Team, and for our son Andrew Dean, who keeps Mountain Quest running while we play with thoughts and words and dive into the abyss of the unknown.

With Appreciation and Love, Alex, David, Arthur, Theresa and John.

Preface

As we move in and out of life situations, there are verbal cues, often conveyed by signs, that catch our attention and somehow miraculously remain in memory throughout our lives, popping in and out as truisms. Although we may not realize how true they were at the time, one of those sayings in an early office setting was: "Change. Your life depends on it!" Then, some 10 years later, a sign appearing on the check-in desk of the dental clinic on Yokosuka Naval Base, clearly referring to our teeth, read: "Ignore them, and they will go away."

So often we feel like victims, with some new challenge emerging from here or there, something interrupting our best laid plans, some stress or weight that sprouts discomfort or confusion. Yet we have a choice to be pulled along into the fray, dive into the flow and fully participate in the decisions and actions, or even to be the wave-setters, co-creating the reality within which we live and breathe.

Never in the history of humanity has the *need to change* so clearly manifested itself into our everyday existence. While the potential for catastrophic destruction has loomed over us since the mid-20th century, we are still *here*, admittedly a world in turmoil on all fronts—plagued with economic, political, eco-system, social, cultural and religious fragmentation—but also a humanity that is awakening to our true potential and power. Just learning how to co-evolve with an increasingly changing, uncertain and complex external environment, we are now beginning to recognize that it is the change available *within* our internal environment *and energetic connections to each other and the larger whole* that offer up an invitation to an incluessent future, that state of Being far beyond the small drop of previous possibility accepted as true, far beyond that which we have known to dream (Dunning, 2015).

In this work, we introduce the overarching concepts of **profundity** and **bifurcation** as related to change. Profundity comes from the Old French term *profundite* which emerges from the late Latin term *profunditas* or *profundus*, meaning profound (Encarta, 1999). Profundity insinuates an intellectual complexity leading to great understanding, perceptiveness and knowledge. There is a focus on greatness in terms of strength and intensity and in depth of thought. We believe that the times in which we live and the opportunity to shape the future of humanity demand that each of us look within, recognizing and utilizing the amazing gifts of our human mind and heart to shape a new world.

Bifurcation comes from the Latin root word *bifurcare*, which literally means to fork, that is, split and branch off into two separate parts (Encarta, 1999). In terms of change, this concept alludes to a pending decision for each decision-maker, each human, and perhaps humanity at large. We live in two worlds, one based on what we understand from Newtonian Physics and one based on what we don't understand but are able to speculate and feel about the Quantum Field. As change continues with every breath we take and every action we make, there is choice as to how we engage our role as co-creator of reality.

In this book, we explore very different ways to create change, each building on the former. There is no right or wrong—choice is a matter of the lessons we are learning and the growth we are seeking—yet it is clear that there is a split ahead where we will need to choose our way forward. One road continues the journey that has been punctuated by physical dominance, bureaucracy, hard competition and a variety of power scenarios. A second road, historically less-traveled, recognizes the connections among all humans, embracing the value of individuation and diversity as a contribution to the collective whole and the opportunities offered through creative imagination. This is the road that recognizes the virtues of inclusiveness and truth and the power of love and beauty, and moves us along the flow representing Quantum entanglement.

A number of themes are woven throughout this work; for example, the idea of "NOW", the use of forces as a tool for growth, the power of patterns, earned and revealed intuition, bisociation and creativity, stuck energy and flow, the search for truth, and so many more. We take a consilience approach, tapping into a deep array of research in knowledge and learning, with specific reference to recent neuroscience understanding that is emerging, pointing the reader to additional resources. And we look to psychology, physics, cell biology, systems and complexity, cognitive theory, social theory and spirituality for their contributions. Humans are holistic, that is, the physical, mental, emotional and intuitional are all at play and working together. Recognize that you are part of one entangled intelligent complex adaptive learning system (Bennet et al., 2015b), each overlapping and affecting the other, whether consciously or unconsciously, in every instant of life. As we move from science to philosophy, facts to psychology, management to poetry, and words to pictures, you will no doubt feel a tugging in the mind/brain, and perhaps some confusion. Such was the case for one of the authors when studying micro-economics and Shakespeare tragedies back to back! The good news is that this can result in a great deal of expansion and availability of a wide variety of frames of reference from which to process incoming information.

Through the past half a century, all of the authors have engaged in extensive research—much of it experiential in nature—which has led us to break through life-long perceived limits and shift and expand our beliefs about Life and the world of which we are a part. The advent of self-publishing virtual books has opened the door to share this learning globally. The concepts forwarded in the earlier works of all of the authors lay the foundation for this book.

While this book is quite large, it wrote itself. In the movie Amadeus (1984), when a complaint is lodged against his work saying there are just too many notes, Mozart responds that there are just exactly as many notes as are needed. In this book, there are exactly as many chapters as are needed, no more, no less. As you move through the information and concepts available in this text, we ask that you stay open to new ideas, ways of thinking and perceiving, and—using the discernment and discretion emerging from your unique life experiences—reflect on how these ideas might fit into your personal theory of the world. It is our hope that these ideas will serve as triggers for a greater expansion of thought and consciousness, which every individual brings to the larger understanding of who we are and how, together as One, we operate in the world.

To begin, we offer the following assumptions:

Assumption 1: Everything—at least in our physical reality—is energy and patterns of energy. We live in a vast field of energy in which we are continuously exchanging information, which is a form of energy.

Assumption 2: Creativity—nurtured by freedom, purpose and choice—is a primary urge of the human. Knowledge serves as an action lever for co-creating our experiences.

Assumption 3: Knowledge is partial and incomplete. Knowledge produces forces, whether those forces are used to push forward an idea that benefits humanity, or whether those forces are to push against another's beliefs and values (knowledge), which can escalate to warfare.

Assumption 4: The human mind is an associative patterner, that is, continuously re-creating knowledge for the situation at hand. Knowledge exists in the human brain in the form of stored or expressed neural patterns that may be selected, activated, mixed and/or reflected upon through thought. Incoming information is associated with stored information. From this mixing process, new patterns are created that may represent understanding, meaning and the capacity to anticipate (to various degrees) the results of potential actions. Thus, knowledge is context sensitive and situation dependent, with the mind continuously growing, restructuring and creating increased organization (information) and knowledge for the moment at hand.

Assumption 5: The unconscious mind has a vast store of tacit knowledge available to us. It has only been in the past few decades that cognitive psychology and neuroscience have begun to seriously explore unconscious mental life. Polanyi felt that tacit knowledge consisted of *a range* of conceptual and sensory information and images that could be used to make sense of a situation or event (Hodgkin, 1991; Smith, 2003). He was right. The unconscious mind is incredibly powerful, on the order of 700,000 times more processing speed than the conscious stream of thought. The challenge is to make better use of our tacit knowledge through creating greater connections with the unconscious, building and expanding the resources stored in the unconscious, deepening areas of resonance, connecting to the larger information field, and learning how to share our tacit resources with each other.

Assumption 6: People are multidimensional, and rarely do they hold to a single belief, a consistent logic, or a specific worldview. As identified in the recent model of experiential learning (Bennet et al, 2015b), there are five primary modes of thinking, each of us with our preferences—concrete experience, reflective observation, abstract conceptualization, active experimentation and social engagement—and each of us has a dozen or more subpersonalities offering a variety of diverse thoughts and feelings that rise to the occasion when triggered by our external and internal environments (Bennet et al., 2015a). *The human experience is a neuronal dance with the Universe, with each of us in the driver's seat selecting our partners and directing our dance steps.*

Assumption 7: We are social creatures who live in an entangled world; our brains are linked together. We are in continuous interaction with those around us, and the brain is continuously changing in response. Thus, in our expanded state we are both individuated and One, bringing all our diversity into collaborative play for the greater good of humanity.

Assumption 8: We live in times of extreme change in the human mind and body, in human-developed systems, and of the Earth, our human host. Through advances in science and technology, most of what we need to learn and thrive in these times is already available. We need only to open our minds and hearts to the amazing potential of our selfs.

There are still vast workings of the human mind and its connections to higher-order energies that we do not understand. The limitations we as humans place on our capacities and capabilities are created from past reference points that have been developed primarily through the rational and logical workings of the mechanical functioning of our mind/brain, an understanding that has come through extensive intellectual effort. Yet we now recognize that *knowledge is a living form of information*, tailored by our minds specifically for situations at hand. The totality of knowledge can no easier be codified and stored than our feelings, nor would it be highly beneficial to do so in a changing and uncertain environment. Thus, in this book, given the limitations of our own perceptions and understanding, we do not even pretend to cover the vast amount of information and knowledge available in the many fields connected to change. We *do* choose to consider and explore areas and phenomena that move beyond our paradigms and beliefs into the larger arena of knowing, and to move beyond the activity of our cognitive functions to consider the larger energy patterns within which humanity is immersed.

This extensive book is initially being published in five Parts as five separate books, which will be available in both kindle (from Amazon) and PDF (from MQIPress) formats. In support of the Intelligent Social Change Journey, these Parts are:

Part I: Laying the Groundwork

Part II: Learning from the Past

Part III: Learning in the Present

Part IV: Co-Creating the Future

Part V: Living in the Future

Each part has a separate focus, yet they work together to support your full engagement in the Intelligent Social Change Journey. A Table of Contents for all five parts is Appendix B. An overarching model of the ISCJ is Appendix A. This model can also be downloaded for A4 printing at the following location: www.mqipress.net

Workshops on all five Parts of *The Profundity and Bifurcation of Change* or, specifically, on The Intelligent Social Change Journey facilitated by the authors are available. Contact alex@mountainquestinstitute.com ... arthur.shelley@rmit.edu.au ... Theresa@quantumleapalchemy.com ... or John@ExplanationAge.com

The Drs. Alex and David Bennet live at the Mountain Quest Institute, Inn and Retreat Center situated on a 430-acre farm in the Allegheny Mountains of West Virginia. See www.mountainquestinn.com and www.mountainquestinstitute.com They may be reached at alex@mountainquestinstitute.com Dr. Arthur Shelley is the originator of *The Organizational Zoo*, Dr. Theresa Bullard is the Founder of the Quantra Leadership Academy as well as an International Instructor for the Modern Mystery School, and Dr. John Lewis is author of *The Explanation Age*. Taking a consilience approach, this eclectic group builds on corroborated resources in a diversity of fields while simultaneously pushing the edge of thought, hopefully beyond your comfort zone, for that is where our journey begins.

Introduction to
The Intelligent Social Change Journey

The Intelligent Social Change Journey (ISCJ) is a developmental journey of the body, mind and heart, moving from the heaviness of cause-and-effect linear extrapolations, to the fluidity of co-evolving with our environment, to the lightness of breathing our thought and feelings into reality. Grounded in development of our mental faculties, these are phase changes, each building on and expanding previous learning in our movement toward intelligent activity.

We are on this journey together. This is very much a *social* journey. Change does not occur in isolation. The deeper our understanding in relationship to others, the easier it is to move into the future. The quality of sympathy is needed as we navigate the linear, cause-and-effect characteristics of Phase 1. The quality of empathy is needed to navigate the co-evolving liquidity of Phase 2. The quality of compassion is needed to navigate the connected breath of the Phase 3 creative leap. See the figure below.

In the progression of learning to navigate change represented by the three phases of the ISCJ, we empower our selfs, individuating and expanding. In the process, we become immersed in the human experience, a neuronal dance with the Universe, with each of us in the driver's seat selecting our partners and directing our dance steps. Let's explore that journey a bit deeper.

In Phase 1 of the Journey, *Learning from the Past*, we act on the physical and the physical changes; we "see" the changes with our sense of form, and therefore they are real. Causes have effects. Actions have consequences, both directly and indirectly, and sometimes delayed. Phase 1 reinforces the characteristics of how we interact with the simplest aspects of our world. The elements are predictable and repeatable and make us feel comfortable because we know what to expect and how to prepare for them. While these parts of the world do exist, our brain tends to automate the thinking around them and we do them with little conscious effort. The challenge with this is that they only remain predictable if all the causing influences remain constant ... and that just doesn't happen in the world of today! The linear cause-and-effect phase of the ISCJ (Phase 1) calls for sympathy. Supporting and caring for the people involved in the change helps to mitigate the force of resistance, improving the opportunity for successful outcomes.

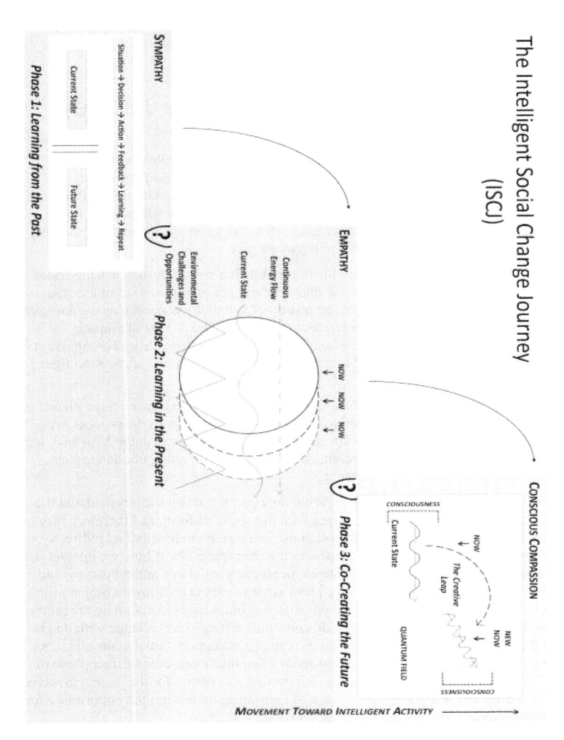

Figure ISCJ-1. *The Baseline Model.*

As we expand toward Phase 2, we begin to recognize patterns; they emerge from experiences that repeat over and over. Recognition of patterns enables us to "see" (in our mind's eye) the relationship of events in terms of time and space, moving us out of an action and reaction mode into a position of co-evolving with our environment, and enabling us to better navigate a world full of diverse challenges and opportunities. It is at this stage that we move from understanding based on past cause-and-effect reactions to how things come together, to produce new things both in the moment at hand and at a future point in time.

Phase 2, *Learning in the Present*, takes us to the next level of thinking and feeling about how we interact with our world, including the interesting area of human social interactions. Although complex, the somewhat recognizable patterns enable us to explore and progress through uncertainty and the unknown, making life more interesting and enjoyable. In Phase 2 patterns grow into concepts, higher mental thought, and we begin the search for a higher level of truth. Sustainability in the co-evolving state of Phase 2 requires empathy, which provides a direct understanding of another individual, and a heightened awareness of the context of their lives and their desires and needs in the moment at hand. While not yet achieving the creative leap of the intuitional (represented in Phase 3), we are clearly developing higher mental faculties and instinctive knowledge of the workings of the Universe, which helps cultivate intuition and develop insights in service to our self and society.

The creative leap of Phase 3, *Co-Creating the Future*, requires the ability to tap into the larger intuitional field that energetically connects all people. This can only be accomplished when energy is focused outward in service to the larger whole, requiring a deeper connection to others. Compassion deepens that connection. Thus, each phase of the Intelligent Social Change Journey calls for an increasing depth of connection to others, moving from sympathy to empathy to compassion.

<<<<<<<<>>>>>>>

INSIGHT: **Each phase of the Intelligent Social Change Journey calls for an increasing depth of connection to others, moving from sympathy to empathy to compassion.**

<<<<<<<<>>>>>>>

The ISCJ Baseline Model accents the phase changes as each phase builds on/expands from the previous phase. As the journeyer moves from Phase 1 to Phase 2 and prepares for the creative leap of Phase 3, the mental faculties are developing, the senses are coming into balance, and there are deepening connections to others. This will feel familiar to many travelers, for this is the place where we began. The model shows our journey is a significant change of mind, body and spirit as we operate on different cognitive and emotional planes as we progress through the developmental phases. Some people are aware of the changes they are undergoing and seek to accelerate the learning, while others resist the development, hoping (perhaps somewhat naively) to simplify the way they interact with the world.

Babies are born connected, to their mothers and families, and to the larger energies surrounding them and within them. This represents Phase 3. As one author exclaimed when exploring this reversal of the Phase 1, 2 and 3 models, "This really brings it all together for me. There is something that we admire in babies that we would like to become, and this framework makes sense of that feeling." If, and when, we return to Phase 3 in the round-trip journey of life, it will be with experience in our backpack and development of the mental faculties under our cap.

Sometime around the fourth grade, as most grade school teachers will attest, the ego pokes its head out, and, through social interactions, the process of individuation has begun, with a focus on, and experiencing in, the NOW. This represents Phase 2 of our change model, a state of co-evolving. In the pre-adolescent child, intuitional connections are subsumed by a physical focus accompanied by emotional flare-ups as the child is immersed in learning experiences, interacting and learning from and with their environment.

By the time the mid-teens come around, the world has imposed a level of order and limits, with a focus on cause-and-effect. In some families and cultures this may take the form of physical, mental or emotional manipulation and control, always related to cause-and-effect. If you do that, this will happen. For others, cultural or religious aspects of expectations and punishment may lead to the cause-and-effect focus. For the mid-teen perceived as overactive and unruly in the schoolroom, the limiting forces may be imposed through Ritalin or other drugs, which may have even started at a much earlier age. Regardless of how it is achieved, learning from the past—the Phase 1 model—becomes the starting point of our lives as we move into adulthood. From this starting point, we begin to develop our mental faculties.

The Overarching ISCJ Model

To help connect the dots, we have prepared a larger version of the Intelligent Social Change Journey, which is at Appendix A. The Overarching ISCJ Model focuses on the relationships of the phases with other aspects of the journey. For example, three critical movements during our journey, consistent with our movement through the phases, are reflected in expanded consciousness, reduction of forces and increased intelligent activity. *Consciousness* is considered a state of awareness and a private, selective and continuous change process, a sequential set of ideas, thoughts, images, feelings and perceptions and an understanding of the connections and relationships among them and our self. *Forces* occur when one type of energy affects another type of energy in a way such that they are moving in different directions, pressing against each other. Bounded (inward focused) and/or limited knowledge creates forces. *Intelligent activity* represents a state of interaction where intent, purpose, direction, values and expected outcomes are clearly understood and communicated among all parties, reflecting wisdom and achieving a higher truth. We will repeat this definition where appropriate throughout the book.

<<<<<<<◇>>>>>>>

INSIGHT: **The ISCJ is a journey toward intelligent activity, which is a state of interaction where intent, purpose, direction, values and expected outcomes are clearly understood and communicated among all parties, reflecting wisdom and achieving a higher truth.**

<<<<<<<◇>>>>>>>

Immediately below each phase of the Overarching ISCJ model are characteristics related to each phase. These are words or short phrases representing some of the ideas that will be developed in each section supporting each phase. **Phase 1,** *Learning from the Past,* characteristics are: linear and sequential, repeatability, engaging past learning, starting from current state, and cause and effect relationship. **Phase 2,** *Learning in the Present,* characteristics are: Recognition of patterns; social interaction; and co-evolving with the environment through continuous learning, quick response, robustness, flexibility, adaptability and alignment. **Phase 3,** *Co-Creating Our Future,* characteristics are: Creative imagination, recognition of global Oneness, mental in service to the intuitive; balancing senses; bringing together time (the past, present and future); knowing; beauty; and wisdom.

Still exploring the overarching model, at the lower part of the graphic we see three areas related to knowledge in terms of the nature of knowledge, areas of reflection, and cognitive shifts necessary for each phase of change. For ease of reference, we have also included the content of these three areas in Table ISCJ-1.

In Phase 1, *Learning from the Past,* the nature of knowledge is characterized as a product of the past and, as we will learn in Chapter 2, knowledge is context sensitive and situation dependent, and partial and incomplete. Reflection during this phase of change is on reviewing the interactions and feedback, and determining cause-and-effect relationships. There is an inward focus, and a questioning of decisions and actions as reflected in the questions: What did I intend? What really happened? Why were there differences? What would I do the same? What would I do differently? The cognitive shifts that are underway during this phase include: (1) recognition of the importance of feedback; (2) the ability to recognize systems and the impact of external forces; (3) recognition and location of "me" in the larger picture (building conscious awareness); and (4) pattern recognition and concept development. These reflections are critical to enabling the phase change to *co-evolving.*

In Phase 2, *Learning in the Present,* the nature of knowledge is characterized in terms of expanded cooperation and collaboration, and knowledge sharing and social learning. There is also the conscious *questioning of why*, and the *pursuit of truth*. Reflection includes a deepening of conceptual thinking and, through cooperation and collaboration, the ability to connect the power of diversity and individuation to the larger whole. There is an increasing outward focus, with the recognition of different world views and the exploration of information from different perspectives, and expanded knowledge capacities. Cognitive shifts that are underway include: (1) the ability to recognize and apply patterns at all levels within a domain of knowledge to predict outcomes; (2) a growing understanding of complexity; (3) increased connectedness of choices, recognition of direction you are heading, and expanded meaning-making; and (4) an expanded ability to bisociate ideas resulting in increased creativity.

In Phase 3, *Co-Creating Our Future*, the nature of knowledge is characterized as a recognition that with knowledge comes responsibility. There is a conscious pursuit of larger truth, and knowledge is selectively used as a measure of effectiveness. Reflection includes the valuing of creative ideas, asking the larger questions: How does this idea serve humanity? Are there any negative consequences? There is an openness to other's ideas, a questioning with humility: What if this idea is right? Are my beliefs or other mental models limiting my thought? Are hidden assumptions or feelings interfering with intelligent activity?

Cognitive shifts that are underway include: (1) a sense and knowing of Oneness; (2) development of both the lower (logic) and upper (conceptual) mental faculties, which work in concert with the emotional guidance system; (3) recognition of self as a co-creator of reality; (4) the ability to engage in intelligent activity; and (5) a developing ability to tap into the intuitional plane at will.

Time and space play a significant role in the phase changes. Using Jung's psychological type classifications, feelings come from the past, sensations occur in the present, intuition is oriented to the future, and thinking embraces the past, present *and* future. Forecasting and visioning work is done at a point of change (McHale, 1977) when a balance is struck continuously between short-term and long-term survival. Salk (1973) describes this as a shift from Epoch A, dominated by ego and short-term considerations, to Epoch B, where both *Being and ego co-exist*. In the ISCJ, this shift occurs somewhere in Phase 2, with Beingness advancing as we journey toward Phase 3. Considerable focus to time and space occurs later in the book (Chapter 16/Part III).

Phase of the Intelligent Social Change Journey	ISCJ: Nature of Knowledge	ISCJ: Points of Reflection	ISCJ: Cognitive Shifts
PHASE 1: Cause and Effect (Requires Sympathy) • Linear, and Sequential • Repeatable • Engaging past learning • Starting from current state • Cause-and-effect relationships	• A product of the past • Knowledge is context-sensitive and situation-dependent • Knowledge is partial and incomplete	• Reviewing the interactions and feedback • Determining cause-and-effect relationships; logic • Inward focus • Questioning of decisions and actions: What did I intend? What really happened? why were there differences? What would I do the same? What would I do differently?	• Recognition of the importance of feedback • Ability to recognize systems and the impact of external forces • Recognition and location of "me" in the larger picture (building conscious awareness) • Beginning pattern recognition and early concept development
PHASE 2: Co-Evolving (Requires Empathy) • Recognition of patterns • Social interaction • Co-evolving with environment through continuous learning, quick response, robustness, flexibility, adaptability, alignment.	• Engaging knowledge sharing and social learning • Engaging cooperation and collaboration • Questioning of why? • Pursuit of truth	• Deeper development of conceptual thinking (higher mental thought) • Through cooperation and collaboration ability to connect the power of diversity and individuation to the larger whole • Outward focus • Recognition of different world views and exploration of information from different perspectives • Expanded knowledge capacities	• The ability to recognize and apply patterns at all levels within a domain of knowledge to predict outcomes • A growing understanding of complexity • Increased connectedness of choices • Recognition of direction you are heading • Expanded meaning-making • Expanded ability to bisociate ideas resulting in increased creativity
PHASE 3: Creative Leap (Requires Compassion) • Creative imagination • Recognition of global Oneness • Mental in service to the intuitive • Balancing senses • Bringing together past, present and future • Knowing; Beauty; Wisdom	• Recognition that with knowledge comes responsibility • Conscious pursuit of larger truth • Knowledge selectively used as a measure of effectiveness	• Valuing of creative ideas • Asking the larger questions: How does this idea serve humanity? Are there any negative consequences? • Openness to other's ides; questioning with humility: What if this idea is right Are my beliefs or other mental models limiting my thought? Are hidden assumptions or feelings interfering with intelligent activity?	• A sense and knowing of Oneness • Development of both the lower (logic) and upper (conceptual) mental faculties, which work in concert with the emotional guidance system • Applies patterns across domains of knowledge for greater good • recognition of self as a co-creator of reality • The ability to engage in intelligent activity • Developing the ability to tap into the intuitional plane at will

Table ISCJ-Table 1. *The three Phases from the viewpoints of the nature of knowledge, points of reflection and cognitive shifts.*

Cognitive-Based Ordering of Change

As a cognitive-based ordering of change, we forward the concept of logical levels of learning consistent with levels of change developed by anthropologist Gregory Bateson (1972) based on the work in logic and mathematics of Bertrand Russell. This logical typing was both a mathematical theory and a law of nature, recognizing long before neuroscience research findings confirmed the relationship of the mind/brain which show that we literally create our reality, with thought affecting the physical structure of the brain, and the physical structure of the brain affecting thought.

Bateson's levels of change range from simplistic habit formation (which he calls Learning I) to large-scale change in the evolutionary process of the human (which he calls Learning IV), with each higher-level synthesizing and organizing the levels below it, and thus creating a greater impact on people and organizations. This is a hierarchy of logical levels, ordered groupings within a system, with the implication that as the levels reach toward the source or beginning **there is a sacredness, power or importance informing this hierarchy of values** (Dilts, 2003). This structure is consistent with the phase changes of the Intelligent Social Change Journey.

<<<<<<<◇>>>>>>

INSIGHT: **Similar to Bateson's levels of change, each higher phase of the Intelligent Social Change Journey synthesizes and organizes the levels below it, thus creating a greater impact in interacting with the world.**

<<<<<<<◇>>>>>>

With Learning 0 representing the status quo, a particular behavioral response to a specific situation, Learning I (first-order change) is stimulus-response conditioning (cause-and-effect change), which includes learning simple skills such as walking, eating, driving, and working. These basic skills are pattern forming, becoming habits, which occur through repetitiveness without conceptualizing the content. For example, we don't have to understand concepts of motion and movement in order to learn to walk. Animals engage in Learning I. Because it is not necessary to understand the concepts, or underlying theories, no questions of reality are raised. Learning I occurs in Phase 1 of the ISCJ.

Learning II (second-order change) is deuteron learning and includes creation, or a change of context inclusive of new images or concepts, or shifts the understanding of, and connections among, existing concepts such that meaning may be interpreted. These changes are based on mental constructs that *depend on a sense of reality* (McWhinney, 1997). While these concepts may represent real things, relations or qualities, they also may be symbolic, specifically created for the situation at hand.

Either way, they provide the means for reconstructing existing concepts, using one reality to modify another, from which new ways of thinking and behaviors emerge.

Argyris and Schon's (1978) concept of double loop learning reflects Level II change. Learning II occurs in Phase 2 of the ISCJ.

Learning III (third-order change) requires thinking beyond our current logic, calling us to change our system of beliefs and values, and offering different sets of alternatives from which choices can be made. Suggesting that Learning III is learning about the concepts used in Learning II, Bateson says,

> In transcending the promises and habits of Learning II, one will gain "a freedom from its bondages," bondages we characterize, for example, as "drive," "dependency," "pride," and "fatalism." One might learn to change the premises acquired by Learning II and to readily choose among the roles through which we express concepts and thus the "self." Learning III is driven by the "contraries" generated in the contexts of Learning I and II. (Bateson, 1972, pp. 301-305)

<<<<<<<<>>>>>>>

INSIGHT: **There is a freedom that occurs as we leave behind the thinking patterns of Phase 2 and open to the new choices and discoveries of Phase 3.**

<<<<<<<<>>>>>>>

Similarly, Berman (1981, p. 346) defines Learning III as, "an experience in which a person suddenly realizes the arbitrary nature of his or her own paradigm." This is the breaking open of our personal mental models, our current logic, losing the differential of subject/object, blending into connection while simultaneously following pathways of diverse belief systems. Learning III occurs as we move into Phase 3 of the ISCJ.

Learning IV deals with revolutionary change, getting outside the system to look at the larger system of systems, awakening to something completely new, different, unique and transformative. This is the space of *incluessence*, a future state far beyond that which we know to dream (Dunning, 2015). As Bateson described this highest level of change:

> The individual mind is immanent but not only in the body. It is immanent in pathways and messages outside the body; and there is a larger Mind of which the individual mind is only a sub-system. This larger Mind is comparable to God and is perhaps what people mean by "God," but it is still immanent in the total interconnected social system and planetary ecology. (Bateson, 1972, p. 465)

Table ISCJ-2 below is a comparison of the Phases of the Intelligent Social Change Journey and the four Levels of Learning espoused by Bateson (1972) based on the work in logic and mathematics of Bertrand Russell, and supported by Argyris and Schon (1978), Berman (1981), and McWhinney (1997).

Phase of the Intelligent Social Change Journey	Level of Learning [NOTE: LEARNING 0 represents the status quo; a behavioral response to a specific situation.]
PHASE 1: Cause and Effect (Requires Sympathy) • Linear, and Sequential • Repeatable • Engaging past learning • Starting from current state • Cause and effect relationships	**LEARNING i:** **(First order change)** • Stimulus-response conditioning • Incudes learning simple skills such as walking, eating, driving and working • Basic skills are pattern forming, becoming habits occurring through repetitiveness without conceptualizing the content • No questions of reality
PHASE 2: Co-Evolving (Requires Empathy) • Recognition of patterns • Social interaction • Co-evolving with environment through continuous learning, quick response, robustness, flexibility, adaptability, alignment	**LEARNING II (Deutero Learning)** **(Second order change)** • Includes creation or change of context inclusive of new images or concepts • Shifts the understanding of, and connections among, existing concepts such that meaning may be interpreted • Based on mental constructions that depend on a sense of reality
[Moving into Phase 3] **PHASE 3: Creative Leap** (Requires Compassion) • Creative imagination • Recognition of global Oneness • Mental in service to the intuitive • Balancing senses • Bringing together past, present and future • Knowing; Beauty; Wisdom	**LEARNING III: (Third order change)** • Thinking beyond current logic • Changing our system of beliefs and values • Different sets of alternatives from which choices can be made • Freedom from bondages **LEARNINNG IV:** • Revolutionary change • Getting outside the system to look at the larger system of systems • Awakening to something completely new, different, unique and transformative • Tapping into the large Mind of which the individual mind is a sub-system

Table ISCJ-Table 2. *Comparison of Phases of the ISCJ with Levels of Learning.*

An example of Learning IV is Buddha's use of intuitional thought to understand others. He used his ability to think in greater and greater ways to help people cooperate and share together, and think better. Learning IV is descriptive of controlled intuition in support of the creative leap in Phase 3 of the ISCJ, perhaps moving beyond what we can comprehend at this point in time, perhaps deepening the connections of sympathy, empathy and compassion to unconditional love.

How to Best Use this Material

This book has, quite purposefully, been chunked into five smaller books, referred to as Parts, which are both independent and interdependent. Chunking is a methodology for learning. The way people become experts involves the chunking of ideas and concepts and creating understanding through development of significant patterns useful for identifying opportunities, solving problems and anticipating future behavior within the focused domain of knowledge. Figure ISCJ-2 shows the relationship of the Parts of this book and their content to the Intelligent Social Change Journey. *Remember*: the ISCJ is a journey of expansion, with each Phase building on—and inclusive of—the former Phase as we develop our mental faculties in service to the intuitional, and move closer to intelligent activity. As such, one needs to experience the earlier phases in order to elevate to the upper levels. Early life experiences and educational development during these earlier stages create the foundation and capacity to develop into higher levels of interactions and ways of being.

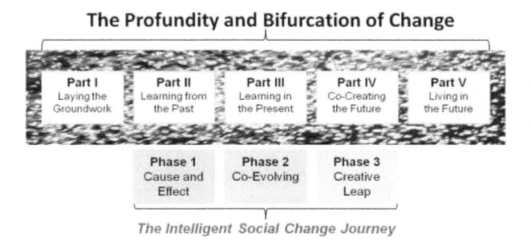

Figure ISCJ-2. *Relationship of Parts and Phases of the ISCJ.*

While many different ideas have been introduced in the paragraphs of this Introduction to the Intelligent Social Change Journey, you will discover that all of these ideas are addressed in depth during the course of this book, and each Part is inclusive of tools, references, insights and reflective questions provided in support of your personal learning journey. We also cross-reference, both within the Parts, and across all of the Parts.

This is a journey, and as such *the learning is in the journey*, the reflecting on and application of the learning, not in achieving a particular capability or entering the next Phase at a specific point in time. Similar to the deepening of relationships with others, the growth of understanding and expansion of consciousness takes its own time, twisting and curving forwards and backwards until we have learned all we can from one frame of reference, and then jump to another to continue our personal journey. That said, we suggest that those who are impatient to know the topics within this book, but reluctant to read such an extended text, jump to Chapter 11/Part III, which provides readiness assessment statements and related characteristics reflecting the high-level content of this book.

For your reference, the Overarching ISCJ model can be downloaded for printing in A3 format at www.MQIPress.net The corresponding author may be reached at alex@mountainquestinstitute.com

PART II

Laying the Groundwork

Introduction to Part II

In the beginning there was only the *intrasomatic* processing of information, at first through *feeling* (simple organisms such as amoebas) and then through *seeing, hearing, smelling* and *tasting,* all occurring in the NOW. With evolution, came development of memory, enabling organisms to recall events of the past in order to handle events occurring in the present. It was the human who developed *extrasomatic* information processing, that is, ways to share information and knowledge, initially through signing and oral language (myths, stories and songs) and later through the amazing sharing of information enabled by technology (Csikszentmihalyi, 1993). Now, learning from the past was largely available to those who chose—and had the capability—to do so.

In our linear conscious thought, everything seems to have a beginning and an end, and in between there is a flow from one event to the next, with a reaction for every action, an exchange of energy, and for every effect an originating cause. However, because of the separation of time and space, it is often difficult to determine cause and effect relationships among events. An event is the way that energy responds to some other energy. We don't have the memory, much less the understanding, of old events. However, this is an ability that can be developed. The more conscious a person is, the quicker the effect joins with the cause, because **consciousness causes time and space to join.**

The more something is forced, with a negative energy outcome, the longer it takes to join events in time and space and bring them into balance. For example, let's say an Executive Board of seven has to vote on five potential opportunities, with each of the five opportunities connected to the personal passion of a different Board member. As the Board meeting extends into the late night, rather than call for a vote, the arguments escalate. The longer this goes on, the more forces that are being built up in terms of anger and frustration, and the more time and space required to bring the Board back into balance such that they can move toward intelligent activity.

You may have noticed that the three phases of the Intelligent Social Change Journey roughly parallel the focus of change consistent with the development of humanity. Phase 1, responding to the linear, experiential nature of life from the beginning of human thought, represents the primary understanding of change into the 20th century. Phase 2, representing the need for, and understanding of, co-evolving with our environment, emerged as we moved into the 21st century. Phase 3, while dotted throughout history as the intuitive flash or punctuated equilibrium, is just coming into our awareness and titillating our imagination as we move into the Golden Age of Humanity, ushering in the expansion of human consciousness.

This book, Part II: *Learning from the Past,* focuses on Phase 1 of the Intelligent Social Change Journey (Figure II-1). Building on Lewin's work (1947), this is a logical model related to cause and effect, learning from the past through feedback loops, making any necessary changes, and acting. As used here, cause, derived from the Latin *causa* meaning motive or reason, is what makes something happen (Encarta, 1999). The causes of things can reach into the future, that is, *causes can create ripples of change.* Effect, derived from the Latin *effectus* or *efficere* meaning to accomplish or work out, refers to a result, a changed state as a result of an action (Encarta, 1999). We don't know something has happened until it is past. Thus, the effects of things are determined by looking at the past.

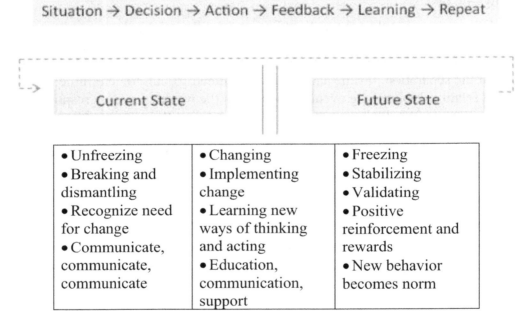

Situation → Decision → Action → Feedback → Learning → Repeat

Current State		Future State
• Unfreezing • Breaking and dismantling • Recognize need for change • Communicate, communicate, communicate	• Changing • Implementing change • Learning new ways of thinking and acting • Education, communication, support	• Freezing • Stabilizing • Validating • Positive reinforcement and rewards • New behavior becomes norm

CHARACERISTICS: sequential, repeatable, learning from the past, current state starting point

Figure II-Intro 1. *Phase 1 of the Intelligent Social Change Journey.*

Thus, Phase 1 assumes that **for every effect there is an originating cause**, yet because of the separation of time and space, it is often *difficult to determine* the cause and effect relationship. It is not easy to remember the details of, much less understand, events of the past. Further, since each person experiences life through a different frame of reference, it is difficult to get a consensus of what exactly happened, much less determine the cause.

In Part II (Phase 1 of the Intelligent Social Change Journey) ...

Each of us experiences cause and effect regularly throughout a lifetime. From the time we are a child touching something hot, as a teenager when we don't study for a test or are grounded, or as an adult when we receive a bonus for outstanding contribution to winning a contract. Thus, the chapters in Part II attempt to capture some of the experiential learning associated with recognition of these cause-and-effect patterns, preparing us to move into the current era of co-evolving with our environment. Note that cause and effect are still very much with us, and provide the foundation necessary to develop our lower mental mind based on logic, and from that repeated learning to move into development of concepts based on patterns of events.

Before launching into the chapters related to Phase 1, we provide the **Introduction to the Intelligent Social Change Journey** (ISCJ), which was primary in *The Profundity and Bifurcation of Change Part I*. The ISCJ is a journey toward intelligent activity, which is a state of interaction where intent, purpose, direction, values and expected outcomes are clearly understood and communicated among all parties, reflecting wisdom and achieving a higher truth.

To expand our understanding of Phase 1 of this journey, in this Part we explore:

Chapter 7: Looking for Cause and Effect. We first consider the relationship of causes, effects, conditions and motives. While recognizing the importance of understanding the linear and logical relationships of cause and effect, we explore why this understanding is not enough.

Chapter 8: A Kaleidoscope of Models. In 1947 Kurt Lewin proposed a three-step change model that is foundational to Phase 1, *Learning from the Past*. This three-stage process was unfreezing (breaking, dismantling), change (a period of confusion) and freezing (crystalizing). This was an early model in change theory; and there have been thousands of published models since that point in time! Although it would be impossible to comprehensively cover this field, we present a kaleidoscope of models representative of the diversity of models ranging from the mid-1950's into this century. In essence, we're all change agents, and since each and every one of us is unique, there are just as many approaches to life and living.

Chapter 9: Modalities of Change. What are modalities of change? This chapter explores the relationship of experiencing, learning, engaging, visioning, imagining and conceptualizing for change. To move toward the future, we benefit from first picturing and then *thinking* the future. We specifically address positive thinking, arguably the greatest tool the individual can employ throughout life, and introduce the concept of cognitive conveyors—specifically, desire, courage and drive—concepts filled with a combination of thought, emotion and feelings that weave themselves through the modalities of change.

Chapter 10: Grounding Change. Change is easier, and occurs more fluidly, when we are grounded; only we must ask: Are we choosing the right things to ground upon? We explore three interpretations of the concept of grounding: (1) giving a foundation, teaching someone the basics; (2) fixing something on or in something else for a foundation; and (3) connecting with the ground. Examples of physical, mental, emotional and spiritual grounding are offered.

Chapter 11: Assessing Readiness. In terms of the new weltanschauung or world view, this chapter offers the opportunity to assess your readiness for change from both an individual and organizational viewpoint. We stimulate a conversation that enables co-creation of a vision. Then, 55 readiness assessment statements help explore your readiness maturity level, enabling you to challenge whether you have the openness and comfort to move into the future.

Chapter 12: The Change Agent's Strategy. Implementing change at every level of the organization follows the growth path of knowledge and sharing. This has proven to be an effective approach to implementing a Phase 1 to Phase 2 change journey as used in the U.S. Department of the Navy to implement Knowledge Management.

We begin.

Chapter 7
Looking for Cause and Effect

SUBTOPICS: CAUSES AND CONDITIONS ... MOTIVES ... LINKING CAUSE AND EFFECT ... WHY CAUSE AND EFFECT IS NOT ENOUGH ... FINAL THOUGHTS

FIGURES: 7-1. A SAMPLE FISHBONE DIAGRAM

TOOLS: 7-1. PERSONAL PLANE-ING PROCESS; 7.2. THE FIVE WHYS

Looking from different frames of reference or world views strongly impacts our understanding of cause and effect. For example, the "cause" of things is considered quite differently in context with each of the four archetypal realities (deterministic, social, mythic and sensory). These worldviews will be explained in more detail in Chapter 13/Part III. McWhinney explains:

> In the deterministic worldview, the innate or primary qualities of the situation set the "cause" or motivation of the action; in the social reality, the intended outcomes "cause" the outcome; and in the mythic cause and effect are one ... reflect on the misunderstandings that follow from questions that ask "why?" "Why did you do that?" The sensory says, "*because* I was tired." To which the social responds, "*because* you didn't care." (McWhinney, 1997, p. 68)

As can be seen, what we focus on is driven by our preferred world view. The differences pointed out by McWhinney are very important to understanding cause and effect.

Perhaps a simpler way to think about this is by using our understanding that the human operates on three planes at all times, the physical, mental and emotional. For example, let's say you come upon an accident where a large truck has plowed into three cars. If you ask "why?" from the physical viewpoint, you note that the truck ricocheted off the center guard and toppled over, spilling the contents on the road, which in turn caused cars to swerve and run into each other. If you ask "why?" from an emotional viewpoint, you are looking at the victims being loaded into ambulances while simultaneously noting the police testing the unharmed truck driver for alcohol level, and his inability to walk a straight line. You are angry. If you ask "why?" from the mental level, you also note that the road is slick, or perhaps that the following cars were too close and were speeding, which can be discerned from the tire marks; or perhaps that the truck driver's brakes failed, as a mechanic has discovered. As can be seen, determining the cause-and-effect relationship of events can be quite difficult, and highly dependent upon from which plane you look.

****

TOOL 7-1: Personal Plane-ing Process

The intent of this exercise is to isolate your sensing capabilities on each plane (physical, mental, emotional) in order to explore cause and effect from different points of view.

STEP 1: Bound the event or situation for which you are seeking a cause, that is, clearly understand the effect that you perceive. Understand this effect to the best of your capabilities. *Ask:* Why is it important to understand the cause? How is this effect harmful or helpful? What is important about this event to me or my organization? Capture your responses on paper for later reference. NOTE: There may be multiple physical effects, in which case you need to go through this process separately for each effect.

STEP 2: Start with the physical plane, which is related to what can be seen, heard, smelled, tasted or touched in the material world. Utilizing all these senses, as appropriate, explore the effect fully. Create a chart with four vertical columns. At the top of the left-hand column write "senses" and underneath that column list each of your five physical senses, taking advantage of the full page, leaving plenty of room between each sense. At the top of the second column write the word "physical". Now, focusing on the *physical effect* of the event or situation for which you are seeking a cause, go down the list and capture your observations from the viewpoint of each of your senses. Be sure you capture the situational context of the physical. This would mean noting other physical objects that may have a relationship to the effect you are exploring. Note that smell and taste are interrelated; you may be able to taste a smell. In the case of our accident example, that may relate to a gas leak or burnt rubber.

STEP 3: At the top of the third column write "mental." Now, focusing on the mental aspects of the effect, go down the list and capture your thoughts from the viewpoint of each of your senses. This will build on your physical observations. *Ask:* How does all this incoming data relate? Are there clear relationships? Is there something that is missing? Is there an indicator that begs more reflection? When you have exhausted the possibilities in terms of mental thought, move on to the next step.

STEP 4: At the top of the fourth column write "emotional." Now, explore the effect from the emotional plane, going down the list and capturing your thoughts from the viewpoint of each of your senses. During this step you can also bring in your sixth sense of connection, thinking from your heart. For example, using the sense of sight, how does this effect make you feel? Do my physical and mental responses feel right? What feels wrong? In terms of what I see, how might the people involved in this event feel? As answers emerge from these and similar questions that come to mind from the viewpoint of each sense, write down your responses.

STEP 5: Now, take a step backwards and explore the relationships among your responses. *Ask:* What have I learned from this exercise? Have any clear causes surfaced? Are there any potential causes that need to be further explored?

If there are multiple effects, after completing this exercise for each effect, look for patterns. Given the chance, for example taking a systems view of the data that has emerged from this process, the human mind is quite capable of identifying patterns which may prove surprising.

STEP 6: Act on your learning. If the effect is undesirable, ensure that it does not occur again. If the effect is desirable, explore ways you can ensure that it continues.

****

In addition to focusing from your three operational planes (physical, mental and emotional), you are also utilizing your personal information circuit informed by your five senses of form (seeing, hearing, smelling, tasting and touching) and potentially your two inner senses (connection and co-creation, both informed by your mental development and emotional guidance system). What does that mean?

In Step 4 of the Personal Plane-ing Process, the inner sense of connection (the sixth sense) was employed in the act of "feeling" how others perceived the effect. Determining cause and effect relationships involving others—and in our interactions with the world other people are always involved—at a minimum requires sympathy for other's role in the situation, whether on the cause or effect side of your consideration. If you have developed a capacity for empathy, a deeper connection to others, you will be able to develop a deeper understanding of their relationship to the cause or effect of a situation or event.

And now, we move to your seventh sense of co-creating, which has also already come into play as you engage in the Personal Plane-ing Process. From a neuroscience perspective, we now know that thoughts change the structure of the brain, and the brain structure influences the creation of new thoughts (Bennet et al, 2015b). As detailed in Chapter 25/Part IV, spatial attention to a specific thing, person or event increases the intensity of the related neuronal firings, which in turn affects the conscious experience of focus, amplifying the contrast in the experience and making it less faint and more salient (Carrasco et al., 2004). Your attention to, and exploration of, the effect will drive, whether consciously or unconsciously, your decisions and actions in the future when you perceive related or similar situations are occurring, are about to occur, or have occurred. Personal Plane-ing is all about learning, taking full advantage of the multidimensional aspects of the human to provide a baseline for exploring a situation in depth from various viewpoints.

Causes and Conditions

To explore cause and effect more fully, we refer to the recent work of Carroll (2016, p. 54) who says that while we look at the world through the lens of cause and effect, reasons why, purposes and goals, "None of those concepts exists as part of the fundamental furniture of reality at its deepest. They emerge as we zoom out from the microscopic level to the level of the everyday." He refers to the second law of thermodynamics, which says that the total entropy (disorder or randomness) of a closed system never decreases; that it either stays constant or increases as time passes. Austrian physicist Ludwig Boltzmann took this concept and said that while it applied at the microscopic level of atoms, that there were many arrangements of atoms that appear the same at the level of observation. With Boltzmann's insights in mind,

> ... it makes perfect sense that entropy tends to increase over time. The reason is simple: there are far more states with high entropy than states with low entropy. If you start in a low entropy configuration and simply evolve in almost any direction your entropy is extraordinarily likely to increase. When the entropy of a system is as high as it can get, we say that the system is in *equilibrium*. In equilibrium, time has no arrow. (Carroll, 2016, p. 58)

Carroll adds the assumption is that the initial state of the Universe was low entropy, taking us all the way back to the Big Bang. This brings us to the ekinological belief that *today is based on a special condition in the far past* (Carroll, 2016). In futures thinking, if a perceived problem does not have a solution, then that perceived problem is *not* a problem, it is a *condition* of the system (Linstone, 1977). Carroll differentiates the relationship of cause and effect and the relationship of early conditioning with the future. Specifically, he explains,

> The laws of physics take the form of rigid patterns: if the ball is at a certain position and has a certain velocity at a certain time, the laws will tell you what the position and velocity will be a moment later, and what they were a moment before. When we think about cause and effect, by contrast, we single out certain events as uniquely responsible for events that come afterward, as "making them happen." (Carroll, 2016, p. 63)

What Carroll is pointing out is that cause and effect implies a responsibility for events, while physics is simply an arrangement in a certain order, a condition of the system, with no specific cause or responsibility. "Different moments in time in the history of the Universe follow each other, according to some pattern, but no one moment causes any other." (Carroll, 2016, p. 63)

As can be seen, by clear definition of these terms, Carroll has differentiated between cause and effect and ordered patterns, yet there is still the question that comes to mind, wouldn't this early conditioning be considered a cause of these ordered patterns? Yet, since knowledge is highly context sensitive and situation dependent, we agree with Carroll that it is useful to consider context in characterizing a situation, as well as to apply modal reasoning—thinking about what could happen as well as what did happen—to explore events in different ways.

<<<<<<<◇>>>>>>>

INSIGHT: **Cause and effect implies a responsibility for events; when there is no specific cause or responsibility, what is perceived as an effect is a *condition* of the system, with no specific cause or responsibility.**

<<<<<<<◇>>>>>>>

What this philosophical argument points out to us is that, when considering cause and effect from the point of conditioning, a deeper understanding of the situation at hand can be gained. In our accident example, the element of "conditioning" might include the truck driver's penchant for drinking, which began at a young age in rebellion to an overly strict and abusive father. Conversely, a direct cause-and-effect relationship might be identified as the truck company postponing a required safety inspection of this truck scheduled two weeks previously. Applying modal reasoning, we might reach further with this thought and realize that the faulty brakes would have been recognized during an inspection, or, that if the contents of the truck had been more secured, the larger accident could have been avoided. This thinking might lead to discovery of new approaches to securing loose loads.

Motives

Further, there are layers of causes, or motives, for any single action. When humans engage in introspection, they have the ability to detect reasons, or motives, for specific actions. However, Nietzsche says that this quest for motives is largely misguided, and that there is no specific set of motives for action. As Nietzsche says,

> Cause and effect: there is probably never such a duality, in truth a continuum faces us, from which we isolate a few pieces, just as we always perceive a movement only as isolated points, i.e., do not really see, but infer ... (GS 112 in Katsafanas, 2016)

We agree. The human is a complex adaptive system, with a large number of interrelated elements with nonlinear relationships, feedback loops and dynamic uncertainties very difficult to understand and predict. This suggests that our *conscious motives* in terms of cause and effects are artificial, and that there is always another layer below that which we identify. While we can single out motives, and justify them, there is always another layer hidden below. As Nietzsche describes,

Everything which enters consciousness is the last link in a chain, a closure. It is just an illusion that one thought is the immediate cause of another thought. The events which are actually connected are played out below our consciousness: the series and sequences of feelings, thoughts, etc., that appear are symptoms of what actually happens! – Below every thought lies an affect. Every thought, every feeling, every will is not born of one particular drive but is a total state, a whole surface of the whole consciousness, and results from how the power of all the drives that constitute us is fixed at that moment ... (SA 12:1[61]/WLN 60 in Katsafanas, 2016).

Thus, according to Nietzsche, there is no single cause and effect, but rather a set of interconnected and interacting forces, all playing a role but with no single cause responsible for the effect (Katsafanas, 2016).

****

TOOL 7-2: The Five Whys

This is a simple yet effective approach to explore cause-and-effect relations to specific situations or problems. You are searching for root causes.

STEP 1: Have the issue or situation firmly in your head.

STEP 2: *Ask:* Why did this occur?

STEP 3: When an answer emerges, *ask:* Why? again ...

STEP 4: In an iterative fashion, *ask* Why? of each answer until there are no more answers to be had. This approach is called the "five" whys since that is generally far down enough to fully understand the cause-and-effect relationship among the elements of the system. However, it is not necessary to stop at five. Continue asking why? of each answer until you cannot come up with any more answers.

****

The Five Whys can be used separately or as part of a Fishbone Diagram, also known as a cause-and-effect diagram, which breaks down root causes that potentially cause an effect in successive levels of detail. You draw a straight arrow, which represents the event or situation, pointing to the "effect", and then draw slanted sublines coming off of it, with each subline representing one of the answers of asking *Why?* at the primary level. These responses (sublines) are generally grouped into areas such as people, processes, management, equipment, materials, environment, etc., as appropriate. Then, you draw sub sublines off of the sublines, each of which represents the result of asking *Why?* at the subline level, and so forth. As can be visualized (see Figure 7-1), and so named by Kaoru Ishikaw who is credited with originated this approach, the resulting graphic looks very much like the skeleton of a fish. Note that the Five Whys and the Fishbone Diagram are most effective when used with cooperative and collaborative groups with a diversity of experiences and ways of thinking.

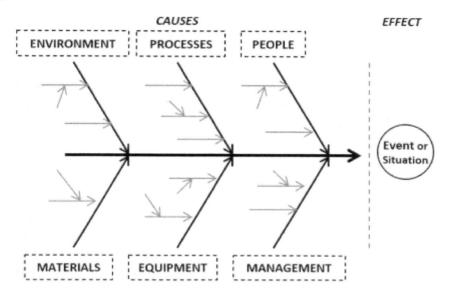

Figure 7-1. *A Sample Fishbone Diagram.*

Linking Cause and Effect

As can be seen through the examples above, the good news is that linking cause and effect is an ability that can be developed. While we agree with Nietzsche that there is rarely a single cause and effect relationship, the more awareness and mental acuity an individual has developed in a specific domain of knowledge, the quicker that individual is able to join cause and effect to any degree of accuracy.

People can sense some causes and effects individually through the senses, but cannot easily share that sensing or consciousness with one another. Rather, *the mental faculties become the vehicle for knowledge sharing.* Thinking together, we *may* be able to simultaneously understand the cause and effect of the cause.

Clearly, time and space also play an important role in several respects. First, they serve as a forcing function to develop our mental faculties. We cannot sense time in relationship to activity unless we are focusing from the mental plane. Mental thinking in relationship to the whole part of time is explored in Chapter 26/Part IV. Second, as noted above, the longer the period of time that passes between cause and effect, the more difficult it is to make connections among cause and effect. However, as over time layers of connections begin to emerge, there *is* the ability to develop patterns from these layers, patterns that become formulas, or concepts, that connect the relationships among actions, a higher truth that applies to multiple examples. (See Chapter 24/Part IV on Knowledge and the Search for Truth.)

Patterns also play an important role in the understanding of self. The maturing self will recognize consistencies in their choices, that is, choices made in different situations that head them in the same direction or toward the same outcome. By understanding these consistencies, an individual develops a deeper understanding of self and expands consciousness. But we're getting ahead of ourselves. Patterns play an essential role in moving us from a limited Phase 1 approach to the co-evolving of Phase 2.

Why Cause and Effect is Not Enough

In a simple world in simple situations, it may be possible to make cause and effect connections. However, when the environment becomes more and more complex, it becomes difficult, if not impossible, to see any linear cause and effect relationships. This is not only due to the large number of entangled elements, but also to the property of emergence.

Emergence, a global or local property of a complex system, results from the interactions and relationships among its agents (people in organizations), and between the agents and their environment. These characteristics represent stable or quasi-stable patterns, often qualitative in nature, within a system in disequilibrium that may exert a strong influence within the system. Examples are culture, trust, attitudes, organizational identity and team spirit.

An emergent property is often said to be more than the sum of its parts, although it would be more accurate to say that the emergent property has *different characteristics* than the sum of its parts. For example, each individual can learn, and so can organizations. However, organizational learning is different than individual learning. Organizational learning requires individuals to work together to accomplish a task with the results created by combining each individual's knowledge with the capability gained *through their mutual (and often interdependent) interactions*. The same results could not be obtained by adding the contributions of each individual together, because, since knowledge is created in the instant at hand, the interactions change what each individual knows, learns, and does. It is this *interactive gain* that produces "synergy" or emergent characteristics of an organization. Thus, the sum of individual learning and organizational learning becomes the total learning of the organization (Bennet and Bennet, 2004). As can be seen, because an emergent property can be quite different than the elements in the organization from which it emerged, it is difficult to trace its origins, that is, to identify a cause and effect factor.

The environment we live and work in today is increasingly more complex, with complexity begetting complexity. This is described more fully in Chapter 13/Part III,

The New Reality. With this increasing complexity, coupled with a faster-paced society, time and space are separated, and causes and effects are quite often lost in the noise. Thus, it becomes necessary to approach change through a new lens, which involves an expansion from Phase 1 to Phase 2 of the Intelligent Social Change Journey, from which viewpoint most successful organizations of today operate. As can be seen, while some decision-makers get stuck in the cause-and-effect loop regardless of its effectiveness, this movement towards co-evolving with our environment is a natural progression.

Final Thoughts

We were very careful with the way the final heading is titled, that is, "Why Cause and Effect is Not Enough." We reiterate that every phase of the Intelligent Social Change Journey builds on the previous phase; it does *not* replace it. There is a lot of learning that occurs through the use of tools such as the Personal Plane-ing Process and the Five Whys, and situations where they can be successfully used to connect cause and effect, leading to intelligent decisions. Remember, that in our round-trip journey back towards the intuitional—which is and has always been available within us, just waiting to be rediscovered—**the mental is in service to the intuitive**. We are here learning new skills and developing our mental faculties, and each Phase of the journey enables us to do just that.

Questions for Reflection:

How do you best explore cause-and-effect relationships?

Are the causes of situations always important to understand?

Chapter 8
A Kaleidoscope of Models

One free man says frankly what he thinks and feels in the midst of thousands who by their actions and words maintain just the opposite. It might be supposed that the man who has frankly expressed his thought would remain isolated, yet in most cases it happens that all, or the majority, of the others have long thought and felt the same as he, only they have not expressed it. And what yesterday was the novel opinion of one man becomes today the general opinion of the majority. And as soon as this opinion is established, at once by imperceptible degrees but irresistibly, the conduct of mankind begins to alter.
– Leo Tolstoy

SUBTOPICS: THEORIES OF CHANGE ... WE BEGIN A FEW YEARS EARLIER ... THE NEW CENTURY ... FINAL THOUGHTS

FIGURE: 8-1. A KALEIDOSCOPE OF CHANGE MODELS. THE EXPANDING MODELS ARE REFLECTIVE OF DEEPER SCIENTIFIC AND EPISTEMOLOGICAL THOUGHT.

Without an overarching paradigm for change, how do you choose strategies that will lead to successful sustained change? The ability to effectively choose the way ahead is based not only on knowing the domain of knowledge in which you swim, but also in understanding theories and models of change. A theory is considered a set of statements and/or principles that explain a group of facts or phenomena to guide action or assist in comprehension or judgment (American Heritage Dictionary, 2006; Bennet & Bennet, 2010a). Based on beliefs and/or mental models and built on assumptions, theories provide a plausible or rational explanation of cause and effect relationships. Taken from the Greek word *theoria*, which has the same root as theatre, theory means to see or view or to make a spectacle (Bohm, 1980).

Bohm sees theories as a form of insight, a way of looking at the world, clear in certain domains, and unclear beyond those domains, continuously shifting as new insights emerge through experience. We agree, and would add that theories offer sparks of opportunity. As can be seen through the examples below, there are many directions from which to explore change. The good news is that there are also similarities or threads that emerge that become a foundation for, or part of, new theories.

<<<<<<<◇>>>>>>>

INSIGHT: **Theories are a form of insight that offer sparks of opportunity.**

<<<<<<<◇>>>>>>>

Good theories and the methodologies connected to those theories provide the opportunity for responding to a wide range of situations, allowing us to reflect on possibilities and so better anticipate the results of our actions. When used by an arrogant mind ("I'm right", "you're wrong" and "I'm not listening"), they can also prove limiting (see Chapter 4/Part I).

In this chapter, we rapidly move through several dozen (or more) change theories that emerged in the latter part of the last century and through the first decade of the current century. While this quick review is by no means complete—nor could it be since change affects every aspect of our knowledge—it is somewhat representative of the types of theories and their corresponding models which emerged; hence we present, for your consideration now and as a resource in the future, a *kaleidoscope of models*. What you will notice is that the expanding models of change reflect the deeper scientific and epistemological thought emerging such as relativity theory, Quantum mechanics, the uncertainty principle, chaos theory and a growing understanding of tacit knowledge.

As we move through these models, we are going to add a few of our thoughts, and encourage you to note your own responses as well. This side conversation will be highlighted and the font will be blue.

Theories of Change

The *profound change* attributed to W. Edwards Deming, which was the translation of profound knowledge from theory to action, concentrated on complexity, variation, and the use of the scientific method as a tool for learning and improvement. Deming moved to axioms in the 1980s, which "comprise a kind of unified field theory for whole-system improvement reflecting Deming's system of profound knowledge" (Delavigne & Robertson, 1994, p. 5). This system of change was also referred to as *Neo-Taylorism*, or "new" Taylorism, which followed on the heels of huge paradigm shifts in science including the relativity theory of Albert Einstein, the Quantum mechanics theory of Max Planck, the uncertainty principle of Werner Heisenberg, the chaotic process of Poincare, the epistemology developed by C. I. Lewis and Percy Bridgman, and the understanding of statistics by Walter Shewhart. The changes taught by Deming were:

1. Every system has variation; hence, the information needed to create optimum systems is unknown and unknowable.

2. Using the scientific method, we learn what's unknown but knowable faster.

3. By observing the operation of the system, built-in flaws can be detected and isolated.

4. Complexity can be reduced and entropy lowered by removing the built-in flaws. (Delavigne & Robertson, 1994, p. 47-48)

We begin a few years earlier …

Salter (1974) says that *social change* begins with a cognitive process. Some sort of problem or issue is identified, isolated and diagnosed and a solution or solution set is developed and actions taken. This, however, is not done from the outside in, but *from the inside out*. [Ah! The beginnings of the individual change model presented in Chapter 6/Part I.] As Salter (1974) describes, "We are not and cannot be outside our social 'problems'. We are inside them—they are the medium in which we swim" (Slater, 1974, p. 150). In addressing what he perceives as misconceptions regarding change, Slater points out that the social system within which we live is both static and empty, that is, it is a "motionless container that must be filled with plans, programs and energy" (McWhinney, 1997, p. 53). Social change is linear, recycling the past in Darwinian evolutionary fashion, and requires obtaining power, using the power that may be part of the problem, with the ultimate power achieved by surrendering that which one has the power to enforce. McWhinney (1997) contends this cannot be accomplished with a narrow focus. For example, solving a problem "requires the use of logics from at least two different realities—one reality describes the given world, the other directs the change. The resolution of major issues is likely to require a complex interworking of many such sets of two or more realities." (p. 57).

Watzlawick et al. (1974) address the principles associated with change. They come from the viewpoint of psychotherapy and incorporate concepts of human communication, interactional therapy, the pathogenic and therapeutic effects of paradoxes (double binds) and of action-oriented rather than origin-oriented techniques of problem resolution. "It examples how, paradoxically, common sense and 'logical' behavior often fail, while actions [appearing] 'illogical' and 'unreasonable' … succeed in producing a desired change" (Watzlawick et al., 1974, p. xiii).

Goodman (1979) introduced the concept of *turning points* for both the agents of change and victims of change. She says there is a strong hope that we are able to hold on to what is best about the past while moving into a better future. [This is the foundation of Appreciative Inquiry and Positive Organizational Behavior emerging in the 1990's (see Chapter 9).] Balanced against this, there is a great fear of losing something vital to us, perhaps even without knowing it. The scale of change ranges from the most superficial to the most critical, with different responses from different people. Some make changes eagerly and easily, and others find change insurmountable. Some have a sense of exhilaration, and others feel profoundly disrupted. The hardest change is when the meaning of our lives is threatened. Carol Dweck (2012) proposed in her book Mindset that some people are predisposed with an open mindset that has them comfortable with exploration and others are comparatively closed. [Perhaps this just represents where people are in the Intelligent Social Change Journey.]

Jacobs (1981) provides a model based on the twelve keys to successful change. As she notes, you don't have to look very far for these keys because they are always a part of you. The twelve keys are: Your past changes, your strengths for coping with change, your fantasy of success—and failure, your priorities, your goals, your motivation for change, your fear and resistance to change, time for mourning your loss, support for the change, timing and readiness, and a plan of action. It is important to identify and take credit for accomplishments on the way to each goal. This is generally completing a long series of small, simple actions. Jacobs says that change involves motion and dynamics, that is, bursts of energy and abrupt stops, enormous leaps and shifts of direction, with a slow but steady forward thrust. As Jacobs (1981, p. 31) describes,

> Think of changemaking as a dance which you choreograph. Its sequences are interrelated and overlapping, requiring your sensitive orchestration. Sometimes you'll have difficulty in feeling grounded, because the motion takes over and carries you along. At other times you'll lose your perspective and wonder in what direction you're going ... Try to sense the flow of movement in your life: the speed, direction and focus of the dance of years. Notice how you keep the momentum going.

[Note the need for grounding and the idea of getting into the flow. These elements are discussed in Chapter 10 and Chapter 18/Part II, respectively.]

Kanter (1983) introduced the concept of *participation management* skills and environment to make possible the full use of new ideas coming from within the corporation. She contrasts the difference between segmentalists, who are anti-change with narrow perspectives [stereotypically like banks and traditional financial or risk averse organizations], and integrative companies, which have a wide-open, team-oriented environment where innovation occurs throughout the organization [such as Gore, where employees elect the bosses].

Dyer (1984) offers that there are *specific strategies* for meeting change head on. There are three factors in any change effort: Type A Factors are targets of change (those that can be handled directly); Type B Factors are targets of influence (those someone else must handle); and Type C Factors are targets for coping (those we don't seem to be able to change). It is critical that the target of change is clearly identified. Action planning is the next stage.

Lippitt et al. (1985) focus on how to analyze the changes needed within an organization and how to then implement those changes efficiently, effectively and with the support of all involved (cover flap). They purport that there are certain common elements to any *planned change* effort. These include: advocacy, time, collaboration and cooperation [the highest virtues on the physical plane], systems approach, interrelationships of changes to other aspects of the system, and emotion and rationality. From a consultant's viewpoint, the change process moves through the following steps: initiation, selection of instruments, preconditioning the client, problem identification and description, data collection, feedback to employees, recommendations to management, evaluation and general learnings.

Kirkpatrick (1985) presents a step-by-step change model that provides a *systematic approach* to managing change. Quite simply and pragmatically, the steps are: (1) determining the need or desire for a change; (2) preparing a tentative plan; (3) analyzing probable reactions; (4) making a final decision; (5) establishing a timetable; (6) communicating the change; and (7) implementing the change. Further, he says the three keys to successful change are: empathy, communication and participation. [We agree. Note that this work was published in 1985, yet these are keys to successful change that continue today. (See Chapter 35/Part V for a discussion of empathy leading to compassion.]

Martel (1986) divides all change into two distinct kinds: *structural and cyclical*. Structural changes are permanent and irreversible, and are seen in information, education and communications and work, income and attitudes. Cyclical changes are temporary and recurring and include business cycles and organizational and social behavior. Change is not random. As Martel (1986, p. 11-12) describes, "There are distinct kinds of change; and these have patterns—with dimensions of direction, magnitude, pace and duration that can be seen and measured." [These are similar to amplitude, frequency and direction, the three ways to consider forces introduced in Chapter 3/Part I.] These patterns are recognizable, and "as we come to understand and use change, we will be better prepared for the future, increasingly able to make tomorrow's world the world we want."

Morgan (1988) forwards that *managerial competencies* need to expand to include development of attitudes, values and mindsets that "allow managers to confront, understand, and deal with a wide range of forces within and outside their organizations, as well as in the development of operational skills" (Morgan, 1988, p. xi). The competence mindset includes: developing skills in reading the environment, fracture analysis, and scenario building; approaching the future proactively; recognizing the importance of leadership and vision; viewing people as a key resource and valuing knowledge, creativity; developing corporate cultures that encourage creativity, learning and innovation; replacing organization hierarchies with flatter, decentralized, self-organizing structures; using information technology as a transformative force; developing skills and attitudes to manage complexity; and reshaping the environment through development of contextual competencies. [A good set!]

Mink et al. (1993) offer a comprehensive model for instituting, managing and assessing change, the *Total Transformation Management Process* (TTMP). TTMP is a *human systems approach* to organizational change. It is an integrated process for implementing system-wide change, optimizing the organization's capacity for the exchange of human energy, minimizing constraints caused by structure, processes, policies and technology, and fostering openness and communication within and without the organization.

Tomasko (1993) asks organizations to apply *design logic* to reorganization. This suggests (1) *Resizing*, that is, adjusting the organization to fit the demands of the future; (2) *Reshaping*, that is, designing the basic building blocks and arranging them to have a positive impact on competitive advantage; and (3) *Rethinking* the basics of how to manage the organization. Tomasko asserts that reinforced jobs, horizontal organizations, dual hierarchies and jobs-as-assignments require skillful design. As Erich Fromm wrote at the outset of the Second World War:

> True freedom is not the absence of structure—letting the employees go off and do whatever they want—but rather a clear structure that enables people to work within established boundaries in an autonomous and creative way." (Tomasko, 1993, p. 184)

[This sounds very much like the adage "Good fences make good neighbors."]

Jacobs (1994) promotes a participatory philosophy of enterprise management, *real time strategic change*. The foundation of this approach lies in interactive large group meetings where hundreds (or thousands) can collaborate to co-create the organization's future. When change occurs simultaneously throughout the organization, there is the benefit of leverage and synergy. Three questions form the basis for achieving more informed and, ultimately, more effective change. These are: "Who is involved in developing these broad, whole picture views? What perspectives are included? And how do these views, once integrated, become the basis of information used to support people in making changes?" (Jacobs, 1994, pp. 24-25)

Thompson (1994) says that in order to manage change you must understand the *five life cycle* changes of organizations and how to manage each one most effectively. In Stage 1, the emerging stage, you ask: Is your organization developing resources for growth? Do you have a clear focus and direction for the future? In Stage 2, the expanding stage, you ask: Has your primary goal shifted to return on investment? Are you developing the effective processes and systems needed for growth? In Stage 3, the maturity stage, you ask: Are your key products and services in place? Have you established market position? Are you attracting and holding customers? In Stage 4, the entrenched stage, you ask: Are you innovating? If not, are you stagnating? How can you find new opportunities for creativity? In Stage 5, the complex stage, you ask: What role does diversification play in your growth plans? How can you encourage yourself and your employees to challenge the historic assumptions that may be holding you back? (back flap)

Pasmore (1994) offers the concept of *strategic change* that is not a one-size-fits-all program, but rather a blueprint for a flexible, high performance organization in which people are active participants in managing change both within the organization and in the marketplace. This includes bold new nonlinear organizational models with constant changes in leadership and a fractal organization design. [Fractal means a repeating pattern that appears at every level; for example, in a geometric figure.]

Youngblood (1994) forwards that *Total Process Management* (TPM) provides a single methodology that integrates the best of both Total Quality Management and Business Process Reengineering, providing a *complete* approach to managing organizational change. This means that TPM is both gradual and rapid, analytic and creative, incremental and dramatic, micro and macro, can be wide-spread and used by project teams, and includes both problem solving and reinventing. [Whew! That's asking a lot.] TPM has a seven-part methodology: (1) establish commitment to performance improvement; (2) create performance improvement capability; (3) evaluate the current environment; (4) conduct benchmarking; (5) establish customer-driven stretch goals; (6) brainstorm innovations; and (7) implement innovations (p. 65).

As we continued this shifting glance at change theory, we recognized that there are many collections by various authors. For example, *The Change Management Handbook* (Berger et al., 1994) brings together 30 contributions to change management theory, all focused on the ability to anticipate and respond to both unexpected and foreseeable change. Collections of this nature abound, and will continue to emerge as we enter the 21st century and beyond. While we fully appreciate their contribution to change theory, we have selected to use full-length books on various aspects of change to represent the kaleidoscope of change. See Figure 8-1.

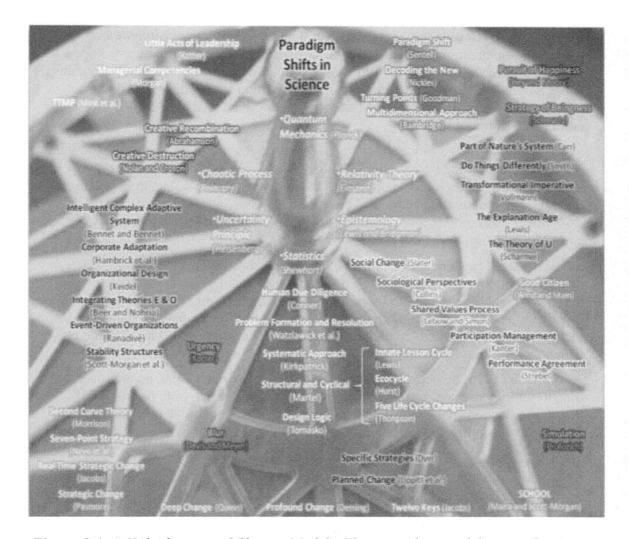

Figure 8-1. *A Kaleidoscope of Change Models. The expanding models are reflective of deeper scientific and epistemological thought.*

   Continuing our representative review, Nolan and Croson (1995) introduce the concept of *creative destruction*, a revolutionary transformation of the organization. Built on a set of 20 management principles for the information economy—concerning aspects of leadership, rewards, organization of tasks, communication, cycle time and value creation—Nolan and Croson provide a six-stage blueprint for transforming from the old to the new. This blueprint includes: downsizing, seeking dynamic balance, developing a market access strategy, becoming customer driven, developing a market foreclosure strategy, and pursuing a global scope.

Keidel (1995) introduces a new theory and language of *organizational design* based on seeing organizational patterns. Keidel explains that organizational issues are a balance of three variables: individual autonomy, hierarchical control and spontaneous cooperation. When we frame issues as tradeoffs among these three variables, underlying patterns become visible that make intelligent analyses, choices and commitments possible.

Hurst (1995) offers a model of change—the *organizational ecocycle*—to show how organizations become systematically vulnerable to catastrophe. He argues that managers must deliberately create crises through acts of "ethical anarchy" to break open the constraints of success. Renewal, he says, demands the restoration of excitement and emotional commitment to change a performance-focused organization back into a learning organization.

Described as *deep change*, Quinn (1996) forwards that this is the path to self-understanding, which for both individuals and the organization is a key to revitalization. "By finding our own moral core and beginning to see ourselves and our organizations in new and more productive ways … we can transform ourselves from victims to powerful agents of change." (Quinn, 1996, front jacket) The simple power is that of self-knowledge coupled with a willingness to take risks.

Vollmann (1996) presents the *Transformation Imperative* model, an approach to transformation and how to make it happen. An enterprise can only be truly transformed when change programs are deep and fully integrated across the organization. Vollmann (1996, jacket) poses four key questions that must be asked of every transformation initiative:

(1) Is it integrated with the long-term goals of the company?

(2) Is it consistent with the company's culture?

(3) Is it feasible based on available resource—and could they be applied better elsewhere? And (4) Is it desirable for all who must implement it?

Carr (1996) forwards that surprise, chance, and constant change are not unexpected anomalies, but *part of nature's system*. [He could have helped write our first chapter!] As Carr (1996, pp. 2-3) describes, "Evolution has complex, subtle mechanisms that include but extend far beyond the well-known concepts of random mutation and natural selection." He contends that people make choices, and individual actions are intentional, thus the evolution of organizations is ultimately caused by the interaction of intentional human beings. "For organizations, human choice is the vital link between the world of potentials and the world of actuality" (Carr, 1996, p. 8). [See Chapter 25/Part IV on Intention and Chapter 38/Part V on Choice.]

Bainbridge (1996) acknowledges that designing for change requires *upheaval* in many different parts of an organization. He presents a *multidimensional approach* to change, showing how changes in one area can be harnessed to make rapid progress elsewhere. By design, control can be maintained and risk minimized while achieving genuine change. The simple process design is: *Design, Define, Develop, Dismantle and Deploy*. Unexpected obstacles may include: key people moving on, energy fading, projects faltering, takeovers occurring, IT becoming a curse, operational issues taking priority, straying from the path, and paralysis by analysis. The answers are planning and communication. The cruxes of communication are: listen; multiple messages, multiple channels; hearts and minds; don't underestimate the audience; illustrate and interpret; and harness the side effects.

Morrison (1996) introduces the *second curve* theory; that is, anticipating the pace of change, identifying your company's new direction, and knowing when to jump onto the second curve. Morrison says that working the second curve means understanding paradox, living with conflicting goals and technologies, and getting comfortable with new rules and new business methods. As Morrison (1996, p. 3) describes, "Staying put may be a mistake, but jumping too soon to a premature second curve can also get you in trouble. You have to balance the risks and rewards with the pace of change."

Frost (1996) supports change based on a *participatory management* style, what is known as the Scanlon Plan. There are four principles to the plan that bring with them optimal synergistic relationships among employees and management: identity (education), participation (responsibility), equity (accountability) and management competence (commitment), with all of these based on integrity. As Frost (1996, p. 135) concludes, "Changing forever gives us the continuing opportunity to become responsible for making a difference."

Kotter (1996) says that *little acts of leadership* are a force for change. He sees leadership, orchestrated by people with profound insight, as a process that creates change. A central aspect of this leadership is direction setting, with alignment following close behind, that is, getting people to understand, accept and line up with the chosen direction. Kotter provides an *action plan for change* and an eight-stage process that every company must go through to achieve its goals. The eight stages are: (1) establish a sense of urgency, (2) create the guiding coalition, (3) develop a vision and strategy, (4) communicate the change vision, (5) empower employees for broad-based action, (6) generate short-term wins, (7) consolidate gains and produce more change, and (8) anchor new approaches into the culture. Mental habits that support lifelong learning include risk taking, humble self-reflection, solicitation of opinions, careful listening and openness to new ideas (p. 183). [That set sounds quite familiar; but then, it is from Kotter!]

<<<<<<<◇>>>>>>>

INSIGHT: A reminder from Kotter: **Little acts of leadership are a force for change.**

<<<<<<<◇>>>>>>>

Nevis et al. (1996) present a *seven-point strategy* for transforming organizations. Inherent in this transformation is the *creation of a new social reality* based on four assumptions: (1) Social or organizational reality is not a given; it is constructed for a given time through the interactions of people creating common, shared understanding. (2) Social reality is created out of the interplay between the external work and the subjective work of participants as they interact to construct a common understanding; truth is the outcome of multiple realities. (3) A new social reality alters in significant and fundamental ways not only how people work but how they experience themselves. (4) The creation of a new social reality is as much a complex process as it is an analytical process; no single influence is powerful enough to transform an organization. Using the vision as a unifying force, there are, however, multiple ways to influence the system. These include: (1) persuasive communication enabling people to envision a different future; (2) participation in creating a shared reality; (3) expectancy: using the power of self-fulfilling prophecy; (4) role modeling to show how it's done; (5) extrinsic rewards to reinforce transformative behaviors; (6) structural rearrangement to shape the work environment; and (7) coercion (using it legitimately). [This is an excellent treatment, which is quite relevant to today's organization.]

Smith (1997) says that to get different results you must *do things differently*. To do things differently you must think differently. And to think differently you must first think about thinking. He says there are seven levels of change: (1) Effectiveness; (2) Efficiency; (3) Improving; (4) Cutting; (5) Adapting; (6) Doing things different; and (7) Doing the impossible. The corresponding mind shifts in thinking are: (1) Effecting thinking; (2) Efficient thinking; (3) Better thinking, Positive thinking; (4) Refocused thinking; (5) Visual thinking; (6) Lateral thinking; and (7) Imaginative thinking. [Yes!]

Maira and Scott-Morgan (1997) offer a balanced, holistic approach to managing change. The approach recognizes the vital importance of intelligent designed structure as well as the capacity of people to learn and respond effectively. It reconciles such polar opposites as reengineering and learning, efficiency and creativity, action and emotion, strategy and implementation and bottom-line results and investment in the future. You manage for: *SCHOOL*, that is, strategic flexibility, change-readiness, hidden leverage, operational alignment, organizational involvement and learning acceleration. The authors contend that an accelerating organization makes them more responsive to fluctuations in their industries and signals from their customers and suppliers, the strongest defense against an unknowable future.

Lebow and Simon (1997) say that increased productivity and profitability come from motivated workers who find their jobs dignified and fulfilling. They present a *Shared Values Process* that is a quantifiable, a test program that combines the ideal with the practical, the human with the pragmatic, and the honorable with the profitable. The eight people values they advocate are: (1) Treat others with uncompromising truth; (2) Lavish trust on your associates; (3) Mentor unselfishly; (4) Be receptive to new ideas regardless of their origin [the approach of Humility presented as a learning and living tool in Chapter 4/Part I]; (5) Take personal risks for the good of the organization; (6) Give credit where it's due; (7) Be honest in all dealings; do not touch dishonest dollars; and (8) Put the interests of others before your own [key to the expansion of consciousness introduced in Chapter 5/Part I]. Their techniques are a way to continuously improve in communication, innovation, enthusiasm, responsibility-taking, empowerment and team play. (Lebow and Simon, 1997, pp. 63-106)

Conner (1998) says that *change is a human imperative*, both unending and increasingly difficult. [We agree.] This whirlwind of change calls for a new kind of organization, nimble enough to instantly adapt to changing markets in a continuing change cycle of disruption, adaptation, expectation, predictability, control and balance. This work is about adapting to change at a moment's notice. Conner introduces the concept of *human due diligence*—focused on the capacity of the individual to absorb change as a limited resource—to orchestrate major enterprise-wide transitions. New learning is at the core of the nimble organization. As introduced in Chapter 5/Part I, Conner (1998, p. 25) says:

> One of the great myths about humans is that repetition results in expertise. Iteration may lead to heightened proficiency, but only if new learning is associated with each interaction. Recurring episodes of change that lack the benefit of new learning produce little more than redundant experiences; no cumulative value is realized.

Strebel (1998) is about building commitment to ongoing change and how this change can be sustained. The first step is offering every employee an economic, social and psychological contract. Strebel (1998, p. xvii) defines a compact as "a *performance agreement* (as reflected in a budget, action plan, performance review, etc.) plus a psychological contract and an employment contract." [One of the authors used this approach to change in regard to a grown son who wanted to pursue a different career. It was quite effective, and he did well with his new choices.] The second step is to orchestrate the renewal of compacts with a process built on the company's change context, that is, one of the four change processes: top-down turnaround, task force change, widespread participation and bottom-up initiatives. The third step is to move toward an employee-driven compact renewal to give employees a sense that they are taking the initiative for change.

Hey and Moore (1998) advocate that personal change *is creating* organizational change. While the caterpillar doesn't know that it must transform to stay alive, this is the imperative confronting American corporations, political institutions and other public and private organizations. Further, this is occurring on top of a social revolution that is transforming the values and actions of all stakeholders. Hey and

Moore use intelligence-gathering methods to document these unprecedented changes. They discovered that Americans are disconnecting from anachronistic institutions and reassessing their goals and seeking new meaning in their lives, which our corporations have failed to provide. Enlightened leaders are responding to this new environment in new ways, supporting the *pursuit of happiness.* [Happiness is a learning point along the path discussed in Chapter 22/Part IV.] Compass points on *this* journey include the enjoyment of simple pleasures, sociability, civility, openness to alternatives and acceptance and inclusion. [A good set.]

Collins (1998) forwards *sociological perspectives* on organizational change. He asserts that any decision about strategy or planning and managing change is based on some theoretical model of organizations and the processes by which these organizations change. Thus, we owe a debt to these theories and models [Conceptual thinking ... see Chapter 26/Part IV.] He goes on to provide a baseline of social theory, noting that there is not one *answer*, but rather an importance to the process that is used to discover the direction ahead. He encourages a shift from top-down to bottom-up views; a shift from focus on consensus to the study of contradiction and complexity; and a shift from managing change to studying organizations and change. [Excellent encouragement!]

Hambrick et al. (1998) capture pragmatic insights on institutional leadership and governance in the face of *profound and continuous change*. As they describe, "Successful corporate transformation requires vigilance, appetite for change, concerted effort and clarity of purpose from three distinct but interconnected parties: the CEO, the top management team and the board of directors" (Hambrick et al., 1998, cover flap). All three of these leadership teams are vital to effective *corporate adaptation.*

Blur (Davis & Meyer, 1998) offers a new change model in response to speed, intangibles and connectivity, the three forces converging on organizations. This is a world where change is constant; *knowledge and imagination are valuable*; products and services are blended as "offers"; transactions become "exchanges"; and physical markets are much like financial markets. *Adaptability* is paramount, and networks provide the framework for that adaptability. [See the discussion on imagining in Chapter 9.]

Sentell (1998) offers that culture can be used as an action tool to shape and sustain higher performance organizations, and calls for a paradigm shift. A paradigm is "a universally accepted model that provides the context for understanding and problem solving/decision making in a particular field" (Sentell, 1998, p. 6). Sentell asserts that *our paradigm of paradigms is in crisis*, and the only solution is a *paradigm shift.* While this paradigm is still emerging, two important characteristics are: (1) a competency culture, a culture open to the truth where people act rationally, focused more on external performance than internal problems; and (2) a change-capable culture, able to respond rapidly to threats and opportunities by spontaneously embracing change. [See Chapter 24/Part IV, Knowledge and the Search for Truth.]

Profozich (1998) forwards that *business process simulation* is one technology emerging as a vehicle by which change can be responsibly and profitably managed. Simulation—which can be used to test system designs before they are built—is a tool used to predict performance and understand the impact of change. He contends that business process simulation is fast becoming a standard with positive return on investment. Implementation begins with developing a schedule followed by model specification (the application you are simulating; required data inputs; types of analyses you intend to perform; and types of information you intend to report). The following steps include: data management, model development (with animation), "what-if" analysis, final project documentation and final recommendations.

In *Champions of Change*, Nadler (1998) offers managers the opportunity to glimpse successful real-world change strategies and explore how top executives drive change. Core principles include: appropriate involvement, committed leadership, valid information, informed choices and integrated change. Sharing and questioning information at all levels is supported, with the best decision emerging from full and open consideration of the widest range of alternatives.

Wind and Main (1998) offer four operating principles that oversee the changes necessary for organizational success, that is, the organization must be *dynamic*, *integrated*, *effective* and *responsible*. *Dynamic* provides the flexibility and adaptability to cope with radical or discontinuous change. The new and the old are asynchronous; thus, the creation of new markets is the only way to stay on the forefront of change. *Integrated* pulls the pieces together in a balanced way to make a transition occur. This means the capability to integrate strategy and architecture, pursuing cost reductions and efficiencies while pursuing growth. This includes a sense of relationships and how things connect to each other, linking activities together as a total system. *Effective* means ensuring you are on the right track and hanging in there long enough to make good ideas work. Good execution is critical. *Responsible* is about treating employees and the rest of society better than it has.

Further, Wind and Main (1998) say that businesses have two personalities. One is unfair, greedy, ruthless, dishonest. The other is trying to be enlightened, responding to a set of urgent pressures from customers, competitors, technology and society. It is smart and innovative, responding intelligently to customers, balancing the needs of stakeholders, coping with globalization, and creating imaginative ways of getting the best out of employees and making a different in the world. As Wind and Main (1998, p. 322) conclude: "The new enterprise needs to be a good citizen." [See the discussion of good character in Chapter 34/Part IV.]

Ranadivé (1999) advocates that the way to rise above creeping commoditization [Can you even pronounce that word?] and gain competitive advantage is through an organization becoming *event-driven*. Event-driven companies are those who acquire, deploy and wisely exploit real-time information, sensing and responding to events in the NOW. A blueprint is provided to turn the enterprise into an integrated organism, sharing critical business information real-time on a global scale. [NOW, the only change we would make is that what we're after is gaining *collaborative advantage*. Competitive advantage is rapidly becoming a war of the past (and this MUST happen for humanity to move forward). But then, this work was published almost two decades ago!]

The New Century

It was about this time that authors began to lament that everything that could be written had been written. Of course, this is never the case. The human mind is incredibly creative, and the more change was explored and focused upon from a wide diversity of directions, the more patterns of thinking and behaviors were identified. A really exciting advancement, of course, came with the advent of sophisticated brain measurement instrumentation such as functional magnetic resonance imaging (fMRI) and transcranial magnetic stimulation (TMS) that occurred around the turn of the century. Now we could not only observe behaviors and measure responses from the outside, but had the ability to look at what was happening from the inside out. All that had emerged in the previous decade came under new scrutiny and led to new understanding. And still, writers wrote, patterns emerged, and new ideas—tinged with new understanding and a wider variety of viewpoints—flooded the landscape. We continue.

Beer and Nohria (2000) contend that there are two leading theories in organizational change: one based on the creation of economic value (Theory E) and the other on building organizational capabilities for the long haul (Theory O). The key lies in integrating them. In organizing a conference based on breaking the code of change, Beer & Nohria (2000) said one of their greatest revelations was discovering the extent to which *both theories and practice of change are rooted in deeply held assumptions and values*. There was a startling degree of emotion displayed; ideological differences that couldn't be resolved by facts alone. While as scientists they espoused the belief that ideology and values have no place in scientific matters, it was necessary to create an open and honest discussion of underlying values in order to develop a higher-order synthesis. This requires *cooperative and collaborative learning* across the many mental, physical and emotional structures that separate our actions, thoughts and feelings. [Yes!] Beer and Nohria (2000, p. 474-5) say that there are three challenges to continuing the quest to break the code of change. These are (1) Finding a way to make explicit, and openly dialogue on the values underlying the different approaches to change; (2) Creating improved learning partnerships among the various actors producing, disseminating and using change knowledge; and (3) Speeding up the process of creating and mobilizing knowledge, because, just as knowledge is context-sensitive and situation dependent, the context of change is a continuously shifting target. [The reality is that valid and usable knowledge is never a sure thing; there will always be the need for discernment and discretion in the context of the user, with the best knowledge available at the point of action.]

With a focus on innovation, Scott-Morgan et al. (2001) suggest *Stability Structures*, which promote growth and innovation while creating an environment of stability. These structures take the form of the pyramid (support incremental innovation following a strategy of slow adaptation), the cube (clustering innovation into short, efficient bursts), the cylinder (with repetitive innovation built into its processes) and the sphere (which develops the maximum number of options then selects the most stable). [What fun!]

Nickles (2001) is an examination of what living in a wired world means to organizational behavior and individual empowerment. There is a new workforce and a new workplace. Nickles (2001, p. 189) says, **"Certain basic rites of passage mark the ebb and flow of life, and the rituals and customs surrounding them have been woven into the fabric of existence from the beginning of recorded humanity."** [Incredibly eloquent, and true.] An indicator of the domino effect of the Internet is its impact on three critical rites of passage: birth, marriage and death. While acknowledging that the Internet is already very much more than e-commerce, encyclopedic information and casual chat room connecting, Nickles says *its most underestimated power is a unique fusion of anonymity and intimacy*. [Brilliant!]

Abrahamson (2004) outlines a new approach to change—*creative recombination*—which includes a series of small-scale, well-paced changes that put existing organizational assets to new uses. This approach calls for *redeploying* people rather than downsizing; *salvaging* processes rather than reengineering them; *recombining* rather than reorganizing organizational structures; *reviving* rather than reinventing core values; and *leveraging* social networks rather than automating. This offers a refreshing alternative to the concept of creative destruction.

Bennet and Bennet (2004) proposed a new model of the firm that enables organizations to react more quickly and fluidly to a fast-changing, dynamic business environment. This is the co-evolving model that is Phase 2 of the Intelligent Social Change Journey. The Intelligent Complex Adaptive System (ICAS), based on research in complexity and neuroscience—and incorporating networking theory and Knowledge Management —turns the living system metaphor into a reality for organization. See Chapter 14/Part III for additional information on the ICAS.

Kotter (2008) says that what's missing in change strategies is a *sense of urgency*. This is "a distinctive attitude and gut-level feeling that lead[s] people to grab opportunities and avoid hazards, to make something important happen today, and constantly shed low-priority activities to move faster and smarter, now" (cover flap). Increasing urgency is the first step of Kotter's eight-step framework articulated in *Leading Change*. However, as we transition to a world where change is continuous and not just episodic, this urgency must become a core, sustained capability. Kotter notes that true urgency is not frantic wheel-spinning; and that its nemesis, complacency, in all its guises, has an insidious nature. Key tactics for increasing urgency and exposing complacency are: bringing the outside in, behaving with urgency *every day*, finding opportunity in crises, and dealing with "NoNos" or naysayers.

Scharmer (2009) introduced the *Theory of U*, what he calls the "social technology of presencing," which forwards that the awareness, attention and consciousness of people in a social system determine the quality of the system. He says that we each have a blind spot that can keep us from being *present*, which is necessary for profound systemic changes. This theory can be considered as a framework, a method and a way of being, all relating to life and profound change, and sets the stage for exploring the Intelligent Social Change Journey.

Makridakis et al. (2009) address the *illusion of control*, which pervades all aspects of our lives. They contend that chance determines a large part of our lives. In self-delusion, we try to control that which cannot be controlled and to predict that which cannot be predicted. However, when we understand the role of chance and luck, we can mitigate the negative impacts by learning when to cede control and when we can gain more control over specific aspects of our lives.

Walsch (2009, p. 2) forwards that change is *what is*, and there is no way to change that ... "What can be changed is the way you deal with change, and the way you're changed by change." He says that everything is in motion and that change is the natural order of things [see Chapter 1/Part I], and what is different is the amount of time it takes to notice the changes that are occurring [see Chapter 13/Part III]. Walsch says that the mind is a tool, a mechanism, and the soul is what provides the fuel for that mechanism. He provides nine changes to empower us, changes that make a Quantum leap in our approach to change, ways of dealing with and creating it. These are (1) change your decision to "go it alone"; (2) change your choice of emotions [see Chapter 19/Part III]; (3) change your choice of thoughts; (4) change your choice of truths [see Chapter 24/Part IV]; (5) change your idea about change itself; (6) change your idea about why change occurs; (7) change your idea about future change; (8) change your idea about life; and (9) change your identity (Walsch, 2009, p. 7). [See Chapter 26/Part IV on the power of thought.]

Lewis (2014) describes the *Innate Lesson Cycle* as a lesson-based learning cycle for change leadership, which follows the storytelling pattern. Using mental model theory, rather than starting with prescriptive steps, Lewis focuses on an underlying description of change based on "workability beliefs" (does, won't, could) and "response modes" (like punctuation: reactive '!', reflective '.', and questioning '?'). These combined mindsets produce the six phases of ADIIEA (pronounced uh-dee-uh): (1) Automation (does work / reactive); (2) Disruption (won't work / reactive); (3) Investigation (won't work / questioning); (4) Ideation (could work / questioning); (5) Expectation (could work / reflective); and (6) Affirmation (does work / reflective). The required action steps are then inferred, within each phase and to lead change to the next phase.

Schwartz (2015) spent many years of his life researching and working with small groups who have made a large difference in the world. He has discovered that these groups have eight characteristics that are common to them all. He says these 8 *Laws of Change for Transformation* have taught him the *Strategy of Beingness*. These 8 Laws pertain to both groups working collectively, and to each individual in those groups. Paraphrasing, these characteristics are: (1) a shared common *intention*; (2) no cherished outcomes (allowing for *synchronicity*); (3) accepting that goals may not be achieved on your watch; (4) accepting that you may not get credit or acknowledgement for this change; (5) ensuring fundamental equality of individuals within an accepted group hierarchy; (6) commitment to non-violence in word, act and thought; (7) authenticity of all participants, with consistent public and private actions; and (8) acting from the Beingness of life-affirming integrity. [This last "law" requires conscious compassion. See Chapter 35/Part V.] In an open house sponsored by the Alliance for Global Consciousness, Schwartz (2017) makes a plea for moving beyond the social damage caused by the focus on profit above all other social order considerations "with little concern for individual, family, community, national, or planetary wellbeing." His plea is addressed to every individual in the world as he forwards that this "will only happen when individuals make a commitment to be an agent of change towards a more compassionate and life-affirming society."

Final Thoughts

The models above are incomplete. There are so many more contributions, some of which have appeared in published books and articles, and some of which have been shared by their originators through formal and informal conversations. One very interesting, missing model, is YOUR model of change. Each of us has a personal theory of change, bringing those sparks from other's thought that make sense to us into our own thought, then integrating things to fit the situation at hand and potential future needs. Hopefully, through this review, some sparks have been added to your personal theory that will make your Intelligent Social Change Journey more interesting and fulfilling.

Questions for Reflection:

Are any of these elements part of your change strategy?

From the list of models above, are there any new ideas that you might bring into your current change methodology?

Can you recognize any patterns as these models move into the new century?

Chapter 9
Modalities of Change

SUBTOPICS: EXPERIENCING, LEARNING AND ENGAGING ... VISIONING ... IMAGINING ... CONCEPTUALIZING ... POSITIVE THINKING ... WEAVING IN DESIRE, DRIVE AND COURAGE

FIGURES: 9-1. COGNITIVE CONVEYORS CAN BE HARNESSED TO SUPPORT BOTH CREATING THE PICTURE OF THE FUTURE AND TAKING THE ACTIONS TO MOVE TOWARD THAT PICTURE ... 9.2. THE INTELLIGENT COMPLEX ADAPTIVE LEARNING SYSTEM EXPERIENTIAL LEARNING MODEL ... 9-3. IN EARLY HUMAN DEVELOPMENT THE EXPERIENTIAL LEARNING LOOP WAS INTERTWINED WITH FEAR DRIVEN BY THE NEED/DESIRE TO SURVIVE.

TOOLS: 9-1. ENGAGING OUTSIDE WORLDVIEWS ... 9-2. PRACTICING MENTAL IMAGINING

Modalities are specific ways of doing things, that is, forms, protocols or conditions that surround theories and methodologies of change, specific ways of thinking, feeling and acting as we move through continuous waves of change in our everyday lives. For example, from the earliest forms of humans we have been in a continuous cycle of experiencing and learning, irrevocably interrelated, and both of which can be considered modalities of change. When considered together, these two modalities resulted in development of Kolb's (1984) behavioral-based experiential learning model. More recently, inclusive of neuroscience findings occurring since the change of the century, the experiential learning model has been expanded to include the mode of social engagement built on a model of interacting with self and co-evolving with our environment (Bennet et al., 2015b). Social engagement, which could also be considered another modality of change, also relates to learning. Experiencing, learning and engaging insinuate movement toward something.

In addition to experiencing, learning and engaging, we suggest visioning, imagining and conceptualizing as additional modalities of change. These modalities insinuate creating a picture of the future, with experiencing, learning and engaging actively moving you toward that picture. Finally, we address positive thinking, which, as we move through this book, we discover is also one of the greatest tools the mind can employ! We become what we think and feel, what we dream and what we focus upon.

Cognitive conveyors weave their way throughout these modalities of change, supporting both development of the picture of the future and the actions necessary to achieve that picture (see Figure 9-1). Cognitive conveyors are a subset of words that represent concepts filled with a combination of thought, emotion and feelings, and while emotional arousal plays an important role in these concepts, affecting mental activity and having a physiological effect on the body, they are not identified as emotions. Specifically, we will briefly discuss the cognitive conveyors of desire, courage and drive in relationship to the modalities of change introduced in this chapter. Cognitive conveyors and cognitive impeders are discussed in more detail in Chapter 19/Part III.

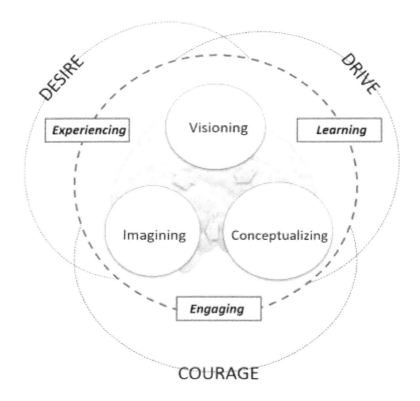

Figure 9-1. *Cognitive conveyors can be harnessed to support both creating the picture of the future and taking the actions to move toward that picture.*

While any serious treatment of these modalities would require books and books, and years and years of dialogue, to even *begin* to uncover the reality of their impact on our personal selfs, or humanity at large, nonetheless we will touch briefly on each of these modalities to bring them to mind for future self-reflection. And perhaps this touching will serve as a reminder that *each of us has choice in how we navigate our ever-changing world.*

Experiencing, Learning and Engaging

Each of these will be considered separately.

Experience consists of the "total response of the learner to a situation or event: what the learner thinks, feels, does or concludes at the time or immediately thereafter" (Boud et al., 1994, p. 18). The *American Heritage Dictionary* (2006) defines experience as an apprehension (ability to understand) of an object, thought, or emotion through the senses or mind; an event, or series of events, participated in or lived through. This describes the relationship between *reflective observation* and *experiential learning*.

Experience is the fundamental way people learn. This discovery process of experience covers much territory, from living in a certain environment to a direct interaction with another person, to a frightening event, to the internal experiences of dreaming, meditation, reading or reflecting on action. All of these are ways that information can come to the attention of the mind, and thereby interact and influence its thoughts and perceptions of the world. Oakshott (1933, p. 9) offers that *experience*, "of all the words in the philosophic vocabulary, is the most difficult to manage." While this is certainly true, individuals can make sense of their experience in many ways, including discussions with friends, collaboration with colleagues, or through communities of practice (Merriam et al., 2007).

Jarvis considers two general situations of experience: *mediated* and *practical*. Mediated experience includes conversations, listening to the media or instruction, lectures, debates, group or team discussions, or reading. Information is communicated primarily through words or pictures (engaging symbols and patterns) and, although there is a direct sense experience between the contributors, it is not a direct experience with the phenomenon itself. Practical experience, on the other hand, is earned knowledge. It occurs when there is a direct, undiluted relationship between the phenomenon and the learner. The signals, patterns, and information from the environment come directly into the learner's embodied senses, thereby initiating bodily sensations that may be perceived by the learner. As Jarvis (2004, p. 92) posits,

> Many writers have focused on experience as a basis for human learning over the years but it has been Kolb's work that has become its popular focus, although one of his main aims was building a theory based on the thinking of those who preceded him.

We will expand on Kolb's work below.

Considering that we all live in and through time, Jarvis also suggests that experience is irrevocably related to learning because learning is the process through which people grow and develop. When adults are actively involved with thinking or action, they are typically unconscious of time (Jarvis, 2004, p. 92). This unawareness of time comes very close to Csikszentmihalyi's detailed research on the autotelic work experience, what he refers to as a flow state (Csikszentmihalyi, 1990). (See Chapter 18/Part III.)

Learning is the creation and application of knowledge, with knowledge considered to be *the capacity (potential or actual) to take effective action* (Bennet and Bennet, 2004), thereby having a direct link to action. Recall from Chapter 2/Part I that knowledge consists of understanding, insights, meaning, intuition, creativity, judgment, and the ability to anticipate the outcome of our actions. Learning and knowledge are two aspects of a continuous cycle as we move through life, with learning enabling the creation of knowledge and applied knowledge (effective action) creating the feedback for continuous learning. Experience is the primary realm for human learning.

From a neuroscience perspective, learning is the identification, selection and mixing of the relevant neural patterns (information) within the learner's mind with the information from an external situation and its environment to create understanding, meaning and anticipation of the outcomes of selected actions (Bennet & Bennet, 2008e). Each learning experience builds on its predecessor by broadening the sources of knowledge creation and the capacity to create knowledge in different ways. When an individual has deep knowledge, more and more of their learning will continuously build up in the unconscious. In other words, in an area of focus, knowledge begets knowledge. The more that is understood, the more that can be created and understood (the more learning that occurs), relegating more to the unconscious in order to free the conscious mind to address the instant at hand. The wider the scope of application and feedback, the greater the potential for patterning (conceptual thinking) and to identify second order patterns (patterns of patterns), which in the largest aggregate leads to the phenomena of Big Data (Mayer-Schönberger & Cukier, 2013).

As the antecedent to all modalities of change, learning is a dynamic process that manifests itself in the continuously changing nature of individuals and organizations, exemplified by innovation, collaboration, culture shifts and personal development. Thus, both the organization and the individuals in the organization are continuously changing. This is not intended as a value statement, rather it is a description of the *natural change process*. Whether change makes an individual or organization better or worse is a value judgment, with values themselves, as knowledge, situation-dependent and context sensitive and therefore subject to change. As Theobald explains, because the pace of change is so great, "it is no longer possible for an individual to get through a full lifetime using the values developed when young … people must constantly re-examine the changing realities that surround them" (Theobald, 1982, p. 162). (Values related to creativity are discussed in Appendix F.)

<<<<<<<◇>>>>>>

INSIGHT: **Learning, an antecedent to all modalities of change, is a dynamic process that manifests itself in the continuously changing nature of individuals and organizations.**

<<<<<<<◇>>>>>>

Experiential learning is the process of acquiring new skills, expertise, attitudes and ways of thinking by doing. We can learn from activities, mistakes, consequences and achievements. Action strengthens retention, the motivation to learn and apply what you learn, *and creativity*. As a working definition, *experiential learning is the creation and application of information and knowledge through experience*, that is, exposure to people and activities and/or active participation in events over time. The experience may be either *primary* (through sense experiences) or *secondary* (mediated experiences) (Jarvis, 2004). These can also be internal experiences in which an individual reflects on or has an internal dialogue with him/her self that leads to deeper knowledge or creative ideas.

Whether we are aware of it or not, *we are engaged in living with all those around us*. As we will consistently bring up in this book as appropriate, we are social creatures who live in an entangled world; our brains are linked together. We are in continuous interaction with those around us, and the brain is continuously changing in response. Over the course of evolution, mechanisms have developed in our brains to enable us to learn through social interactions. We now recognize that an individual cannot evolve or expand without interaction with others. Cozolino (2006, p. 3) suggests that scientists need to understand that neither a single neuron nor an individual human brain exists in nature. "Without mutually stimulating interactions, people and neurons wither and die." The human brain is designed to think socially. For example, think about *your* everyday life and those with whom you interact; we form and reform social groups and relationships every day of our lives.

Mahoney and Restak look at the neuron as a model for corporate success, a design based on networking. "Our identity as social creatures is hardwired into the very structure of our brain ... this pattern of interconnectedness and sociability exists at every level of brain function." (Mahoney & Restak, 1998, p. 42) Similarly, Gazzaniga (2008) feels that, metaphorically, humans are much more of a sociological entity than a single self. The basis of this sociability is the continuous communication occurring among neurons. In 1998 the Nobel Prize in Physiology or Medicine was awarded to three scientists for their work on cell signaling, now described as Redox signaling. Our bodies use this Redox process—the process of exchanging electrons between atoms—to signal and communicate on an atomic level in order to coordinate the defense, repair and replacement of tissue (Naidu, 2013).

Experiential learning requires permeable and porous boundaries in interacting with others and our environment. A powerful form of this learning is through stories. As McWhinney (1997, pp. 227-8) describes,

> We learn from experience when to change tactics, to move from enforcer to persuader, from fantasy to engineering, from doubt to trust, but the deeper and more efficient guidance may come from stories, given by example, read in biography and history, and extracted from myth and epic tales.

The use of story is discussed, and tools provided, in Chapter 17/Part III.

To balance our understanding, there can be significant barriers to deep learning, rethinking assumptions and values that have been taken for granted, and the worldview within which they sit. Our individual mental models—often simplistic, inarticulate and unconscious—interact with complex social dynamics, norms and assumptions. *It seems that we must first embrace an understanding of our self.* As an instructor in a systems and complexity class at a graduate level, one author asked students to do a one-minute learning self-reflection at the end of each class. A student pointed out that in a busy world of acting and responding, self-reflection was a luxury; there was no time for that, so he wasn't sure what to write down. Perhaps reflection has become an act of choice. *Reflection is a necessary part of learning,* whether taking a minute or two after specific experiences or consciously choosing a quiet time or meditation period during the day.

<<<<<<<<>>>>>>>

INSIGHT: **As our individual mental models—often simplistic, inarticulate and unconscious—interact with complex social dynamics, norms and assumptions, it seems that we must first embrace an understanding of our self.**

<<<<<<<<>>>>>>>

The best-known experiential learning model was developed in 1984 by Kolb. Kolb chose to call his model *experiential* learning to tie its intellectual origins to the work of Dewey, Lewin, and Piaget, and to emphasize the strong role of experience in the learning process. Dewey changed historical thinking about education from classical to progressive by bringing the ideas of experience, individuality, and goal attainment into education. Lewin, through his T-groups and group dynamics, highlighted the role of tension between experience and abstract thinking. Piaget discovered the stages of maturation of thinking and the efficacy of tying experience to learning—helping to move learning from information memorization to surface, shallow or deep knowledge. While each of these giants in their field had detractors, the combination of their contributions set the stage for Kolb's detailed analysis of the learning process and the important role of experience within that process.

Putting experience in terms of creating knowledge, Kolb (1984, p. 21) says that, "Knowledge is continuously derived from and tested out in the experiences of the learner." While Kolb differentiates his model from the rationalists and behaviorists, and other cognitive theories of learning, he posits that experiential learning complements both cognitive and behavioral theories. Cognitive theories give heavy emphasis to abstract symbols and their manipulations, and behavioral theories ignore consciousness and subjective experiences in the learning process. Note that at this point in our history, there was no way to understand the workings of the mind/brain from the inside out. It wasn't until the turn of the century that development of sophisticated brain measurement instrumentation enabled a surge in Neuroscience research.

The four adaptive modes of the learning process characterized by Kolb as a cycle are concrete experience, reflective observation, abstract conceptualization, and active experimentation. The Kolb model also contains two distinctive dimensions made up of concrete experience/abstract conceptualization along the vertical axis and active experimentation/reflective observation along the horizontal axis. The learning process derives from the transactions among these four modes and the resolution of the adaptive dialectics between them. Dialectics plays an important role in Kolb's model because each pair of opposite modes is considered to be dialectically related. In his use of the expression *concrete experience*, Kolb intended his approach to be a holistic integrating perspective on learning which considered the combination of experience, perception, cognition, and behavior (Kolb, 1984).

It wasn't until 2002, shortly after the turn-of-the-century explosion of neuroscience research, that Michael Zull, a student of Kolb's, used early learnings from neuroscience to expand the experiential learning model by demonstrating the relationships between the modes of thinking and the physiological sections of the human brain. As Zull (2002, pp. 18-19) says, "Concrete experience comes through the sensory cortex, reflective observation involves the integrative cortex at the back, creating new abstract concepts occurs in the frontal integrative cortex, and active testing involves the motor brain."

As neuroscience research continued to explode, David Bennet, a nuclear physicist and mathematician fascinated with the workings of the mind/brain, went back to school to obtain a Ph.D. (at age 75) in neuroscience and adult learning. As he contends, and using his words:

In this shifting and dynamic environment, life demands accelerated cycles of learning experiences. Fortunately, we as a humanity have begun to look within ourselves to better understand the way our mind/brain operates, the amazing qualities of the body that power our thoughts and feelings, and the reciprocal loops as those thoughts and feelings change our physical structure. **This emerging knowledge begs us to relook and rethink what we know about learning, providing a new starting point to expand toward the future.** [Emphasis added]

In 2015, Bennet published an expanded experiential learning model, the Intelligent Complex Adaptive Learning System, which adds a fifth mode of *social engagement* to Kolb's concrete experience, reflective observation, abstract conceptualization and active experimentation, with these five modes undergirded by the power of self in an ever-shifting environment (Figure 9-2).

Bennet reframes the learning environment, bringing in neuroscience findings in the areas of the unconscious, memory, emotion, stress, creativity, mirror neurons, social interaction, Epigenetics, plasticity, exercise and health, and aging (Bennet et al, 2015b). A significant conclusion is that, should they desire, *adults have much more control over their learning than they may realize.* Much of this work is distributed throughout this book in support of our focus on change.

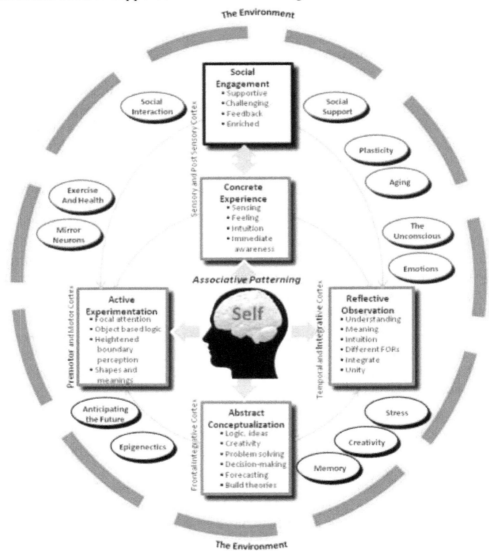

Figure 9-2. *The ICALS experiential learning model.*

Engaging. As a continuous stream of learning, life is meant to be engaged. As introduced above, experience is how we get to know the world, with experience in the NOW quickly linked to our learning from the past and providing meaning. For example, Piaget's (1968) constructivism model of learning was all about *engaged* *learning*, with learning occurring primarily in a social setting among peers. As Conrad and Donaldson (2011, p. 2) explain:

> Piaget believed effective discussions were only possible when there was symmetrical power between the discussants ... because equals were more likely to resolve the contradictions between each other's views than were partners of unequal authority.

The advent of the Internet enabled global engagement. In this setting, everyone becomes a learner and an expert, "with opportunities to seek and share what they know, critique what they learn, and become more engaged and involved with the global community" (Netday and Blackboard, 2006).

The science of sales is a science of engagement that each of us participates in regularly, whether as a seller or as a purchaser. While engagement begins with attention (see Chapter 25/Part IV), engagement moves beyond attention to both getting and *keeping* attention and interest. And, since emotions preempt cognitive thought at the conscious level, and because emotional processing can—and regularly does—take place outside of conscious awareness (LeDoux, 1996), emotions play a large role in engagement. Thus, while engagement is a choice, that choice is largely affected by past experiences, the emotions connected with those past experiences, and the areas of our personal passion.

Visioning

Visioning is a part of all planned change. In the context of a modality of change, we explore visioning as the human capacity to look into the future and perceive a desired state or situation. The human mind is continuously anticipating the outcome of actions. Thus, visioning, when employed by an individual or group of individuals with well-developed mental faculties, would most likely include ideas and processes for achieving that vision.

The future is visioned very much in alignment with Ozbekhan's (1973-4) concept of planning, which establishes a logical future for an organization which can be anticipated by what has occurred in the past and expected environmental changes. (See the discussion of planning in Chapter 16/Part III.) The usefulness of what has occurred in the past is, of course, highly dependent on the needs and wants of the organization and its leadership, and highly reliant on the visioner's experience, education, values, culture, social engagement, recent events and predilections. The property of emergence, holistic characteristics which come along with living in an increasingly complex world and cannot be anticipated, will undoubtedly come into play, perturbing the journey toward that vision. Ozbekhan (1973-4) also noted that there are unexpected and unpredictable events with enough force to change the course of an organization. These events are what makes the future unknowable.

Worldviews, basic sets of beliefs that guide action, play a large role in visioning (Guba, 1990). Hegal suggests that a sign of the mature individual is the ability to hold conflicting world views together at the same time (*Weltanschauungen*) (Stewart, 2000)**, acting and living, and having life enriched by that capability**. This ability to *see the world globally while simultaneously seeing it as a world of unique individuals is critical to the visioning process.*

There are many models for exploring our worldviews. Worldviews, which can also be considered paradigms (Lincoln et al., 2011; Mertens, 2010) or, with a focus on knowledge, epistemologies and ontologies (Crotty, 1998; Malafsky & Newman, 2010), bring with them general philosophical orientations about the world (Creswell, 2014). A simple approach is to perceive a situation from very close up (say 500 feet), from close up (say 1 mile up) and from a distance (say 5 or more miles up). The idea is that the more you can see globally, the less important the small details become and the more of an ecosystem approach or organizational approach rather than an individual or group approach. In Chapter 13/Part III one model for assessing our worldviews in terms of alternative realities (unitary, sensory, mythic and social) is introduced. As another example, and building on Creswell's approach for social sciences research, we will briefly introduce four worldviews described as postpositivist, constructivist, transformative and pragmatic.

The *postpositivist* worldview, or scientific method, challenges the absolute truth of knowledge (Phillips & Burbules, 2000), recognizing that when the behavior and actions of humans are involved there are no absolute claims of knowledge. This worldview is based on a deterministic philosophy where cause and effect are related (Phase 1 of the Intelligent Social Change Journey). Thus, the postpositivist searches out the causes that are influencing outcomes. Taking a reductionist approach, through observation and measurement of an objective reality, the potspositivist seeks to discover a small, discrete set of ideas to test.

The *constructivist* worldview, often called social constructivism, comes from work developed at the Mannheim School of Social Sciences[8-1] and from the work of Berger and Luckmann (1967) in *The Social Construction of Reality* and Lincoln and Guba (1985) in *Naturalistic Inquiry*. Social constructivists look for varied and multiple subjective meanings which emerge from the complexity of views from interactions among and with others (Phase 1I of the Intelligent Social Change Journey).

The *transformative* worldview breaks through structural laws and theories to focus on the lives and experiences of marginalized individuals in society and, specifically, on issues of power, social justice, discrimination and oppression (Neuman, 2009, Fay, 1987; Heron & Reason, 1997; Kemmis & Wilkinson, 1998; Kemmis and McTaggart, 2000; Mertens, 2009, 2010). Building on a theory of beliefs and intertwined with politics and a political change agenda, the transformative worldview supports an action agenda for reform that has the potential to change the lives of the participants and the institutions in which they work and live. Moreover, specific issues need to be addressed that speak to important social issues of the day, issues such as empowerment, inequality, oppression, domination, suppression, and alienation. Transformative research provides a voice for these participants, raising their consciousness or advancing an agenda for change to improve their lives. This worldview represents a united voice for reform and change. (Creswell, 2014, p. 9-10.)

The *pragmatic* worldview looks at actions, situations and consequences with a focus on what works, the discovery of solutions to problems. Morgan (2007), Patton (1990) and Tashakkori and Teddlie (2010) emphasize that it is important to focus on the problem, and then use a diversity of approaches to derive knowledge about the problem. When viewed together, Cherryholmes (1992), Morgan (2007) and Creswell (2014) provide a philosophical basis for the pragmatic worldview that is not committed to any specific system of philosophy and reality. Believing in an external world independent of the mind as well as that lodged in the mind, pragmatists do not see the world as an absolute unity, but rather believe that truth is what works at the time, and that there is freedom of choice (Creswell, 2014).

These four worldviews are highly consistent with the diversity of approaches to co-creating our reality detailed in Chapter 23/Part IV.

****

TOOL 9-1: Engaging Outside Worldviews

This is a process to bring about third-order change (see the Introduction to the ISCJ), which requires giving up well-formed boundaries and beliefs. It can be achieved in two ways: through vesseling and managing the process.

FIRST, *vesseling* provides a psychological setting for people to explore their concepts of reality. This is done by using stories and myths related to the space of realities, enabling participants to step back from assumed realities to *make room* for choosing new worldviews.

SECOND, *managing* the process involves persistent commitment, managing communication, and guiding others to select and provide resources for the modes of change emerging along the path to resolution (McWhinney, 1997). Those modes, of course, include learning and experiential exercises related to differing ways of perceiving events that are occurring. One approach is to engage graphics and pictures for the exploration of ideas. An example of this is provided in Chapter 11 in the discussion of Conversations that Matter.

AN EXAMPLE: When employees who had received high performance evaluations at the *Branch* level were not the recipients of special awards at the

Organizational level, there was anger and an outbreak of "favoritism" gossip. A story was created that related to an art competition with four levels: local, state-wide, regional and national. In each of a diversity of categories, blue-ribbon winners at each level were invited to compete at the next highest level, that is, winners at the local level competed at the state level; winners at the state level competed at the regional level; and winners at the regional level competed at the national level. While there were increasing rewards associated with both participating in and winning the various levels, and a great deal of learning in the experience, the national winners received the highest awards and rewards. In this example, a series of meetings was held at the branch level with leadership and Human Resources people attending. This story was first presented, and then an open discussion encouraged regarding the circumstances of the story and taking place in the context of the story.

Ultimately, the growth of understanding and recognition of choice can move participants closer to intelligent activity. See McWhinney, 1997, for detailed application on using story and myth to engage outside worldviews.

.*************

In the organizational context—which can be extrapolated to a global context—this becomes a shared visioning process built on *unity and shared purpose*. Unity and shared purpose represent the ability of an organization to integrate and mobilize its resources to (1) provide a continuous line of focus and attention and (2) pull together the relevant parts of the organization when and where they are needed to co-evolve with the environment. Senge (1990) emphasizes the importance of a shared vision where employees participate in the development of a corporate vision, and can then make decisions and take actions consistent with the direction set by senior leadership. One can hardly disagree with this so long as the environment is reasonably stable and the vision does not change frequently. However, in our current world and continuing into the future, we can expect more changes within every organization that operates close to the field where knowledge and information are the prime movers. Under these conditions, structures and relationships must be established that support and ensure continuous, rapid two-way feedback between key components throughout the organization.

As a model, let's look at Edelman and Tononi's description of the mechanism that provides unity to consciousness, thereby creating a continuous history of thought and a consistency of identity and action:

> Our analysis leads to several conclusions: First, conscious experience appears to be associated with neural activity that is distributed simultaneously across neuronal groups in many different regions of the brain. Consciousness is therefore not the prerogative of any one brain area; instead, its neural substrates are widely dispersed throughout the so-called thalamocortical system and associated regions. Second, to support conscious experience, a large number of groups of neurons

must interact rapidly and reciprocally through the process called reentry. If these reentrant interactions are blocked, entire sectors of consciousness disappear, and consciousness itself may shrink or split. Finally, we show that the activity patterns of the groups of neurons that support conscious experience must be constantly changing and sufficiently differentiated from one another. If a large number of neurons in the brain start firing in the same way, reducing the diversity of the brain's neuronal repertoires, as is the case in deep sleep and epilepsy, consciousness disappears. (Edelman and Tononi, 2000, p. 36)

Recognize that the brain has roughly 100 billion neurons, each with an average of 1000 connections to other neurons. Information is stored in the connections between neurons and in patterns of connecting neurons, which change continuously, dependent on external sensory inputs and other internal pattern inputs. It is also known that different regions of the brain process different parts of a visual image and that all of the outputs of these processes are combined to make the image a unitary whole so that the perceiver "sees" a self-consistent integrated picture. This ability to maintain different parts of the brain in harmony and to pull them together is exactly the challenge of the future organization, where the external environmental complexity continually impinges on many parts of the firm and may not in itself have coherence or consistency. Evolution's solution to these "binding problems" is to create certain neuron paths that provide continuous two-way communication between key operating networks (Edelman & Tononi,2000). This is what we attempt to do in organizations today with social media and various structural shifts such as the use of teams and communities of practice.

This binding problems is also applicable to our globally-developing humanity. Given a common frame of reference, cooperatively and collaboratively engaging in visioning with global partners is one process that can help. As an after note, holding the vision of what is possible often requires being blind to its improbability. As McWhinney (1997, p. 226) describes,

Consciousness would create a cosmic hell for humanity had we not also been given courage to blind our consciousness in the service of action. To act, **we must reduce our awareness of possibility** [emphasis added]—to go blind to those questions that would inhibit action, to the fear of losing opportunity.

Indeed, courage, a cognitive conveyer, intertwines throughout all the modalities of learning.

Imagining

As intelligent complex adaptive systems, we bring to bear all that it is to be human— our entangled matrix of thoughts, feelings and experiences emerging within and without throughout life—in figuring out and imposing order on the world around us. In an environment of probability, randomness and chaos, is it there or do we artificially impose it? The answer is *Yes*. Are the forces we perceive real or imaginary? *Yes*. Any thought that is perceived, focused and felt, is "real" and—in terms of the perceiving, focusing and feeling—is affecting the self and, consciously or unconsciously, the decisions and actions the self is making and taking.

<<<<<<<<>>>>>>>>

INSIGHT: **Any thought that is perceived, focused and felt is "real"; and, in terms of the perceiving focusing and feeling, is affecting the self and the decisions and actions the self is making and taking.**

<<<<<<<<>>>>>>>>

Gell-Mann (1994) says that we impose artificial order based on false principles of causation, comforting ourselves with the illusion of mastery. "We fantasize that we can manipulate the world around us by appealing to the imaginary forces we have invented" (p. 276). He says that myths, magic and superstition are examples. Yet, it is just those creative imaginings that enabled Einstein to discover relativity, and it is those creative imaginings that have punctuated the spiral of history with sparks of light that opened up new thought. Our beliefs in myth and magic are "part of the grand search for pattern, for creative association, that includes artistic work and that enriches human life" (Gell-Mann, 1994, p. 279).

Along with many of our beliefs, much of our creative imagining occurs in the unconscious realms; as we know, many things the brain does are not available to consciousness. LeDoux (2002, p. 11) offers,

> [This includes] almost everything the brain does, from standard body maintenance like regulating heart rate, breathing rhythms, stomach contractions, and posture to controlling many aspects of seeing, smelling, behaving, feeling, speaking, thinking, evaluating, judging, **believing and imagining**.

However, once the imaginings of our mind move through our conscious stream of thought, there is a choice to accept or reject, believe or not believe, value or devalue, or just flow with those imaginings. MacFlouer (2004-16) notes that when creative imagination is disconnected from the mental faculties, the emergent moving pictures of our mind are unstructured and often conflictive with one another. When these conflicts prevent thought from becoming a functional form, they are considered fantasy. Conversely, creative imagination can also represent actual, or potentially actual, occurrences based upon the situation and context of an event or series of events. Thus, there are two parts of creative imagination: one that is unactionable, yet may provide ideas for future actions, and one that is actionable in the situation and context at hand.

In looking at long-term sustainability and trying to envision that future, Gell-Mann (1997, p. 364) feels that it is vital to make concrete images of the world that is envisioned.

Only then can our imagination escape from the confines of the practices and attitudes that are now causing or threatening to cause so much trouble, and invent improved ways to manage our relations with one another and with the rest of the biosphere.

In fact, Gell-Mann (1997, p. 364) calls for a special team of *imaginative challengers* to keep posing the question: "[W]hat kinds of surprises, technological or psychological or social, could make that fairly distant future totally different from what we might anticipate today?" This requires collective foresight, that is, an understanding of potential branching histories of the future. For example, interlinked transitions to greater sustainability is a major step for humanity toward planetary consciousness. And, after the transitions, as Gell-Mann (1997, p. 366) notes, "Humanity as a whole—together with the other organisms inhabiting the planet— would function, much more than now, as a composite, richly diverse complex adaptive system."

****

TOOL 9-2: PRACTICING MENTAL IMAGINING

In 1970, long before we learned much about the inner workings of our mind/brain, M.R. Kopmeyer, the owner of a publishing company in Louisville, Kentucky, wrote in the Dedication of his book: "May your thoughts be stimulating and our results rewarding ... because your THOUGHTS will determine what you ARE."

Kopmeyer said that, based on the soundest of psychological and physiological principles, the only way to really become an expert—in almost any endeavor—is to practice intensively in your *imagination*. For example, a person cannot possibly think of all that needs to be done in golf to make a perfect drive, stroke or putt while actually doing them. Nor can a person consciously move their hands and fingers when playing the piano or keyboarding. The point is that the conscious mind cannot *think* that rapidly; but the unconscious mind can.

The way you do this, Kopmeyer informs, is to ...

STEP (1): First, physically do the thing you are practicing, and then

STEP (2): Practice each movement over and over again in your *imagination,* impressing *mental pictures* into the unconscious mind.

As Kopmeyer describes:

... relax in an easy chair in a quiet room away from all distractions ... Then you, mentally, take each perfect movement at a time and consciously visualize your performing that movement to perfection. Over and over again ... Practice does not 'make perfect,' as the old saying used to tell us. Only practice of *perfection* makes perfect. And until you become a real expert, you can only *practice perfection* in your *imagination*. (Kopmeyer, 1970, p. 68)

NOTE: As we learn more about our mind/brain, we now refer to the phenomena behind Practicing Mental Imagining as mirror neurons, a form of cognitive mimicry that transfers actions, behaviors and most likely other cultural norms (Zull, 2002). As Blakemore and Frith (2005, pp. 160-161) describe,

Simply observing someone moving activates similar brain areas to those activated by producing movements oneself. The brain's *motor regions* become active by the mere observation of movements even if the observer remains completely still.

Thus, when we *see* something being enacted, our mind creates the same patterns that we would use to enact that "something" ourselves. Mirror neurons link our perception to the priming of the motor systems that engage the same action. In other words, "what we see, we become ready to do, to mirror other's actions and our own behaviors" (Siegel, 2007, p. 347).

Kopmeyer had it right. Neurons scattered through key parts of the brain fire—not only when we are performing a certain action, but when we are watching someone else perform that action (Dobbs, 2007), and imagining that *perfect* action over and over again as movies in our brain.

****

Conceptualizing

At the beginning of the introduction to their book, *Philosophy in the Flesh*, Lakoff and Johnson (1999, p. 3) offer the following: "The mind is inherently embodied. Thought is mostly unconscious. Abstract concepts are largely metaphorical. And these are three major findings of cognitive science." Further, they say that, "All of our knowledge and beliefs are framed in terms of a conceptual system that resides mostly in the cognitive unconscious" (p. 13).

Chris Argyris, an American business theorist, says that a step toward breaking the code of change is to "create knowledge that can be used to create transformational, non-routine, *double-loop changes* [emphasis added] in individuals, groups, intergroups, and organizations" (Argyris, 2000, p. 427). He refers to a theory of action, using theories that are applicable to many cases as well as the situation a hand. This is the realm of pattern recognition and the development of conceptual thinking, that is, *recognizing the relationships among types of things and the patterns of response and change because of those relationships*. For example, adoption of a practice that was considered a "best practice" in another organization, does not mean the same change will occur when applied in another organization. Understanding the pattern allows *the transfer of the pattern and understanding of that success*.

Remember, knowledge is fragmented and piece-meal, partial and incomplete, context-sensitive and situation dependent, and ever changing. It is the thinker who is using the knowledge that makes the difference. (Conceptual thinking is expanded in Chapter 26/Part IV.)

In working with PhD students on research design, the starting point is generally identification of an issue, problem, or challenge within a domain of focus in the current reality. As this is put into words, a conceptual model begins to emerge, from which viewpoint the student searches for current theory to help explain this phenomenon, then reaches out to other systems within the domain of focus to explore their related experiences. Van de Ven (2000) views this as a baseball diamond, with the solution at home base, and the theory, conceptual model and reality represented as 1st, 2nd and 3rd bases, respectively. The 1st base line represents research design and conduct, the 2nd base line represents theory building, the 3rd base line represents problem formulation, and the 4th base line represents problem solving. While arguing that all the bases must be covered to hit a home run, Van de Ven (2000, p. 399) notes that research can begin from any base, "to begin from different starting conditions and preferences and to apply different methods and styles of inquiry." And so it is with change, which can begin from any of the bases, yet in order to hit a home run requires running all the bases, a basic change in our level of thinking and acting.

Positive Thinking

The generation born close to the beginning of the 1900's lived through two world wars with unthinkable atrocities. Little wonder that in 1952 the world welcomed *The Power of Positive Thinking* published by American minister Norman Vincent Peale (1952). Of course, as occurs when new thinking based on experience is widely publicized, this book came under immediate attack by critics. There were two primary reasons: (1) what Peale wrote offered many anecdotes that were unsubstantiated, and (2) it was likened to hypnosis, with the underlying theme of convincing people of his personal beliefs. This is not surprising since Peale, as a minister, had great passion for improving the lives of others! From the viewpoint of neuroscience findings emerging as we entered the 21st century, and what would have been difficult to scientifically prove in the 1950's, there is, indeed, substantial power in positive thinking. As Bennet says, "What we believe leads to what we think leads to our knowledge base, which leads to our actions, which determines success" (Bennet et al., 2015b). Further, what we think and believe impacts our physical bodies. The bottom line is, as Lipton (2005) sums up, "The belief that we are frail, chemical machines controlled by genes is giving way to an understanding that we are powerful creators of our lives and the world in which we live" (p. 17).

<<<<<<<<>>>>>>>>

INSIGHT: **When reflecting on experiences, the power of positive thinking amplifies learning and changes mindsets from seeing problems to creating opportunities.**

<<<<<<<<>>>>>>>>

More recent related movements, which bring positive thinking into the business world, are Appreciative Inquiry (AI) and Positive Organizational Behavior (POB). AI was named in 1990 by David Cooperrider and his colleagues who were studying at the Weatherhead Graduate School of Management at Case Western Reserve University. In its original form, Cooperrider considered AI a mode of action research, which embraces the uniqueness of the appreciative mode. It is much more.

Traditional organizational interventions identify problems and hunt for solutions; the AI approach locates and tries to understand that which is working, learning from it and amplifying it, using it as a complement to other interventions, or, perhaps, offering a way other interventions can be approached. AI is based on the simple premise that organizations (teams, communities, countries) grow in the direction of what they are repeatedly asked questions about and therefore focus their attention upon (Srivastva & Cooperrider, 1990). (See the discussion of attention in Chapter 25/Part IV for confirming neuroscience findings.) The four principles Srivastva and Cooperrider lay down for AI are that action research should begin with appreciation, should be applicable, should be provocative, and should be collaborative.

Since its inception in 1990, AI has become a meme, that is, it has taken on a life of its own, being used as a strategic change approach and in support of knowledge sharing. The principles of AI can also be translated into assumptions, the rules that a group follows when making decisions about behavior or performance (Argyris, 1993). For example, Hammond and Hall (1996, pp. 2-3) translate the principles of AI into the following assumptions:

1. In every society, organization, or group [and within every individual] something works.

2. **What we focus on becomes our reality.**

3. **Reality is created in the moment** and there are multiple realities.

4. **The act of asking questions of an organization or group [or individual] influences the group [or individual] in some way.**

5. People have more confidence and comfort to journey into the future (the unknown) when they carry forward parts of the past (the known).

6. If we carry parts of the past forward, they should be what is *best* about the past.

7. It is important to value differences.

8. **The language we use creates our reality.**

This is a good set of assumptions, and their related actions, to use as we engage in the Conversations that Matter discussed in Chapter 11 on Assessing Readiness for Change.

We find that this set of assumptions, published in 1996, is based on a behavioral model, and was created *prior* to development of mind/brain measurement capabilities. Consider assumptions 2, 3, 4 and 8 referring to focusing, asking questions and the language we use. We now know from an understanding of mind/brain plasticity that thoughts change the structure of the brain, and the brain structure influences the creation of new thoughts (Bennet & Bennet, 2015b). This emphasizes the power of questions not only to trigger thought, but to actually help shape our brains. As the focus in organizations and communities has moved back to people and the knowledge they create, share and use, the empowering aspects of the AI approach can help build self-confidence in—and receptivity to—new ideas, and accelerate behavioral change. Similar to the energy of gratitude, the energy of appreciation is near the 350 (Acceptance) level of consciousness. (See Chapter 5/Part I.) This level is well into Phase 2 of the Intelligent Social Change Journey.

Similarly, from a psychological viewpoint, Positive Organizational Behavior (POB) is defined as "the study and application of positively oriented human resource strengths and psychological capacities that can be measured, developed, and effectively managed for performance improvement in today's workplace" (Luthans, 2002, p. 59). POB forwards that by focusing on positive self-development, organizations can inspire employees and boost organizational performance (Bakker & Schaufelli, 2008; Wright & Quick, 2009). Thus, the individual's positive psychological condition is highly valued in POB (Luthans & Avolio, 2009), with positive psychological capital as a core construct. This construct is concerned with the developmental state of an individual in terms of self-efficacy, optimism, hope and resiliency (Luthans & Youssef, 2004). (Self efficacy is addressed in Chapter 13/Part III; resiliency is discussed in Chapter 14/Part III.)

A popular and inspirational, short-length video weaving its way through organizations world-wide is entitled *Celebrate What's Right with the World*. Dewitt Jones, the host and a former *National Geographic* photographer, shares the direction that came with every assignment. You've guessed it. That direction was: "Go out and celebrate what's right with the world." Thus, began his life-long journey of looking for possibilities, with the change curve that can be accompanied by fear of the unknown becoming a *possibility curve* propelled by curiosity and wonder. He looked and he found, and through his photographs, Jones shared these possibilities with the world. Key concepts in this video are linked to both the AI and POB approaches, simple words accompanied by inspirational photographs and film clips. These concepts include: "Believe it and you'll see it," "Recognize abundance," "Look for possibilities," "Ride the Changes," and "Be your best for the world" (Jones, nd).

The benefits of positive thought to you are immeasurable. The power of thought is reiterated throughout this text and supported by neuroscience findings. As is so succinctly expressed in the January 06, 2017, daily quote from Abraham-Hicks Publications, the bottom line is:

> The more good-feeling thoughts you focus upon, the more you allow the cells of your body to thrive. You will notice a marked improvement in clarity, agility, stamina, and vigor, for you are literally breathing your way to Well-Being, until chronic feelings of appreciation, love, eagerness, and joy will confirm that you have released all resistance and are now allowing Well-Being.

Weaving in Desire, Courage and Drive

Desire, courage and drive represent different combinations of emotional and mental activity called cognitive conveyors, a subset of words that represent concepts filled with a combination of thought, emotion and feelings. The mental activity of "wonder" in the previous paragraph would also fit into this set. While emotional arousal plays an important role in these concepts, affecting mental activity and having a physiological effect on the body, they are not identified as emotions (see Chapter 19/Part III).

Cognitive conveyors weave their way throughout the modalities of change. For example, experiential learning covers much territory from living in a certain environment to a direct interaction with another person, to a frightening event, to the internal experiences of dreaming, meditation, reading or reflection on action. In early human development, this experiential learning loop was intertwined with fear driven by the need/**desire** to survive. Learning from personal experience or the experiences of others would promote change in behavior. While survival today is rarely a matter of being eaten by a tiger, nonetheless fear and desire often remain in the learning loop related to financial success, saving face, bullying, personal desires and selfishness, and even an arrogance of personal entitlement. See Figure 9-3.

We will briefly focus on desire, courage and drive as cognitive conveyors.

Desire. As used here, desire is the expression of a feeling, to want or wish for something (Merriam-Webster,2016). As such, it is closely related to intention (see 25/Part IV). Desire is a sustaining life force, indeed, an animating, *continuously expanding* life force which is unstoppable as long as we live and breathe. Of desire, Bertrand Russell (1950) says: "Desire is a subject upon which ... true views can only be arrived at by an almost complete reversal of the ordinary unreflecting opinion."

What he means is that desire is occurring without our conscious awareness, a bedfellow driving our thoughts and actions.

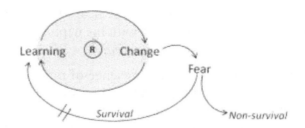

Figure 9-3. *In early human development, the experiential learning loop was intertwined with fear driven by the need/desire to survive. (Recall from Chapter 4/Part I that the personality is charged with keeping us alive, experiencing pleasure, protecting us, avoiding pain, and eliminating fear.)*

Desires can be rational or non-rational. Irvine (2006, p. 11) says that,

> ... many of our most profound, life-affecting desires are not rational, in the sense that we don't use rational thought processes to form them. Indeed, we don't form them; they form themselves within us. They simply pop into our heads, uninvited and unannounced. While they reside there, they take control of our lives. A single rogue desire can trample the plans we had for our lives and thereby alter our destinies.

An example that many people are familiar with is falling in love.

An interesting aspect of desires is that they can change with time as one desire replaces another. This makes sense as we understand ourselves as verbs, forever experiencing and growing and expanding. Further, as we understand that we are social creatures, our desires often flow with what is currently popular or what we perceive will help others admire or respect us, or separate us above the crowd.

People are often caught up in their desires for physical possessions. Though we are all materialists to some extent since that is the world within which we interact, when the desire for material goods becomes primary, energy is focused inwards, not only limiting learning but limiting creativity and reducing consciousness. Materialism is discussed in more length in Chapter 10.

Courage. To be involved in change means dealing with the unknown at some level, and the unknown is the foremost object of human fear. Courage is about choices made and actions taken in an uncertain environment, the courage to think and act. This does *not* mean there is a lack of fear. As psychologist Rollo May says, "Courage is not the absence of despair; it is, rather, the capacity to move ahead *in spite of despair*" (May, 1975). In the latest *Green Lantern* movie (Warner Brothers, 2011), our hero is a test pilot. Following a near fatality, the hero's young nephew asks, "Were you afraid?" The hero's answer is a response heard earlier in the movie from his father, "It's my business not to be." He sits with his nephew and explains that while fear is always close at hand, *courage is a choice.*

Mulford (1989-2007) says that courage and presence of mind have the same meaning, with presence of mind implying command of mind. Conversely, cowardice, or lack of mental control, is rooted in the habit of hurry, a lack of repose. Underlying this hurried mental condition and the acts it promotes is *fear, another word for lack of power to control our minds.* Mental or physical courage determine the degree of success; and the degree of failure is based on timidity, or fear. Further, because fear can become a habit of mind, built up over time, it can become a conditioned response emerging from the unconscious, setting off small and large panic attacks from the smallest emotional perturbation. Living in a continuous environment of the unknown, it is easy to perceive how this could occur.

Opportunities—and change itself—involve risk, often including the letting go of old habits and ways of thinking. (Letting go is addressed in Chapter 20/Part III.) For the human mind focused on the past, the concept of risk brings to mind trials and tribulations resulting from similar situations or circumstances, often events perceived out of your personal control. For the human mind focused on the NOW, the instant at hand, risk may involve the unknown dangers of change, or even the risk of NOT taking action or NOT exploring an opportunity. For the human mind focused on the future, there is the risk of mis-anticipation or false prediction, the risk of fantasy versus factual creative imagination, or the risk of under-resourcing, that is, carrying too much baggage from the past and present to attend to the future.

Courage is required at all levels of change, from the recognition of choice (and responsibility) to understanding the context, and to taking action in a complex situation. There is a paradox here. In order to act, we must be fully committed to a reality while simultaneously recognizing there is uncertainty in that reality. As Rollo May (1975, p. 13) describes, "Courage is not a virtue or value among other personal values like love or fidelity. It is the foundation that underlies and gives reality to all other virtue and personal values." The more recognition of choice, the greater the courage required to act. This is why soldiers and emergency response personnel are trained to act unconsciously, that is, when they do not need to consciously consider alternatives and choice, when the required response to specific situations has been embedded in their unconscious, the less courage is required to act. However, as Admiral Hyman Rickover recognized, "Good ideas are not adopted automatically. They must be driven into practice with courageous patience" (Bennis & Nanus, 1985). This model of making decisions in an environment of uncertainty is an unseeing behavior can be labeled as *satisficing* (Simon, 1947). **Moral courage**

requires a higher level of courage. Moral courage is a perceptual courage (May, 1975), highly dependent on an individual's ability to perceive through the eyes of another.

The good news is that courage can be cultivated and increased at any time through deliberation. As Mulford, (1989-2007, p. 36) says:

> You can have the satisfaction of knowing that in everything you do you have accomplished two things—namely the doing of the thing itself and by the manner of its doing, adding eternally to yourself another atom of the quality of courage. You can do this by the cultivation of deliberation—deliberation of speech, of walking, of writing, of eating—deliberation in everything.

Deliberation and deliberate action deals largely with the little acts of life, sending our thought and subsequent actions in the same direction. Our conscious mind is linear, connecting one thought to the next (as is Phase 1 of the Intelligent Social Change Journey), and in acting we take one step at a time, a single transaction at a time. Thus, in the material world in which we live, we can deliberately deal with one force at a time, and through repeated deliberation and deliberate action create this behavior pattern as a habit, learning to keep our mind present with us at all times.

When an individual is deliberate, the mind is trained to take the time to think and concentrate on that thought, providing time to explore opportunities presented by the situation at hand. We have learned from neuroscience the power of mirror neurons, that, under certain circumstances, anything done in the mind has the same pattern of neuronal firings and as much force as if done with the body. "To train then for courage is to train for deliberate movement in all things, for that is simply training to mass and hold your force in reserve and let out no more than is needed for the moment ... No quality of mind is more needful to success in all undertakings than courage." (Mulford, 1989-2007, p. 41)

Drive. "Drive" is to move toward or through something with mental or physical force, to cause something to happen. While it is often urged forward by our desires, it can also become an automated process or an unconscious emergent force, sometimes beyond our control.

The drive we focus on here is a *choice* connected to desire. Every individual has energy levels that vary with physical health, interest, experiences, age, and so forth. How we focus this energy and the level of energy focused in a particular direction can be a choice. For example, if we get joy out of learning, we can choose to put ourselves in learning situations ranging from the classroom to dialogues with respected and knowledgeable others. In this example, the concept of "drive" would insinuate that we had a goal to achieve and would continue that learning until the goal was achieved.

Note that the same concept can act as a cognitive conveyor or a cognitive impeder. Drive is a good example of that. There is no doubt that the way we have described drive above is a cognitive conveyor, accelerating movement toward a defined goal. However, drive could also very much get in the way, that is, it might be so strong that an individual fails to take the necessary time to think through actions. In this case, drive would serve as a cognitive impeder.

While this was a very brief treatment of desire, courage and drive, it can be seen that these cognitive conveyors strongly affect our thoughts and actions and weave in and out of the changing dramas of our lives. By understanding their importance and impact—which also applies to other cognitive conveyors and impeders—we can consciously harness their energy to bring about the change we choose.

Questions for Reflection:

What are some examples of experiences from which you have learned?

Are there experiences from which you could have learned more?

Are you able to engage the power of positive thinking in your everyday life?

How do you practice mental imaging in your organization?

Other than desire, courage and drive, what other cognitive conveyors have you experienced?

Chapter 10
Grounding Change

SUBTOPICS: HIERARCHY AS A GROUNDING STRUCTURE ... GROUNDING THROUGH RELATIONSHIPS ... GROUNDING THROUGH IDEAS ... GROUNDING THROUGH BELIEFS AND FAITH ... FINAL THOUGHTS

TABLE: 10-1. COMPARISON OF THE INTELLIGENT SOCIAL CHANGE JOURNEY PHASES WITH THE STAGES OF FAITH DEVELOPMENT, STAGES OF MORAL DEVELOPMENT AND LEVELS OF CONSCIOUSNESS.

FIGURES: 10-1. THREE INTERPRETATIONS OF THE CONCEPT OF GROUNDING. 10-2. THE MOVEMENT FROM A FOCUS ON VALUE BUILT ON TRUST AND RESPECT OF PEOPLE TO VALUE BUILT ON THE RELATIONSHIPS OF, RESPECT FOR AND RESONANCE WITH IDEAS ... 10-3. (LEFT) A NOMINAL GRAPH ILLUSTRATING THE HISTORICAL (2000) LEVELS OF KNOWLEDGE USED IN AN ORGANIZATION ON ANY GIVEN DAY. (RIGHT) A NOMINAL GRAPH ILLUSTRATING THE 2016 LEVELS USED IN AN ORGANIZATION ON ANY GIVEN DAY.

TOOLS: 10-1. GROUNDING THROUGH NATURE ... 10-2. RELATIONSHIP NETWORK MANAGEMENT

Change is easier for humans, and occurs more fluidly, when we are grounded. Grounded people have a strong sense of purpose and characterize higher orders of the Intelligent Social Change Journey. Grounding has to do with feeling connected and secure, providing a baseline or foundation, keeping us balanced as we move through life, and has very much to do with our worldview. Grounding can occur physically, mentally, emotionally or spiritually, and comes in all flavors, dependent on the individual's hierarchy of needs. For example, for those who grew up during a societal depression, material possessions or continuously ingesting large meals may be part of their security structure.

As used here, there are **three interpretations of the concept of grounding** that will guide our conversation. First, to ground is to give someone a foundation, to teach someone the basics. Second, to ground is to fix something on or in something else for a foundation. Third, to ground is to connect with the Earth, the ground (Encarta, 1999). All three of these interpretations carries with it, to a different degree, the idea of attachment, connecting something to something else. See Figure 10-1.

In the first context, each individual is born into a family, an environment, a religion, a culture from which emerge their first learnings. As poet Cindy Scott (2016) so eloquently writes:

You become grounded when you are born and cradled against your mother's breast. You become grounded when your caregiver, someone who loves you, reaches down when you fall, and lifts you up. You become grounded when you fall in love, and hold hands through the trials of life. You become grounded when you choose a family, and they choose you and become the center of your world. And you become grounded when you find your inner self, and discover you are part of something larger.

Grounding has very much to do with our personal identity. Identity in this context is considered the essential self, the set of characteristics recognized as belonging uniquely to an individual.

Figure 10-1. *Three interpretations of the concept of grounding.*

In our physical, mental, emotional and spiritual bodies, each of us has at our core a pivot point, a fulcrum, around which everything else revolves and upon which other parts of us depend. For example, in our physical body it may be our strength, agility, and/or excellent metabolism. Mentally it may be our ability to see connections and patterns among disparate things. Emotionally it may be our compassion. Spiritually it may be our belief in service to others demonstrated by our actions. These pivot points serve as our ground for other activities, which may find expression as, continuing our example above, respectively, a major league baseball player, a Nobel laureate in science, or a Mother Teresa, who conveys both compassion and service to others.

As individuals grow through their development cycle, they move from being *egocentric* to *sociocentric* to becoming *worldcentric.* This represents Phase 1, Phase 2 and Phase 3 of the Intelligent Social Change Journey, respectively. In this progression, we first associate our identity with the physical body and self, and then identify our selfs in relationship to others. Then, as we take on various roles in life, these roles in the larger world become the focus of our identity. As we increase our connections to the larger world, which literally occurred with the advent of the Internet at the end of the century, we become global in nature, and our identity becomes worldcentric. From this point, there is only a short distance to go to experience the World Soul. As Wilber (1996, p. 203) contends,

> It's only a small step further to actually experience your central identity, not just with all human beings, but all living beings. The global or worldcentric awareness simply steps up another notch, escapes its anthropocentric prejudice, and announces itself as all sentient beings. You experience the World Soul.

This same progression occurs in organizations.

<<<<<<<<>>>>>>>

INSIGHT: **For individuals and organizations, being grounded enables effective change. You can't effectively change without knowing your beginning and your destination, and understanding the relationships and connectedness that are making you who you are.**

<<<<<<<<>>>>>>>

In the second context, people often ground themselves with material goods. Since we all exist in physical reality—however we perceive that reality—we are all materialists to some extent. And it is quite likely that most of us have special material goods that help ground us, providing feelings of comfort, safety and continuity. For example, an heirloom ring that's been passed down for generations, or a musical instrument that you periodically play, serving to release tension and bringing you into a place of peace.

However, if materialism advances and becomes primary in an individual, there are a number of characteristics that emerge. These include superficiality, exclusion, covetousness, fear, and consumption.

First, the property of superficiality. Recall the discussion in Chapter 2/Part I on the levels of knowledge. Surface knowledge changes very rapidly, with no stable or settled value. This is similar to material possessions. When they are an idea in our heads, we work to achieve that idea. When they become an object in the physical, they separate from us. Remember, we are verbs, not nouns, continuously learning and experiencing, and expanding our desires.

Second, the property of exclusion. As *The Hindu* (2001) explains,

> Matter is neutral; whereas materialism is loaded with negativity. Matter in materialism serves as the medium of separation between individuals and

communities. Between the rich and the poor, there is a wall thicker than the Great Wall of China ... It is like the mental revolution that preceded the circumnavigation of the globe. Ferdinand Magellan dared to embark on his adventure because, unlike his contemporaries, he saw the sea as something that 'connected' the continents. Others assumed that the sea 'separated' the continents! ... [M]aterialism is a throw-back to the pre-Magellan era in the geography of the soul. (*The Hindu*, 2001)

Third, the property of covetousness. With money as compressed energy the arbitrator among people, work becomes a means to that which can be bought, owned and controlled, leading to the degradation of human worth and perverse logic of corruption. And along the way, there is loss of value and meaning, and consciousness.

Fourth, the property of fear. As we expand our material possessions and ground ourselves with them, we become trapped by irrational fears of potential loss and lurking dangers, living in a domain of compromised freedom. Our possessions now own us.

Fifth, the property of consumption, the pulling inward of which degrades creativity, which is an outward flow. Consumerism, the ritual of materialism, has powerful psychosocial and pseudo-religious overtones (*The Hindu,* 2001). Buying and controlling that which you buy becomes a way to placate yourself, overcome adversity, demonstrate your worth, and place yourself above others and beyond the fray of everyday life.

A combination of these properties related to materialism can lead to narcissism, an extreme state of self-love and admiration coupled with extreme selfishness and self-obsession. This is a state that seems to emerge in advanced societies where a focus on wealth and control exists. There was a clear example of this in the 2016 Presidential elections in the United States.

According to Mathew Arnold (1869), in the context of culture materialism leads to Philistinism[9-1], which makes the heart subservient to the stomach, coming with all the incumbent individual and societal problems. Philistinism can also lead to religious fundamentalism, with individuals using religion as a weapon to defend vested interests.

In the context of religion, there are various dogma related to materialism that derive from Judaism, St. Paul and Thomas Aquinas, and move through Puritanism, Quakerism and into Protestantism. Early concerns are wrought with the concept of wasting time—the deadliest of sins—since, "The span of human life is infinitely short and precious ..." (Weber, 1905). A powerful threat that runs through the relationship of materialism and religion is the recognition that wherever riches increase, the essence of religion decreases in equal proportions.

As can be recognized through the short and incomplete discussion above, when materialism becomes the major grounding force for an individual it serves as a separating force, with consumerism (bringing energy in and holding it) the inverse of creativity (an outward expression of energy). It also produces stuck energy, which is discussed in depth in chapter 20/Part III. Thus, materialism brings with it properties that limit learning, development of self and consciousness expansion.

In the third context, nature serves as both an external and internal grounding mechanism. We are part of a larger ecosystem that is Earth, whose energies—water, air, light, sound—surge through our physical bodies. Perhaps we can best understand this through the concept of *holon*, which is a system or entity that is both a self-contained whole in relation to its subsystems while simultaneously a dependent part of a larger whole (Koestler, 1967). When we physically walk through the grass, lean against a tree, or splash in a running stream, we are energetically connecting to these natural sources, all of which are part of the Earth and our larger ecosystem. Dynamic in nature, an ecosystem represents interactions among living organisms and non-living components of the environment in a given area, with each part having a role to play in the natural cycles of life.

The exploration of the unknown represented in Figure 11-1 (Chapter 11)) is grounded in the core of the Earth and looking out toward possible futures. Using this image can stimulate diverse conversations, Conversations that Matter, with increased understanding of the depth of our connections with the larger ecosystem.

A recent movement called *Earthing* is rapidly expanding based on the discovery that grounding to the Earth promotes vibrant health. Hetherington (2015) relates grounding to having an energetic, electrical connection to the earth and, generally, being comfortable in our physical body. Ober et al. (2014) say that when we directly connect with the earth, we receive the gentle energy of Vitamin G. The "G" stands for grounding, a warm tingling that moves through our body, bringing with it balance and well-being. Similar to the body's production of vitamin D when exposed to sunlight, electrons enter the body through exposure to the ground, what Ober et al. (2014) characterize as an electrical nutrient which acts much like antioxidants, working to heal injuries, reduce muscle loss, enhance the immune system, and generally disarming the free radicals, those elements responsible for aging!

Ober et al. (2014) provide evidence that regular contact with Earth's natural surface prevents chronic inflammation in the body. As an example of the effectiveness of grounding in healing, one man who has sticky blood caused by inherited high levels of Lipoprotein, including a history of aneurysms and blood clots, purchased a grounding sheet. Earthing not only eliminated his leg pain, but his blood pressure became normal without medication. There are literally thousands of similar examples available on the Internet, and almost as many products to help people ground themselves! [No endorsements intended.]

****

TOOL 10-1: Grounding through Nature

STEP (1): Find a comfortable place outside to stand quietly in the grass with bare feet. Empty your head (using your creative imagination to do so). Closing your eyes, gently wiggle your toes in the grass. Feel the energy of the Earth rising up through your feet, your legs, your torso, then simultaneously flowing down your arms and up your neck into your head, where it mixes with the white light streaming into your head from above, and then moves back down your body and into the Earth. This cycle repeats. Take deep breaths in rhythm with the energy rising and returning, rising and returning. Continue until you are ready to move.

STEP (2): Open your eyes and walk to a nearby tree, feeling a surge of Earth energy into your being with every footstep. When you reach the tree, spread your palms against the outer bark, close your eyes, and ever so slowly use your creative imagination to move your consciousness into the middle of the tree. There is a pinkness there, and a pulsing. Feel this life pulse of the tree and let your heart beat at the same rhythm. Become one with the tree. When you are ready to move on, thank the tree, slowly bringing your awareness back into your body and opening your eyes.

STEP (3): Walk to some nearby bushes. Sit on the ground or in a chair in front of them, facing them. Feel the solidity of the ground beneath your feet. You are connected. Pick a specific leaf or small clump of leaves on the bush and focus on those. Note that they are alive. Reflect on their size, color, how they are attached to the stem and one another, their beauty. If there is a breeze, watch their movement. Reach out your hand and gently touch the leaves, closing your eyes and pulling their energy into your hand. There is a warmth in their feel, almost a kiss. When you are ready, send loving thoughts to this plant, open your eyes, and gently bring yourself back into a standing position.

STEP (4): Turning your face upwards, feel the light of the sun (day) or the gentle echo of the moon (night) against your face. Invite the light to enter through the pores of your skin. Feel it caressing you, filling you and gently rolling over your skin, and, like the gentle dripping of a soft shower, moving into the earth below you. When you are complete, thank the light and slowly bring yourself back into your reality.

****

Place, regardless of its geographical location, is an important grounding point for people and organizations. For example, people identify with the location of their birth, the resting place of their ancestors, and where other important events in their lives occur. Thus, place serves as a context for identity.

The most effective means of grounding for an individual—grounding not just the physical body but the mind and emotions—is highly dependent on what fits your personal perspective, goals, objectives, background, experience and needed or desired security levels. Further, the means of grounding can shift over time depending on the situation and challenge an individual is facing or perceiving. To further explore the concept of grounding, we first address the concept of hierarchy as a grounding structure; then specifically look at grounding through relationships, grounding through ideas, and grounding through beliefs and faith.

Hierarchy as a Grounding Structure

Hierarchy references structure, "an order of some complexity, in which the elements are distributed along the gradient of importance" (Kuntz, 1968, p. 162). Interestingly enough, there is some leeway here for individuals to create the structure in which they are most comfortable. In a hierarchy, the dominant structural element may be a central point, such as in a circular structure, or have an axial symmetry. Wherever the central point (dominant structure) is located in the hierarchy (middle, top, bottom, etc.), each part is determined by where it is located in relation to that central point. From one perspective, the central point or dominant structure might well be the overarching system itself. For example, in the human body, while working independently to some extent, systems and subsystems all contribute to levels of functioning (and hopefully wellness) of the body.

While it is true that in a radical version of hierarchy the entire pattern may depend directly on one center, most hierarchies consist of groups of subordinate hierarchies who in turn have groups of subordinate hierarchies, with each group having its own particular relation to the dominant center point (Kuntz, 1968). The key concepts here are (1) there is a central theme to the system with a dominant center point, and (2) the function of any one part can only be understood in its relation to the whole.

While dependency (and potentially interdependency) are elements of hierarchies, the relationship of subordinate hierarchies to higher level groups need not be one of control. They are subordinate in terms of location, in terms of focus. For example, in the human body there are subsystems which process matter-energy (such as the mouth, lungs, heart, stomach and liver); subsystems which process information (such as the eyes, postsynaptic regions of neurons, network of neurons interconnecting centers of the central nervous system, temporal auditory cortex, and larynx); and subsystems which process both matter-energy and information (such as the genitalia and skin) (Miller, 1978).

The core pattern stored in the brain could be described as a pattern of patterns with possibly both hierarchical and associative relationships to other patterns. Different models and theories come into play when looking at high-order patterns. The concept of heuristics is an excellent example. Heuristics are speculative formulations (or simple patterns) that serve as a guide to investigate the solution of a problem. For example, horses have a strong hierarchal social structure. They act in accordance to their place in the hierarchy, which simultaneously provides the feeling of safety while honing their periphery awareness in terms of ensuring they acquiesce to any horse higher in the pecking order. To "acquiesce" might be reactive (such as moving out of the way), or proactive (such as staying in the background or taking a later turn at the salt lick). Generally, once established, horses seem to be comfortable with their placement and the repetitive behaviors that come along with that placement, with the subsequent consequence of few "reactive" events, repeatable behaviors and ever-increasing "proactive" behavior. This keen awareness of "each" and "other" goes beyond the comfort of hierarchy.

Horses also operate according to internal signals that are observable, but difficult to understand from the human perspective. For example, as one of the authors watched four of the Mountain Quest Arabians stream down the mountain pasture the other day (different ages, different sizes, different places in the hierarchy of the herd), the beautiful animals matched each other's gaits, gliding in perfect harmony through the grass, simultaneously stopping in an even line perpendicular to where the author stood, turning 90 degrees to the right in unison, and arching their necks back to the right. Watching in amazement, the only thing that appeared to have caught their attention was a soft breeze coming from the direction of their focus. Nostrils flaring and manes blowing, they held this pose for an unbelievable ten seconds before at the same instant breaking the pattern, each moving in their own direction.

Our personal ontology and taxonomy are another example of the use of hierarchy for grounding. To consciously manage our knowledge, we must first define an organizational structure to place information into primary categories (for example, by type, use, importance, etc.) and then by descriptive terms to group like items (for example, finances, strategy, games, etc.). These concept categories are an ontology that maps the main ideas and their relationships. Once we have developed a conceptual map of our knowledge, then we can create a set of terms that will be used to label items according to the concepts described in the conceptual map. This structured set of terms is a taxonomy (Malafsky & Newman, 2008).

Wilber says there are four major stages of transpersonal development or evolution, each with a different world view: the psychic (nature mysticism), the subtle (deity mysticism), the causal (formless mysticism) and the nondual (nondual mysticism) (Wilber, 1996). Each of these basic structures has discrete, identifiable levels, and each is differentiated from the other in terms of architecture, cognitions, self-sense, moral stances, self-needs, etc. While Wilber presents these basic structures as concentric spheres or a nested holarchy, he notes that movement and growth through them is not ladder-like, but rather dependent on the self, potentially with the pattern of forward-movement followed by backward movement. As he describes,

> … the self's center of gravity will tend to organize itself around a predominant higher basic structure. It will tend to identify its center of gravity with this structure; this will be its 'home base'—its major fulcrum—around which it will

organize most of its perceptions, its moral responses, its motivations, its drives, and so on. (Wilber, 1996, p. 201)

Thus, the hierarchy—and an understanding of where we are in that hierarchy—provides the grounding for living life and expansion. Our aware self emerges from a connectome, a hierarchical network of neurons, with groups at one level connected to the next level and grouped, and so forth. While different groups may have different focus points, it is when they come together that we have consciousness. Connectomes have a small-world property, which is based on the concept of the six-degrees-of-separation experiment by psychologist Stanley Milgram (1977). A network has a small-world property "when most nodes are not directly connected to one another, but each one can be reached from any other one by a small number of steps" (Carroll, 2016, p. 332). This structure supports hierarchical behavior that is considered at a critical point, a point between order and chaos, which is where individuals and organizations have the greatest creative potential and can fully take advantage of their complexity.

Grounding Through Relationships

As introduced above, while relationships, and in particular the family, have historically provided identity and grounding, in our global world the old social order that was based on kinship and the tribe has broken down; the new order is built on social engagement and ideas. The historical value-setting roles of such institutions as organized religions and hereditary aristocracies are less central, and perhaps even peripheral.

We are social creatures. While this concept has been around for centuries, recall Cozolino's belief that we are just waking up to the complexity of our own brains, how they are linked together, and that "all of our biologies are interwoven" (Cozolino & Sprokay, 2006, p. 3). As introduced in Chapter 9, studies in social neuroscience have affirmed that over the course of evolution physical mechanisms have developed in our brains to enable us to learn through social interactions. These physical mechanisms enable us to get the knowledge we need for survival (Johnson, 2006). People are in continuous, two-way interaction with those around them, and the brain is continuously changing in response, with a great deal of this communication occurring in the unconscious (Bennet and Bennet, 2010b).

Global connectivity and the Internet are bringing about new modes of social networking. Historically, from the Total Quality perspective we learned about the power of teams, and from the Knowledge Management-perspective we learned about the value of communities, and we began to consider the importance of social capital in both cases. Teams have an action focus, a planned agenda; communities have a knowledge focus, with an emerging agenda. Both surfaced the need for developing and building on trusted relationships in order to leverage knowledge, facilitate learning from each other, and create deeper knowledge.

From a neuroscience perspective, trust in a relationship is very important in enhancing learning. When a secure, bonding relationship in which trust has been established occurs, there is "a cascade of biochemical processes, stimulating and enhancing the growth and connectivity of neural networks throughout the brain" (Schore, 1994, as cited in Cozolino, 2002, p. 191). This process promotes neural growth and learning. Further, Cozolino has found that social interaction and *affective attunement* actually contribute to the evolution and sculpting of the brain, that is, they not only stimulate the brain to grow, but facilitate organization and integration (Cozolino, 2002). The notion of affective attunement is connected to Dewey's observations that an educator needs to "have that sympathetic understanding of individuals as individuals which gives him an idea of what is actually going on in the minds of those who are learning" (Dewey, [1938] 1997, p. 39). As Johnson (2006) explains, "According to social cognitive neuroscience, the brain actually needs to seek out an affectively attuned other if it is to learn. Affective attunement alleviates fear" (p. 65).

The new concept of social networking—one that utilizes the Internet—demands a shift in our perceptions, and a further shift from relationship-based interactions to idea-based interactions, with affective attunement developing through virtual relationships. Virtual networking primarily relies on the resonance of ideas to develop a level of trust. While this is quite different than the personal relationships or connections built up over time among personal and work interactions, those that connect continuously *do* build up a level of trust based on the responses of those with whom they interact. Idea resonance will be discussed further below.

****

TOOL 10-2: Relationship Network Management

A self-empowering tool in social networking is Relationship Network Management.

Our everyday conversations *lay the groundwork for the decisions we will make in the future*. Therefore, since time is a scarce resource, it is critical to choose our interactions wisely. The relationship network is a matrix of people that consists of the sum of an individual's relationships, those individuals with whom the individual interacts, or has interacted with in the past, and have a connection or significant association (Bennet and Bennet, 2004). In short, all those with whom you have had repeated and comfortable conversations.

Whether virtual or face-to-face, relationships are ultimately about people and the way they interact with each other over long periods of time. The fundamental principle of success in relationships parallels Sun Tzu's fundamental principle of success in warfare, i.e., know thyself, know the other, and know the situation. Principles of Relationship Network Management start with the individual (what the individual brings to a relationship in terms of values, ability to communicate, expertise and experience, ideas, and willingness to share and learn). Then we move into understanding the situation (virtual or face-to-face, open or guarded communication, content of exchange, purpose of interactions, etc.), and the other (trusted or unknown, values, communication skills, frame of reference, expertise and experience, and willingness to share and learn).

There are several basic concepts that successful Relationship Network Management is built upon. These include interdependency, trust, openness, flow and equitability, all of which overlap. For example, interdependency includes a state of mutual reliance, confidence, and trust. Note that interdependence does not translate into freedom for individuals to do as they choose. Interdependence means a world of greater constraint or greater conflict, or both, "greater constraint in so far as individuals accept the demands of interdependence; greater conflict in so far as they do not." (Vickers, 1977, p. 40) (See the discussion in Chapter 4/Part I on interdependence.)

Trust is based on integrity and consistency over time, saying what you mean, and following through on what you say, and openness is directly related to trust and a willingness to share. As can be seen, these qualities facilitate the free flow of data, information and knowledge among individuals, across teams and organizations, and around the world. Equitability in terms of fairness and reasonableness means that all those involved in the sharing gain something of value out of the relationship. These qualities are consistent with our definition of intelligent behavior, that is, *a perfect state of interaction where intent, purpose, direction, values and expected outcomes are clearly understood and communicated among all parties, reflecting wisdom and achieving a higher truth.*

There are five steps to managing your relationship network.

STEP (1): Recognize the value of your network. When we recognize the value of our relationship network, we can learn to consciously manage it, and provide the level of grounding needed to operate in the world of ideas.

STEP (2): Identify the domains of knowledge (areas of passion) that are important to you and what you want to achieve in life.

STEP (3): Identify the people with whom you regularly interact, both in your personal and professional life. Note how often you interact with them, the quality of the interaction, and whether they can depend on you and you on them to respond to questions with honest (and valued) opinions. *Ask*: What is at the root of this relationship? How do we complement each other? What do I learn from them? What do they learn from me? Is this relationship knowledge expanding? Consider the principals of Relationship Network Management and assure that each relationship exists within the bounds of those principals.

STEP (4): Carefully compare the list developed in Step (2) with the Network and understanding developed in Step (3). Then, consciously choose to develop, expand, and actively sustain those positive relationships in terms of thought, feelings and actions. Where gaps are identified, that is, where you have no exposure to the domains of knowledge (passion) which are important to you, prepare a plan that will bring that knowledge into your awareness and experience. For example, taking a college class related to that knowledge area will open the door to networking with people with similar interests.

It is critical to choose your network wisely. At some point in the future you will make a decision based on a conversation you had today or last week. Although you may or may not remember the conversation, the resonant content of that conversation is linked into your unconscious to associate with future thought. Thus, your everyday conversations and reflections on those conversations serve as grounding functions for future decisions and actions.

STEP (5) By choice, stay open to sharing and learning through your relationship network. See the tool of Humility provided in Chapter 4/Part I. (A chart for RNM is available in Bennet et al., 2015c.)

****

In the new environment of virtual networking with an ever-increasing amount of information emerging, the self has more responsibility in terms of discretion and discernment. The higher level of consciousness achieved by the self, the more responsibility. This means more discernment and discretion a (D^2). Taken together, D^2 addresses the concepts of selection, valuing and laying aside, that is, the ability to identify and choose what is of value, and the equally difficult ability to lay aside that which is not of value.

The Internet offers a smorgasbord of ideas, and social media sites that serve as sounding boards, and grounding boards, for those ideas. While some of these ideas may be enlightening and serve to trigger your creativity, much of the information moving across the Internet is *noise*, perhaps even propaganda or "flights of fancy". Deciding which is which requires critical thinking in terms of discernment and discretion. (See Chapter 24/Part IV, Knowledge and the Search for Truth.)

For example, based on extensive research, Tapscott points out that while pursuing freedom of choice the Net generation has moved beyond issues of individual privacy. In the course of open exchange with unknown individuals, based on a resonance of ideas, personal details are often shared. Tapscott says, "They're giving away their personal information on social networks and elsewhere and in doing so are undermining their future privacy." (Tapscott, 2009, p. 7) This is a D^2 issue that falls squarely on the self. Or, does this represent a pattern of the future?

Grounding Through Ideas

While focused in the physical, and provided with an often highly-active emotional guidance system, humans are primarily mental beings, with all the modalities of change focused on developing our mental faculties. Note: In Chapter 9 we introduced six modalities of change: experience, learning, engaging, visioning, imagining and conceptualizing, all woven together through desire, drive and courage. Because of this focus, we often identify ourselves with our ideas.

The idea of time is a grounding function. In Phase 1 activity we are very much focused on, and grounded by, the past. When we move into the co-evolving of Phase 2, we are grounding in the present reality, which is one of increasing complexity and uncertainty (see Chapter 13/Part III). When we are able to recognize patterns of patterns, that is, a higher level of truth, we can achieve escape velocity to move beyond the demands and limitations of the present and ground our thinking in the future.

As introduced above and consistent with the increased availability of information—primarily surface knowledge as Knowledge (Informing) and the resultant coupling of knowledge and creativity—an emergent quality of our new paradigm is *idea resonance*. With the rise of bureaucracy in the 1900's, idea resonance was primarily built on relationships, that is, the valuing of ideas and self based on attunement with trusted and respected others who were *personally known* to the decision-maker. As organizations grew more powerful and important in our society, there was an expansion to include value built on *respect and trust of structure*, that is, work associates in "my" organization, and external "experts" (such as those represented in Fortune 500 organizations). These were people identified as successful by "my work associates" and the world in general, and recognized as experts in "my" domain of knowledge (many belonging to companies which have since failed). While this resonance still often included attunement with specific people, there was a larger resonance with purpose and ideas beginning to occur.

In the global social networks of the last decade—and consistent with an expanding focus on innovation—we have moved fully into the venue of idea resonance, that is, ***value built on relationship of, respect for and resonance with ideas***. As we increasingly become aware, "Exposure to a greater diversity of perspectives and knowledge increases the quality of ideas, leading to better innovation results." (Carpenter, 2009) See Figure 10-2.

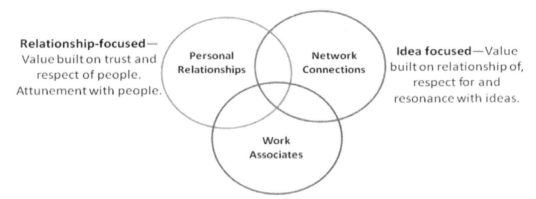

Relationship-focused—
Value built on trust and
respect of people.
Attunement with people.

Personal
Relationships

Network
Connections

Idea focused—Value
built on relationship of,
respect for and
resonance with ideas.

Work
Associates

Relationship and idea-focused—Value built on respect and
trust of structure and people. Resonance with purpose,
structure and ideas. Possible attunement with people.

Figure 10-2. *The movement from a focus on value built on trust and respect of people to value built on the relationships of, respect for and resonance with ideas.*

This global shift toward expansion of, and dependency on, social knowledge is clearly demonstrated by the new generation of decision-makers. Through continuous connectivity and engagement in conversations and dialogue (a search for meaning), the tech savvy generations have developed—and continue to develop—a wide array of shallow knowledge. Recall the discussion of the levels of knowledge in Chapter 2/Part I. Surface knowledge is predominantly, but not exclusively, simple information (used to take effective action), answering the question of what, when, where and who, and generally explicit. Shallow knowledge includes information that has some depth of understanding, meaning and sense-making such that *it requires context*. This is the realm of social knowledge, with conversations through methodical virtual interactions offering the opportunity for creating a shared understanding of greater context and meaning.

Until the end of the last century, conversations for most employees were largely limited by organizational relationships and geographical location. Today, the Internet and travel options provide the opportunity for a diversity of conversations which facilitate the crisscrossing of ideas around the globe. Thus, the ideas that ground us and support our identity are often global in nature and consciousness expanding.

In Figure 10-3, to the left is a nominal graph illustrating the historical levels of knowledge needed/used in an organization on any given day. These levels are consistent with the level of decisions made in an organization (tactical, operational, strategic/ontological) (Bennet & Bennet, 2010; 2013). To the right is a nominal graph illustrating the current levels of knowledge needed/used in an organization on any given day. The increase in shallow knowledge is a result of consistent expanded interactions via social media (Tapscott, 2009).

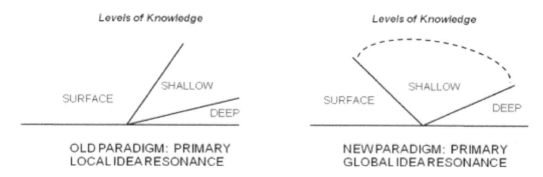

Figure 10-3. *(Left) A nominal graph illustrating the historical (2000) levels of knowledge used in an organization on any given day. (Right) A nominal graph illustrating the 2016 levels used in an organization on any given day*

What does this mean? First, we are moving toward a more connected, transparent world. Little is held back in the everyday tweeting of younger generations. More formally, this transparency is grounded in global organizational protocols and government directives around the world. For example, in 2009 the U.S. Government issued an Open Government Directive in support of the President's Memorandum that set forth three principles for government: transparency, participation and collaboration. Government organizations—and by extension the private, educational and nonprofit sectors that support these government organizations—were provided general and specific directions for achieving behavior changes in support of these principles. A starting place was expanding access to information by making it available online in open formats, and developing policy frameworks supporting the use of emerging technologies, reinforcing the principle that openness is the default position.

Second, there does not appear to be a loss of deep knowledge. This is surprising considering the general characteristic of the new generations to flit rapidly from one idea to another, always connecting things together. However, those who are able to hold a focus on a specific domain of knowledge are actually moving into the realms of deep knowledge earlier in their careers This is because they have greater access to the learned patterns of those who have deep knowledge; thus engaging others' learned patterns through conceptual thinking, mimicry and mirror neurons. Further, as minds expand, the concept of "deep" is also changing to include the ability to tap into the intuitional and having developed the mental faculties sufficiently to be able to grasp and apply that which is acquired.

Third, knowledge as a force is an idea generator, the currency of creativity and innovation, determining the future of organizations by how it is used. As information flows freely and is generally available to all—and as people recognize the power of and creative potential in the mind/brain and learn to tap into that power and creativity—global groups of individuals with a diversity of ideas have the ability to be thought leaders, and collaboratively take effective action in their domains of focus. We recognize that in an increasingly complex environment with a free-flow of data and information, no single individual has enough knowledge to move through the complex decision-making process (Bennet & Bennet, 2013). Success rests in social knowledge creation, the same informal process naturally engaged by tech savvy generations and, now, their children. Social knowledge not only provides a strong grounding network of ideas, but is at the core of collaborative leadership, idea leadership and service to the larger humanity (Bennet, et al., 2015c).

As large numbers of people talk to large numbers of people, pushing out a variety of information and ideas, connecting patterns across knowledge domains and responding to those ideas, it "feels good" to be part of the group. Checking in with our personal guidance system, when emerging ideas begin to "feel good" and are important to a desired outcome, you have idea resonance. Thus, from this viewpoint, our ideas are grounding us.

Grounding Through Beliefs and Faith

We consider a belief as *a feeling* that something is good, right or valuable; a feeling of trust in the worth or ability of someone or something; *a state or habit of mind* in which trust or confidence is placed in some person or thing. Belief is also related to a conviction of the truth, a tenet or body of tenets held by a group. Note that a conviction is both a feeling and a state or habit of mind.

Beliefs change how we perceive the world, and our biology adapts to those beliefs (Lipton, 2005). We each have a unique autobiography that includes different beliefs and personal goals. *What we believe leads to what we think leads to our knowledge base, which leads to our actions* (Bennet et al, 2015b). For example, if we believe that we cannot do something, our thoughts, feelings, and actions will be such that, at best, it will be much more difficult to accomplish that objective. If we believe we *can* accomplish something, we are much more likely to be successful ... and this results from choice, not genes.

This statement presents a chain of logic that ties our beliefs to our actions and our successes—or failures. Our beliefs heavily influence our mindset or frame of reference, the direction from which we perceive, reflect, and comprehend an external experience or situation. Thus, beliefs influence how we interpret and feel about the information that comes into our senses, what insights we develop, what ideas we create and what parts of the incoming information of which we are most aware. From these reflective observation and abstract conceptualization processes, we create our understanding and meaning of the external world. How we see the external world and how we emotionally feel about external events drives our actions and reactions. How we act and react to our external environment influences whether we are successful or not, that is, whether we achieve our goals or not. As Lipton (2005, p. 143) sums up, "Your beliefs act like filters on a camera, changing how you see the world. And your biology adapts to those beliefs."

To understand the connection between beliefs (patterns in the mind) and the physiology of the brain, consider the following story that is used in Chapter 19/Part III to help us understand that we own our emotions: You have just received a phone call from the local police telling you that your daughter has been killed in an automobile accident. Now envision your feelings, emotions, and behavior, the changes in your body, your actions, and so on. These are all real and can be observed and measured. Ten minutes later you receive a second call from the same policeman who tells you that there was a mistake and it was not your daughter who was killed. Now imagine the change in your behavior and feelings. All of this was created by your own thoughts and feelings. Your daughter was perfectly fine and healthy the entire time. The changes were created by beliefs and thoughts within your own mind.

As can be seen, beliefs and biology are not independent; they are intimately connected through the relationship of patterns of the mind (in the brain) and the physiology of the brain. Patterns of neuronal firings and changing synaptic strengths can, and do, create and release hormones that change the body. Since creating and associating thoughts in the mind are the domain of learning, and these thought patterns exist in the physiological structure of the brain, learning and neuroscience are irrevocably interrelated.

Thus, *positive and negative beliefs affect every aspect of life* (Bennet et al, 2015b). This is a finding that has widespread application. When we recognize how powerful our beliefs are, we hold the key to freedom and we can change our minds (Lipton, 2005). We can experience, interpret, and anticipate our responses to external events, and decide on our response as we choose. Our thoughts can change our brains; our brains can change our body. Without the benefit of what we know today from neuroscience, Henry Ford had it right! Reiterating,

> Henry Ford was right about the efficiency of assembly lines and he was right about the power of the mind ... Your beliefs act like filters on a camera, changing how you see the world. And your biology adapts to those beliefs. When we truly recognize that our beliefs are that powerful, we hold the key to freedom ... we can change our minds. (Lipton, 2005, p. 143)

Begley (2007) gives us a clue as to how to do this: "By meditative exertion and other mental exercises, you can actively change your feelings, your attitudes, and your mind-set" (p. 14). (See Chapter 19/Part III.) For example, Buddhism avows that the mind has a formidable power of self-transformation.

While there is no doubt that in some areas genes play a significant role in our development, findings from neuroscience research provide evidence that individuals have the opportunity and challenge to make independent decisions and take actions to significantly influence and direct their learning and personal development. For example, and as introduced above, Epigenetics suggests that if the learner chooses positive and relevant beliefs toward learning that individual will indeed be able to learn (Begley, 2007; Bownds, 1999; Lipton, 2005; Rose, 2005). Thus, the power of will and **choice of beliefs** are in the hands of the individual. It is no longer reasonable to sidestep personal responsibility under the guise that genes control destiny.

<<<<<<<<>>>>>>>

INSIGHT: **It is no longer reasonable to sidestep personal responsibility under the guise that genes control destiny.**

<<<<<<<<>>>>>>>

Many of the same words used to define *beliefs* are used to define *faith*, that is, faith can be considered a *strong belief or trust* in someone or something, or *accepting something without question*. Further, faith can be a specific reference to belief in the existence of God, or refer to strong religious feelings or beliefs, or a system of religious beliefs (Merriam Webster, 2016).

In *Urantia* (1954) it is forwarded that belief has attained the level of faith when it *motivates life* and shapes the *model of living*. This does not insinuate that the acceptance of a specific teaching as true is belief, not faith. Neither is certainty or conviction considered faith. As explained, "A state of mind attains to faith levels only when it actually dominates the mode of living. Faith is a *living attribute* [emphasis added] of genuine personal religious experience." (*Urantia*, 1954, p. 1114) This living experience is expanding, liberating and personal. It is inclusive of noble beliefs and an exalted system of philosophy as well as spiritual meanings, divine ideals and supreme values, both God-knowing and man-serving. (See the discussion of nobility in Chapter 22/Part IV and the discussion of good character in Chapter 34/Part V.)

The term faith may also carry with it the idea of obligation from loyalty (connected to trust). As an epistemological theory (Fideism), faith is independent of reason, that is, reason and faith are separate approaches, with faith having a higher truth value in natural theology. In other words, Fideism *questions the ability of reason to arrive at some larger truths*. Conversely, it is made clear in *Urantia* (1954) that faith does not shackle the creative imagination, nor does it sustain unreasonable prejudice toward the discoveries of scientific investigation. As can be seen, the idea of faith has numerous connotations used in different ways, and is dependent on context.

Fowler (1995) sees faith as a universal feature of human living, an activity of trusting, committing, and relating to the world. From this perspective, and highly aware of the forces at play in our lives, Fowler (1995, p 4) says, "Faith is a person's or group's way of moving into the force field of life. It is our way of finding coherence in and giving meaning to the multiple forces and relations that make up our lives."

<<<<<<<<◇>>>>>>>

INSIGHT: **Faith is a universal feature of human living, an activity of trusting, committing, and relating to the world.**

<<<<<<<<◇>>>>>>>

Fowler proposes six stages of faith-development which correlate to development of the self across the life-span and appear to somewhat parallel Kohlberg's six stage of moral development, which were explored in Chapter 2/Part 1 in relationship to levels of knowledge comprehension. According to Kohlberg, moral development is hierarchical, with each subsequent stage of six stages reorganizing and integrating the preceding one and consequently providing a comprehensive basis for moral decisions (Kohlberg, 1981). You may recall that although the sequence an individual moves through these stages is presumably fixed, the *rate* at which an individual progresses through the stages varies considerably, dependent on experience and learning capacity. An individual does not necessarily progress through all six stages during the course of life; in fact, an individual can become content—and fixed—in a specific stage for a lifetime. This is the same case for the six stages of faith-development. We will briefly review the six stages of faith-development and their direct relationship with both moral development of the self (Kohlberg, 1981) and development of the levels of consciousness (Hawkins, 2002) introduced in Chapter 5/Part I.

The first faith stage is *intuitive-projective*, when the young child uses speech and symbolic representation to organize sensory experience into meaning units. They assume that the experiences and perceptions they have are the *only perspective*. This is a fantasy-filled, imitative phase with the emergent birth of imagination and "the ability to unify and grasp the experience-world in powerful images as presented in stories that register the child's intuitive understandings and feelings toward the ultimate conditions of existence" (Fowler, 1995, p. 134). In terms of moral development, the first stage of Kohlberg's sequence is externally based with a punishment orientation, that is, concerned more with the power of authorities and avoiding punishment than with doing the right thing, looking from the viewpoint of the consequences of actions (Fowler, 1995).

The second faith stage is *mythic-literal*, when the ten-year-old, capable of both inductive and deductive reasoning, constructs an orderly, linear and dependable world. The self is emerging and choice is coming into play. Story is the primary way of providing unity and value to experience. As Fowler (1995, p. 149) describes, "The new capacity or strength in this stage is the rise of narrative and the emergence of story, drama and myth as ways of finding and giving coherence to experience." In terms of moral development, Kohlberg suggests that moral judgment emerges around the age of 7, with the construction and coordination of thought relating the self and others in what he calls *instrumental exchange*, that is, concern with balancing self-interest with the interests, rights and needs of others. In this second stage of conventional reasoning, individual acts are performed to satisfy personal needs.

The third faith stage is *synthetic-conventional*, which comes along with puberty and all of its changes on the physical and emotional planes. Operational thinking emerges along with the ability to reflect upon one's self. This is a social stage, a conformist stage, where identity is not yet grasped and beliefs and values not yet objectified and examined. Fowler (1995, p. 173) sees the emergent capacity of this stage as "the forming of a personal myth—the myth of one's own becoming in identity and faith, incorporating one's past and anticipated future in an image of the ultimate environment unified by characteristics of personality." Similarly, in moral development, the third stage of Kohlberg's model is focused on interpersonal relationships, with the individual making decisions by internalizing the rules to meet their own desires or achieve the approval of significant others. As noted in Chapter 2/Part I regarding Kohlberg's model, and as also applies to Fowler's model, with the exception of stage 1 of the faith development model, all of these early stages are rooted in Phase 1 of the Intelligent Social Change Journey. They have linear connections and cause-and-effect relationships: " I do this for my personal gratification; and I do that to please my significant other."

In stage four of Kohlberg's model, morality becomes more of *doing one's duty*, implying that the internalized rules are maintained for their own sake rather than the sake of others. The fourth faith stage is *individuative-reflective*, development of a system of meaning which represents a critical distancing from previous values and emergence of identity with an executive ego. The ascendant strength is the

> ... capacity for critical reflection on identity (self) and outlook (ideology). Its dangers inherent in its strengths: an excessive confidence in the conscious mind and in critical thought and a kind of second narcissism in which the now clearly bounded, reflective self over-assimilates 'reality' and the perspective of others into its own world view. (Fowler, 1995, p. 182)

The fourth stages of faith development and moral development relate to a growth of critical reflection and the assimilation of the perspectives of others into a personal reality. This occurs as we expand to Phase 2 of the Intelligent Social Change Journey. While rules and consequences (cause and effect) are recognized, critical thought is underway that is moving beyond the focus of self.

The fifth faith stage is *conjunctive*, a way of seeing, knowing and committing that moves beyond logic, seeing both sides of an issue simultaneously. As Fowler (1995, p. 185) describes, "Conjunctive faith suspects that things are organically related to each other; it attends to the pattern of interrelatedness in things, trying to avoid force-fitting to its own prior mind set." This is a field of ironic imagination, which is defined as,

... a capacity to see and be in one's or one's group's most powerful meanings, while simultaneously recognizing that they are relative, partial and inevitably distorting apprehensions of transcendent reality. (Fowler, 1995, p. 198)

Seeing the organic interrelatedness in things relates to the co-evolving of Phase 2 of the ISCJ model, with thought progressing "beyond logic" to larger concepts. Similarly, during stage five of the moral development model (contractual orientation), individuals begin understanding abstract moral principles and consider each situation differently. While at this stage individuals develop their own rules and principles for good decision-making and behavior, they recognize the need for flexibility and relativism in those rules of behavior, and the protection of all individuals.

In stage six of moral development, personal commitment instead of social consensus represents the basis for individual choices among moral possibilities (Berzonsky, 1994). At this stage an individual's conduct is driven by their own ideals and somewhat independent of the reaction of others. This is the stage that Kohlberg latter described as the *universal ethical principle orientation*. As Kohlberg says,

The formulation of and action in terms of universalizable moral principles ... require a moral imagination informed enough and detached enough from one's own interests to accurately take the perspective of every person or group affected by a policy or action being considered. (Fowler, 1995, p. 84)

Note the relationship of Kohlberg's stage six description to the definition of intelligent activity, which is *a state of interaction where intent, purpose, direction, values and expected outcomes are clearly understood and communicated among all parties, reflecting wisdom and achieving a higher truth.* (See Chapter 2/Part I and, specifically, Figure 2-3 in that chapter.)

The sixth faith stage is *universalizing faith*, a state that is often considered as not attainable. As Fowler (1995, p. 200) describes, "The self at Stage 6 engages in spending and being spent for the transformation of present reality in the direction of a transcendent actuality." This is the actuality of unconditional love, universalizing compassion in a universal community, and with a selfless passion to serve others and a desire to transform the world.

In summary, except for the first stage of faith development, which is pre-cognitive, all of the characteristics of the early stages of faith development and moral development fall solidly into Phase 1 of the Intelligent Social Change Journey. The "adult" journey of both faith development and moral development begins at stage four, which is where there is a closer relationship to the Phase 2 characteristics of the ISCJ. Stage 5 of the developmental models refer to "things organically related to each other" and the "interrelatedness of things". They also describe a higher level of mental thought "beyond logic" and the need for flexibility and relativism and the protection of all individuals. These characteristics sit solidly in co-evolving, Phase 2 of the ISCJ.

Phase of the Intelligent Social Change Journey	Stage of faith development (Fowler, 1995)	Stage of moral development (Kohlberg, 1981)	Levels of Consciousness (Hawkins, 2002)
NON-COGNITIVE	STAGE ONE: Intuitive-Projective • Speech and symbolic representation to organize sensory experience into meaning		
PHASE 1: Cause and Effect (Requires Sympathy) • Linear, and Sequential • repeatable • Engaging past learning • Starting from current state • Cause-and-effect relationships	STATE TWO: Mythic-literal • Inductive and deductive reasoning • Orderly, linear and dependable world	STAGE ONE: • Power of authority and punishment • Consequences of actions STAGE TWO: Instrumental Exchange • Conventional reasoning • Balancing self-interests w/others	20-150: Move through Shame, Guilt, Apathy, Grief, Fear, Desire and Anger (Dependent on individual)
	STAGE THREE: Synthetic-Conventional • Reflection on self • Social, conformist stage	STAGE THREE: • Interpersonal relationships focus • Internalized rules meeting desires and for approval of significant others	175: Pride 200: Courage [Moving out of negativity]
PHASE 2: Co-Evolving (Requires Empathy) • Individuated human • Recognition of patterns • Social interaction • Co-evolving with environment through continuous learning, quick response, robustness, flexibility, adaptability, alignment	STAGE FOUR: Individuative-Reflective • Developing system of meaning • Executive ego; Critical thinking • Incorporating others' perspectives STAGE FIVE: Conjunctive • Way of seeing, knowing and committing beyond logic • Seeing both sides of an issue simultaneously • Interrelatedness of things • Ironic imagination	STAGE FOUR: Doing one's duty • Internalized rules maintained for their own sake rather than for the sake of others STAGE FIVE: Contractual Orientation • Understand abstract moral principles • Consider each situation differently • Develop rules and principles for good decision-making and behavior • Recognize need for flexibility and relativism in rules of behavior and protection of all individuals	250: Neutrality 310: Willingness 350 Acceptance 400: Reason 500: Love [Interest in spiritual awareness]
PHASE 3: Creative Leap (Requires Compassion) • Creative imagination • Recognition of global Oneness • Mental in service to intuitive • Balancing senses • Bringing together past, present and future • Knowing; Beauty; Wisdom	STAGE SIX: Universalizing Faith • Transcendent actuality • Unconditional love • Universalizing compassion • Selfless passion to serve others • Desire to transform the world	STAGE SIX: Universal Ethical Principle Orientation • Universalizable moral principles • Personal commitment • Conduct driven by own ideas • Informed Moral imagination • Accurately take perspective of others	540: Joy 600: Peace [Good of mankind becomes primary goal] 700-1,000: Enlightenment

Table 10-1. *Comparison of ISCJ with faith, moral development and consciousness.*

If an individual achieves stage 6 of the moral development model, they have individuated while simultaneously taking actions based on universalizable moral principles, with the ability to "accurately take the perspective of every person or group affected by a policy or action being considered" (Fowler, 1995). This is a state of *personal commitment to universal ethical principles*. The faith development model portrays stage 6 in even stronger terms. As described by Kohlberg, this is a transcendent state based on **unconditional love**, **compassion** in a universal community, and with a **selfless passion to serve others** and a **desire to transform the world.** This stage correlates with the 500 level and above of consciousness introduced in Chapter 5/Part I, specifically characterized by spiritual awareness for both the self and others, and at the 600-level moving into the search for enlightenment for the good of mankind (Hawkins, 2002). (As a virtue, the progression from sympathy to empathy to compassion to unconditional love is discussed in Chapter 35/Part V.)

The close relationship of growth and expansion among moral development, faith development and the Intelligent Social Change Journey is not a coincidence. The ISCJ is a journey that encompasses all aspects of what it is to be human, and there is growth and expansion from all of those aspects. As we have come to recognize over the past century, the human is holistic, that is, our physical, mental, emotional and spiritual natures work together to create a whole human. One cannot be separated out from the other three. Thus, faith development and moral development, along with consciousness expansion, are all interconnected with the Intelligent Social Change Journey.

Final Thoughts

When we consider that everything is composed of energy and patterns of energy, the energetic connections among all things are not surprising, nor should the human connections to each other and the Earth come as a surprise. We are continuously exchanging energy with others and our environment. Nor, as introduced above, is it a surprise that material goods help ground us, especially if they have emotional connections to our foundations of family.

We as humans often tend to take something good to the extreme, throwing us out of balance as we act and interact in a changing, uncertain and complex environment. Understanding those things that ground us, that keep us balanced in life, is important both for our comfort, and for our sustainability as a living system.

Questions for Reflection:

When asked *who* you are, how do you describe yourself? Is it name, or job title, or do you share your purpose for being?

As I move through the circumstances of life, am I able to shift my grounding to freely move into change?

What role do my beliefs play as I move through the phases of moral development, and what specific beliefs indicate where I am on this journey?

Chapter 11
Assessing Readiness for Change

How do we perceive ourselves and in what context?
How do we know where we most effectively operate and from where our success comes?
How do we make sensible and strategic decisions on what we are becoming?

SUBTOPICS: A STARTING POINT ... ASSESSING READINESS ... PRIMING THE PUMP ... THE STATEMENTS ... PART I ... PART II ... PART III ... PART IV ... PART V ... SCORING

FIGURE: 11-1. EXPLORING THE UNKNOWN TO CO-CREATE MORE KNOWN.

TOOL: 11-1. CO-CREATING CONVERSATIONS THAT MATTER

Every life is a journey, and at every point in this journey we are in the process of becoming something else. So it can be difficult to secure a robust foundation from which we take our next steps. There can be vastly different perspectives on where we are at any point in time. What is known to one is unknown to others, or perceived very differently. What seems real to one person can be totally unreal to another. *Your truth* is considered just a perception by others, and vice versa. For example, one person's terrorist is another's war hero, an unfortunate reality that we collectively face in challenging times.

Differences in perception of reality, belief and truth often cause conflict between those who differ. Historically, these differences have caused arguments, ill feelings and even wars. However, if we can get past considering differences as barriers, and tune our mindset to *view differences as potential for creative living and innovation*, we can expand and accelerate what we individually and collectively are capable of achieving. By engaging others in this mindset, we can also *amplify the value* of what we achieve by helping those around us achieve more as well.

This takes trust, in others and in ourselves. (Trust is addressed in Chapter 13/Part III.) The challenge is to lead life in an inclusive way that sets the environment in which people are stimulated to openly share differences, with the confidence that this will generate constructive ideas. This concept, referred to as *Creative Friction* (Shelley, 2017) is a pathway to accelerated learning, development and innovation. It leads to inclusion of greater diversity of perspecctives and smoother integration of change.

A Starting Point ...

A starting point to assessing our readiness to move into the future is co-creating an idea of what that future looks like. Figure 11-1 is one of many images designed to stimulate *Conversations That Matter* (Shelley 2017) around the concept of visioning the future. It is designed not to define the path, but to engage people to explore their perspectives of what the *range of paths* may be, and to share pespectives on their current point in this journey. This process occurs with the tenents of Appreciative Inquiry in mind (see Chapter 9).

  It is not uncommon for people in the same organization (and even on the same team) to perceive their current positon to be very different parts of this image. Experiences using this image (and others with a different focus) have demonstrated the power of exploring individually, and then in pairs or small groups, before engaging in whole group wider discussion, which maximises the range of perspectives available through divergent thinking before convergent dialogue begins. Cycling between divergent (focusing on openly exploring and option generating) conversation and convergent interactions (focusing on merging, prioritizing and reducing ideas and concepts) enables us to optimise the outcomes. This iterative approach has been successfully adopted in several design and problem solving approaches such as Design Thinking.

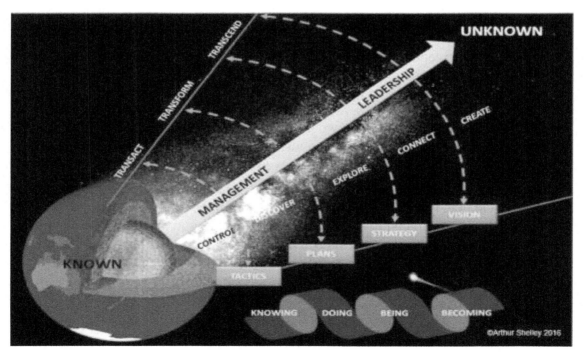

Figure 11-1. *Exploring the unknown to co-create more known.*

The wider the scope of participants in the conversations, the greater the outcomes can be. For example, recent successes with stimulating open conversatons includes the public gamification of the design of biochemicals. Researchers have found that novice voices can add new perspectives. Some novel RNA (Ribo Nucleaic Acid) molecues have been designed and folding patterns solved by providing a gamified environment asking online gamers to solve the "puzzle" (faster than supercomputers were able to achieve). Another example is mapping of astronomical bodies by enabling thousands of amateur astronnomers to add data to the collective library. The learning happens much faster, and the extensive data generated enables astronomers to shift their focus from data gathering to data analysis, from which emeges the real understanding and discovery.

****

TOOL 11-1: Co-Creating Conversations That Matter

The process for facilitating co-creative converations that matter is quite simple.

STEP (1): Show the image or object in question (for example, Figure 11-1), and

STEP (2): *Ask* a question. The questions can be changed depending on the desired oucomes. The question can be completely open-ended, such as: "Tell me what you think about this image?" Or, it can be somewhat leading to get a different focus, such as: "Where do you think our organization fits into this image and why?"

Best results come when you ask each person to write down a few quick bullet points. (You want them to capture their initial FEELING about the question before the thinking mind begins to over analyze ... that can wait for the wider conversation.)

STEP (3). Engaging intelligent rules of etiquette for dialogue, start the wider conversation. There is an amazing set of themes that come out of such conversations. Some people inherently see the pessimistic side of their situation and highlight barriers to progress. Some do the opposite and talk of the positives, perhaps even over-estimating the quality of what is being done. Some see the component parts of the organization, while others take a more holoistic or systems point of view. The key is to engage participants in exploring the reasons behind the differences to share why there are multiple perspectives. This is where the insights come from as ideas shared stimulate others to respond and new knowedge is co-created.

The specific image itself is not the critical factor. Although Figure 1.1 has been deliberately designed to stimulate conversations around strategic leadership, knowledge and realtionships in visioning the future, it can be used for other conversations with great effect. Equally, other simpler artifacts can also trigger rich conversations. Combining a creative and out-of-context stimulant with a provocative question and open and inclusive facilitation generates optimal outcomes, leveraging the diversity of views of engaged participants to create new knowledge and insights, which form new options. Synergies emerge from connections between thoughts and ideas, with each component critical to the richness and success of the interaction.

The key to remember about such interactions is that, as the facilitator, your aim is not to lead the participants to a predetermined outcome, but to co-create a set of options that did not exist before, and then intermix these to generate a range of options to co-create a future that does not yet exist. Now, it is time to explore the group's readiness for change.

****

We have provided similar conversation starters in this book through a range of imagess, all of which stimulate insights if paired with a provocative question.

Assessing Readiness

For the purposes of this discussion, it is assumed a vision of the future is in place, and that the intent of an individual or organization is consistent with that vision. See the Conversations that Matter approach provided above.

Understanding and assessing readiness for change is a vital component of change leadership. Since new knowledge is based on our existing knowledge base through the associative patterning process, it is important to relate new thought to previously developed, and accepted, thought. Three important aspects to consider are:

(1) Individuals and organizations have a threshold within which they operate. This threshold of awareness is the functioning space within which knowledge and events make sense (Bennet & Bennet, 2006a). If a desired future state is so far above this threshold, the value of it cannot be perceived. If it is well below this threshold, it is so well known that there is no additional value in pursuing it. (See Chapter 5/Part I for a deeper discussion of this threshold.)

(2) Individuals and organizations have established ranges of potential results that are considered "acceptable." For an individual, this is highly dependent on beliefs, desires and experiences (our personal culture). For an organization, this is highly dependent on leadership, vision and culture.

(3) Individuals and organizations have an absorptive capacity, that is, the ability to recognize, assimilate and apply new knowledge related to *the direction* of individual or organizational desires and goals.

At this particular point in the history of humanity—in the midst of a conscious expansion of our human capacity and understanding—the rules are changing; indeed, we are beginning to recognize higher patterns and truths that heretofore have been unrecognizable, far beyond the upper thresholds of all but a few advanced humans such as an Einstein, Leonardo Da Vinci, Pope John Paul II, the 14th Dalai Lama, Mother Teresa, Bill Gates, Thomas Edison, Eleanor Roosevelt, Mozart, Nelson

Mandela, Martin Luther King, Desmond Tutu and others of whom you are aware who have touched us in service to creating a better world.

Readiness assessments can help individuals or organizations determine how to leverage past successes and learn from past failures to strengthen change approaches and determine the readiness of the individual or organization to embrace new learning. They can also help inculcate new ideas through the process of seeding. The latter is the intent of this exercise.

<<<<<<<◇>>>>>>

INSIGHT: **At this particular point in the history of humanity, the rules are changing. We are beginning to recognize higher patterns and truths that heretofore have been unrecognizable.**

<<<<<<<◇>>>>>>

As introduced in Chapter 9, learning is the antecedent to all modalities of change, a dynamic process that manifests itself in the continuously changing nature of individuals and organizations. It is exemplified by innovation, collaboration, culture shifts and personal development. It is commonly recognized that the world is changing at a rapid pace and in uncertain directions (see Chapter 13/Part III). This is often referred to as a non-linear, dynamic, complex world in which predictability is rare, if existent at all. In such a world we can no longer rely on the logic of the past to achieve future success (primarily a Phase 1 focus). As we move away from predictable patterns susceptible to logic, we are increasingly reliant on our "gut" instinct, an internal sense of knowing that can tap into the intuitional plane. Yet, this knowing can only serve us if we "know" what to do with it, how to act. Development of our mental faculties is essential to acting. To prepare ourselves to understand current situational assessments and potential future opportunities and threats, it is essential we learn to **identify, understand, interpret, make decisions, and take appropriate action** to counter new threats and recognize and embrace new opportunities utilizing this sense of *knowing*, which is, to some extent, available to each human.

Initially, there are three critical problem areas to address. The first is a thorough and deep understanding of ourselves, i.e., our goals, objectives, values, limitations, internal defenses, and weaknesses of thought and action. By knowing ourselves we learn to engage our capabilities and support our strengths, thus ensuring that the data, information, and knowledge coming to us is properly identified and interpreted. The second critical element is that of knowing the other. This includes areas such as culture, goals and objectives, thinking patterns, internal inconsistencies, capabilities, strategies, tactics, and political motivations.

After understanding ourselves and working to understand the other, to whom we are inextricably connected, the third critical area is that of *knowing* the situation in as an objective and realistic manner as possible, that is, *understanding the situation in context*. The current dynamics of our environment, the multiple forces involved, the complexity of relationships, the many aspects of events that are governed by human emotion, and the unprecedented amount of available data and information make situational awareness a challenging but essential phenomenon. Fully engaging the senses and situational awareness is discussed in Chapter 29/Part IV.

While knowing ourselves, knowing the other and knowing the situation are critical elements in all of the phases of the Intelligent Social Change Journey, the way these concepts are translated are quite different in each phase. For example, from the Phase 1 cause-and-effect viewpoint these three elements may well determine the outcome of a hard competition, or the ultimate competition of warfare. Knowing ourselves and knowing the other are primary themes throughout Sun Tzu's famous master text on *The Art of War*:

> So it is said that if you know others and know yourself, you will not be imperiled in a hundred battles; if you do not know others but know yourself, you win one and lose one; if you do not know others and do not know yourself, you will be imperiled in every single battle.

Recall that as we expand through the three phases of the ISCJ, there is a movement from sympathy to empathy to compassion, deepening our connections to others as we move toward intelligent activity. In Phase 2 this deepening serves to strengthen our ability to cooperate and collaborate, critical in successfully co-evolving. Deeply embedded within Phase 2, knowing ourselves, knowing the other and knowing the situation, lays the framework and foundation for making effective decisions and taking right actions, providing, of course, that we have developed our physical capabilities, *built our mental faculties, and are fully utilizing our emotional guidance system to respond with agility and flexibility to surprise situations and opportunities*. As we move toward Phase 3, the perceived "separation" between our self and the other becomes a recognized "connectivity" while simultaneously individuating and honoring diversity. Thus the context of knowing ourselves, knowing the other, and knowing the situation is quite different, with a focus on *the sharing and bisociation of ideas, and innovation in service to the global world*.

Priming the Pump

One major learning throughout serving many years as change agents, is the need to measure for the future, not the past. To do this we vision the future as if it is here today, and perceive the processes and outcomes that are occurring from that frame of reference.

Similarly, thought patterns and behaviors in this future environment will be different than those we experience in today's world. Thus the 55 statements that follow in this chapter represent looking at change from the viewpoint of the future, reflecting the ability to use all three phases of the Intelligent Social Change Journey model: the cause and effect, linear, logical Phase 1 approach; the co-evolving, co-creating based on conceptual thought and the search for truth of the Phase 2 approach; and the balancing of senses, tapping into the intuitional and creative leap of the Phase 3 approach. This is a first step to laying aside our mental models and fully engaging a holistic approach to change. Since there are so many concepts—and their application—connected to the full and successful use of these phases, this Part serves as an initial exposure, an overview or for some a review, of important concepts developed throughout this book.

All statements and the concepts they represent are not equal, and may or may not apply at any given time to the stage or extent of desired change. For example, an individual or organization may be ready for the creative leap in one domain of knowledge or situation, and lacking in another area where the mental preparation in terms of recognition of patterns, conceptual thinking and developing an understanding of truth has not yet been achieved. However, all of these concepts— and more as we continue learning about ourselves, others, and the Universe in which we live—will eventually emerge in the journey of change.

The Statements

We have chosen to use a simple, comfortable five-point Likert scale, which allows for a neutral response (3) so that the responder can, whether in the conscious or unconscious, just sit with an idea for a period of time. Remember, all of these concepts will emerge as you move through this book, each unfolding on the other. And after the book is finished, it is hoped that these statements will serve as a reminder of key ideas. There are 55 core statements.

There are two five-point Likert scales for you to use with each question. The first is focused on your cognitive availability. It asks how open or closed you are to the concept that is presented. Your response would be one of the following:

(1) Closed → (2) Somewhat Closed → (3) Neutral → (4) Somewhat Open → (5) Very Open

Now look at the same concept from the viewpoint of your feelings, how comfortable you are with the concept. Your response would be one of the following:

(1) Very Uncomfortable → (2) Some Discomfort → (3) Neutral → (4) Somewhat Comfortable → (5) Very Comfortable

Choose your response based on both your mental faculties and your feelings prior to reading the short paragraph following each statement. After you have made your choices (usually your first response is the best one), think about or write down the rationale for your choice. This will help you understand why you think/feel the way you do.

The paragraph below each statement will provide a surface level of understanding regarding the concept, and will point to the Chapter/Part where additional information can be found. The intent of these short paragraphs is to stimulate and titillate. There are no right or wrong responses; each person is quite different. However, you are planting new ideas into your subconscious as you move through this exercise, and that may just trigger a past thought or experience that makes sense. Above all, please have fun as you navigate these potentially new, yet somehow familiar, ideas!

PART I: Laying the Groundwork

1. The interpretation and meaning of incoming information is very much a function of pre-existing patterns in the brain.

Characteristics: Incoming information is associated with related patterns you have in your mind, experiences and the patterns associated with those experiences. The new pattern focused on the situation at hand is built on these associations, that is, relationships with other patterns already in your mind that provide meaning. [See Chapter 1/Part I.]

Choose: (1) Closed → (2) Somewhat Closed → (3) Neutral → (4) Somewhat Open → (5) Very Open

Choose: (1) Very Uncomfortable → (2) Some Discomfort → (3) Neutral → (4) Somewhat Comfortable → (5) Very Comfortable

Provide rationale/supporting evidence:

2. I recognize that my knowledge is incomplete and imperfect and choose to be a continuous learner.

Characteristics: Knowledge is context sensitive and situation dependent. Any small shift in the context or situation may require shifting or expanding knowledge, which in turn drives different decisions and actions to achieve the desired outcome(s). Further, no single person can know all there is to know regarding a specific subject. Thus, interacting with others who have expertise in a domain of knowledge and continuously learning from each other provides the best opportunity for making wise decisions. [See Chapter 2/Part I.]

Choose: (1) Closed → (2) Somewhat Closed → (3) Neutral → (4) Somewhat Open → (5) Very Open

Choose: (1) Very Uncomfortable → (2) Some Discomfort → (3) Neutral → (4) Somewhat Comfortable → (5) Very Comfortable

Provide rationale/supporting evidence:

3. In all situations I move toward intelligent activity.

Characteristics: Intelligent activity is a state of interaction where intent, purpose, direction, values and expected outcomes are clearly understood and communicated among all parties, reflecting wisdom and achieving a higher truth. When knowledge is connected to other knowledge, shared and expanded, the people who are sharing move toward intelligent activity, with the result of taking action that has a higher potential for effectiveness, spurring on creativity, and helping others serve themselves and others. The concept of "effectiveness" is now a shared intent, with the "goodness" of the result perceived by multiple individuals, organizations or countries. [See Chapter 2/Part I.] Intelligent activity removes forces. [See Chapter 3/Part I.]

Choose: (1) Closed → (2) Somewhat Closed → (3) Neutral → (4) Somewhat Open → (5) Very Open

Choose: (1) Very Uncomfortable → (2) Some Discomfort → (3) Neutral → (4) Somewhat Comfortable → (5) Very Comfortable

Provide rationale/supporting evidence:

4. Cooperation and collaboration reduce forces and enable the free flow of creativity.

Characteristics: Cooperation and collaboration not only reduce forces, helping to bring everyone together heading in a common direction with a shared understanding, but they are also critical to achieving intelligent activity. The reduction of forces allows the free flow of ideas. [See Chapter 3/Part I.]

Choose: (1) Closed → (2) Somewhat Closed → (3) Neutral → (4) Somewhat Open → (5) Very Open

Choose: (1) Very Uncomfortable → (2) Some Discomfort → (3) Neutral → (4) Somewhat Comfortable → (5) Very Comfortable

Provide rationale/supporting evidence:

5. I recognize the power of forces and am able to successfully mitigate or leverage those forces to move forward with new ideas.

Characteristics: Forces are a part of our everyday world. A Force Field Analysis can be used to help identify forces in place that support or work against a solution, issue or problem. It helps illustrate the driving forces that can be reinforced or the restraining forces that can be eliminated or reduced. It also helps identify positive forces that can be strengthened to propel a project forward. [See Chapter 3/Part I.]

Choose: (1) Closed → (2) Somewhat Closed → (3) Neutral → (4) Somewhat Open → (5) Very Open

Choose: (1) Very Uncomfortable → (2) Some Discomfort → (3) Neutral → (4) Somewhat Comfortable → (5) Very Comfortable

Provide rationale/supporting evidence:

6. Humility is not only an excellent learning approach, but it helps reduce forces.

Characteristics: The greatest barriers to learning and change are egotism ("I am right") and arrogance ("I am right, you are wrong, and I'm not listening"). When we respond to others with humility, we take the stance "you are right", *listening* to what is being said and trying to understand their viewpoint. This approach offers greater opportunity for learning and hearing others' ideas offers greater opportunity for the bisociation of ideas, enabling creativity and supporting innovation. [See Chapter 4/Part I.]

Choose: (1) Closed → (2) Somewhat Closed → (3) Neutral → (4) Somewhat Open → (5) Very Open

Choose: (1) Very Uncomfortable → (2) Some Discomfort → (3) Neutral → (4) Somewhat Comfortable → (5) Very Comfortable

Provide rationale/supporting evidence:

7. I need not be a victim to my unconscious; my conscious self can exercise choice.

Characteristics: In the early part of our lives the personality—working from the unconscious—helps ensure our survival, experience of pleasure and avoidance of pain. As the self develops, we move into the position of making conscious choices. [See Chapter 4/Part I.]

Choose: (1) Closed → (2) Somewhat Closed → (3) Neutral → (4) Somewhat Open → (5) Very Open

Choose: (1) Very Uncomfortable → (2) Some Discomfort → (3) Neutral → (4) Somewhat Comfortable → (5) Very Comfortable

Provide rationale/supporting evidence:

8. The amount of meaning in life is directly related to an individual's level of consciousness.

Characteristics: We never just see some "thing". The mind automatically mixes the external scenes with our own history, feelings and goals (the associative patterning process) to give it context and meaning. In other words, meaning is created out of external events and signals complexed with internal resources. [See Chapter 5/Part I.]

Choose: (1) Closed → (2) Somewhat Closed → (3) Neutral → (4) Somewhat Open → (5) Very Open

Choose: (1) Very Uncomfortable → (2) Some Discomfort → (3) Neutral → (4) Somewhat Comfortable → (5) Very Comfortable

Provide rationale/supporting evidence:

9. I realize that I operate simultaneously on the physical, emotional, mental and spiritual planes, and I seek to integrate all of these perspectives into changing my thoughts and actions.

Characteristics: As we moved through the 20th Century into the 21st Century, there was recognition that people were complex adaptive systems, and that the entangled physical, mental, emotional and spiritual systems could not be separated out from each other but are integral parts of the larger whole. [See Chapter 6/Part I.]

Choose: (1) Closed → (2) Somewhat Closed → (3) Neutral → (4) Somewhat Open → (5) Very Open

Choose: (1) Very Uncomfortable → (2) Some Discomfort → (3) Neutral → (4) Somewhat Comfortable → (5) Very Comfortable

Provide rationale/supporting evidence:

10. Awareness, understanding, believing, feeling good, owning and having the knowledge and confidence to act are part of my personal change strategy.

Characteristics: Although change and adaptation are natural characteristics of the brain, so is the search for safety, security and comfort. To embrace change I need to be aware, understand, believe its truth, feel good about it, feel ownership of it, and be empower, that is, having the knowledge to change and the courage to act on that knowledge. All of these aspects of us need to be involved in change. [See Chapter 6/Part I.]

Choose: (1) Closed → (2) Somewhat Closed → (3) Neutral → (4) Somewhat Open → (5) Very Open

Choose: (1) Very Uncomfortable → (2) Some Discomfort → (3) Neutral → (4) Somewhat Comfortable → (5) Very Comfortable

Provide rationale/supporting evidence:

PART II: Learning from the Past

11. When we recognize patterns among events, it becomes increasingly easier to connect cause and effect.

Characteristics: The longer the period of time that passes between cause and effect, the more difficult it is to make connections among them. However, as over time layers of connections begin to emerge, there is the ability to develop patterns from these layers, patterns that become formulas, or concepts, that connect the relationships among actions, a higher truth that applies to multiple examples.

Choose: (1) Closed → (2) Somewhat Closed → (3) Neutral → (4) Somewhat Open → (5) Very Open

Choose: (1) Very Uncomfortable → (2) Some Discomfort → (3) Neutral → (4) Somewhat Comfortable → (5) Very Comfortable

Provide rationale/supporting evidence:

12. I am aware of a wide variety of change models and methodologies and understand which are most applicable for my purposes.

Characteristics: There are as many models of change as there are people considering change, many overlapping and many applicable only to specific situations. Strategic change programs often fail to deliver because of a lack of alignment between approach and context.

Good theories and the methodologies connected to those theories provide the opportunity for responding to a wide range of situations, allowing us to reflect on possibilities and so better anticipate the results of our actions. [See Chapter 8.]

Choose: (1) Closed → (2) Somewhat Closed → (3) Neutral → (4) Somewhat Open → (5) Very Open

Choose: (1) Very Uncomfortable → (2) Some Discomfort → (3) Neutral → (4) Somewhat Comfortable → (5) Very Comfortable

Provide rationale/supporting evidence:

13. I work to achieve balanced thought, that is, to engage different worldviews and frames of reference when assessing threats and opportunities.

Characteristics: The sign of a mature individual is the ability to hold conflicting world views together at the same time, acting and living, and having life enriched by that capability. This is the ability to see the world globally while simultaneously seeing it as a world of unique individuals. [See Chapter 9.]

Choose: (1) Closed → (2) Somewhat Closed → (3) Neutral → (4) Somewhat Open → (5) Very Open

Choose: (1) Very Uncomfortable → (2) Some Discomfort → (3) Neutral → (4) Somewhat Comfortable → (5) Very Comfortable

Provide rationale/supporting evidence:

14. I have the courage to think, feel and live my dreams.

Characteristics: Courage is required at all levels of change, from the recognition of choice (and responsibility) to understanding the context, and to taking action in a complex situation. [See Chapter 9.]

Choose: (1) Closed → (2) Somewhat Closed → (3) Neutral → (4) Somewhat Open → (5) Very Open

Choose: (1) Very Uncomfortable → (2) Some Discomfort → (3) Neutral → (4) Somewhat Comfortable → (5) Very Comfortable

Provide rationale/supporting evidence:

15. I understand the important aspects of my life that provide the foundation of who I am becoming.

Characteristics: Grounded people are confident about who they are, who they are connected to, and where they belong. They understand what value they contribute to others, and have a strong sense of identity. So how do they know this and achieve a sense of harmony with self? [See Chapter 10.]

Choose: (1) Closed → (2) Somewhat Closed → (3) Neutral → (4) Somewhat Open → (5) Very Open

Choose: (1) Very Uncomfortable → (2) Some Discomfort → (3) Neutral → (4) Somewhat Comfortable → (5) Very Comfortable

Provide rationale/supporting evidence:

16. I am part of a network of colleagues and friends where trust and openness provide a platform for knowledge sharing.

Characteristics: Cooperation, collaboration and knowledge sharing represent the highest virtue on the physical plane, and form a foundation of trust building. [See Chapter 10.]

Choose: (1) Closed → (2) Somewhat Closed → (3) Neutral → (4) Somewhat Open → (5) Very Open

Choose: (1) Very Uncomfortable → (2) Some Discomfort → (3) Neutral → (4) Somewhat Comfortable → (5) Very Comfortable

Provide rationale/supporting evidence:

17. Through the sharing of ideas with others, I expand my consciousness and enable the generation of larger ideas.

Characteristics: I share my ideas freely with others and listen carefully to the ideas of others. This is the stuff of creativity When ideas flow freely there is the opportunity to not only learn but to bisociate those ideas and have new ideas emerge. [See Chapter 12.]

Choose: (1) Closed → (2) Somewhat Closed → (3) Neutral → (4) Somewhat Open → (5) Very Open

Choose: (1) Very Uncomfortable → (2) Some Discomfort → (3) Neutral → (4) Somewhat Comfortable → (5) Very Comfortable

Provide rationale/supporting evidence:

PART III: Learning in the Present

18. When I do not have direct knowledge, I seek trusted sources to achieve my objectives.

Characteristics: Trust is relative. Applicability, accountability and authorization are elements which I consider when either giving or receiving trust. [See Chapter 13/Part III.]

Choose: (1) Closed → (2) Somewhat Closed → (3) Neutral → (4) Somewhat Open → (5) Very Open

Choose: (1) Very Uncomfortable → (2) Some Discomfort → (3) Neutral → (4) Somewhat Comfortable → (5) Very Comfortable

Provide rationale/supporting evidence:

19. For long-term sustainability, people and organizations (as complex adaptive systems) must change and adapt to co-evolve with their environment.

Characteristics: Complex adaptive systems are in a constant state of change with high degrees of interdependence. As each element of a complex adaptive system changes, others need to adapt to remain aligned. [See Chapter 14/Part III.]

Choose: (1) Closed → (2) Somewhat Closed → (3) Neutral → (4) Somewhat Open → (5) Very Open

Choose: (1) Very Uncomfortable → (2) Some Discomfort → (3) Neutral → (4) Somewhat Comfortable → (5) Very Comfortable

Provide rationale/supporting evidence:

20. My organization proportionally increases learning activities in order to cope with increasing complexity as we evolve.

Characteristics: Greater levels of learning assist with decreasing resistance to change. [See Chapter 14/Part III.]

Choose: (1) Closed → (2) Somewhat Closed → (3) Neutral → (4) Somewhat Open → (5) Very Open

Choose: (1) Very Uncomfortable → (2) Some Discomfort → (3) Neutral → (4) Somewhat Comfortable → (5) Very Comfortable

Provide rationale/supporting evidence:

21. We are well prepared to lead complex changes over space and time to create a new future.

Characteristics: Reflective planning is necessary for iterative enhancement and providing superior outcomes. We leverage time as a critical resource in the planning process. [See Chapter 16/Part III.]

Choose: (1) Closed → (2) Somewhat Closed → (3) Neutral → (4) Somewhat Open → (5) Very Open

Choose: (1) Very Uncomfortable → (2) Some Discomfort → (3) Neutral → (4) Somewhat Comfortable → (5) Very Comfortable

Provide rationale/supporting evidence:

22. I effectively construct and leverage stories to influence my intelligent social change journey.

Characteristics: Stories are proactively collected and shared to co-create thinking about the future. Stories are used to ensure a cohesive value system and influence our social development. [See Chapter 17/Part III.]

Choose: (1) Closed → (2) Somewhat Closed → (3) Neutral → (4) Somewhat Open → (5) Very Open

Choose: (1) Very Uncomfortable → (2) Some Discomfort → (3) Neutral → (4) Somewhat Comfortable → (5) Very Comfortable

Provide rationale/supporting evidence:

23. My thoughts and feelings change the structure of my brain and directly impact my actions.

Characteristics: As we are exposed to more diverse and varying conditions, the brain creates new patterns and strengths of connections and thereby changes its physiological structure. It is also true that the structure of the brain—containing a huge number of networks of neurons—significantly influences how incoming signals representing new thoughts (that is, patterns composed of networks of neurons) are formed. These new patterns entering the brain associate or connect with patterns already in the brain and impact our actions. [See Chapter 18/Part III.]

Choose: (1) Closed → (2) Somewhat Closed → (3) Neutral → (4) Somewhat Open → (5) Very Open

Choose: (1) Very Uncomfortable → (2) Some Discomfort → (3) Neutral → (4) Somewhat Comfortable → (5) Very Comfortable

Provide rationale/supporting evidence:

24. Energy and information flows are aligned to generate optimal performance.

Characteristics: The eight conditions that combine to create the flow experience are: Clear goals; quick feedback; a balance between opportunity and capacity; deepened concentration; being in the present; being in control; an altered sense of time; and the loss of ego. [See Chapter 18/Part III.]

Choose: (1) Closed → (2) Somewhat Closed → (3) Neutral → (4) Somewhat Open → (5) Very Open

Choose: (1) Very Uncomfortable → (2) Some Discomfort → (3) Neutral → (4) Somewhat Comfortable → (5) Very Comfortable

Provide rationale/supporting evidence:

25. I strive to achieve emotional intelligence to fully engage the emotional plane as a guidance system.

Characteristics: Emotional intelligence is the ability to sense, understand, and effectively apply the power and acumen of emotions as a source of human energy, information, connection, and influence. For years, it was widely held that rationality was the way of the executive. Now it is becoming clear that the full spectrum of what it is to be human—including the rational and the emotional parts of the mind—must be engaged to achieve the best performance in our personal lives and in our organizations. [See Chapter 19/Part III.]

Choose: (1) Closed → (2) Somewhat Closed → (3) Neutral → (4) Somewhat Open → (5) Very Open

Choose: (1) Very Uncomfortable → (2) Some Discomfort → (3) Neutral → (4) Somewhat Comfortable → (5) Very Comfortable

Provide rationale/supporting evidence:

26. The best process for "forgetting" is inattention, and the very best way to avoid attending to some memory is to have a stronger, more significant memory replace it.

Characteristics: We understand that reliving an event embeds those memories deeper into long-term memory, much like purposeful rehearsing, making them more impervious to any possible "forgetting" process. Ultimately, from the mind/brain perspective, that which does not get attention eventually does go away (use it or lose it). [See Chapter 20/Part III.]

Choose: (1) Closed → (2) Somewhat Closed → (3) Neutral → (4) Somewhat Open → (5) Very Open

Choose: (1) Very Uncomfortable → (2) Some Discomfort → (3) Neutral → (4) Somewhat Comfortable → (5) Very Comfortable

Provide rationale/supporting evidence:

27. I recognize that I have—and continue to identify—mental models, and I use this information to assess my responses to challenges and opportunities as they emerge.

Characteristics: Mental models—which represent our beliefs, assumptions and ways of interpreting the outside world—are built up over time and through experience, limiting us to familiar ways of thinking and acting. When new insights conflict with these mental models, they fail to get put into practice. Thus, we must continuously review our perceptions and assumptions of the external world and question our mental models to ensure they are consistent with the current reality. [See Chapter 20/Part III.]

Choose: (1) Closed → (2) Somewhat Closed → (3) Neutral → (4) Somewhat Open → (5) Very Open

Choose: (1) Very Uncomfortable → (2) Some Discomfort → (3) Neutral → (4) Somewhat Comfortable → (5) Very Comfortable

Provide rationale/supporting evidence:

28. The development of knowledge capacities provides the opportunity to move beyond our mental models and expand our frames of reference and worldviews.

Characteristics: While knowledge is the structure we experientially build upon, as we now recognize it is always incomplete and continuously changing. Knowledge capacities provide us unique ways to explore emergent knowledge. [See Chapter 21/Part III.]

Choose: (1) Closed → (2) Somewhat Closed → (3) Neutral → (4) Somewhat Open → (5) Very Open

Choose: (1) Very Uncomfortable → (2) Some Discomfort → (3) Neutral → (4) Somewhat Comfortable → (5) Very Comfortable

Provide rationale/supporting evidence:

29. Stimulating behavioral diversity and adaptability builds trust, enhances organizational performance and increases innovation.

Characteristics: Psychometric profilers categorize people into a box. Tools like *The Organizational Zoo* do just the opposite. They remove the box to encourage individual adaptability and cultural diversity. Metaphoric representation of behaviors provides a safe language for behavior conversations. [See Chapter 20/Part III.]

Choose: (1) Closed → (2) Somewhat Closed → (3) Neutral → (4) Somewhat Open → (5) Very Open

Choose: (1) Very Uncomfortable → (2) Some Discomfort → (3) Neutral → (4) Somewhat Comfortable → (5) Very Comfortable

Provide rationale/supporting evidence:

PART IV: Co-Creating the Future

30. Our vision can be viewed as a verb, not just a noun.

Characteristics: A vision is not the title of a document. It is an evolving future state that can be achieved through actionable change initiatives. [See Part IV: CO-CREATING THE FUTURE.]

Choose: (1) Closed → (2) Somewhat Closed → (3) Neutral → (4) Somewhat Open → (5) Very Open

Choose: (1) Very Uncomfortable → (2) Some Discomfort → (3) Neutral → (4) Somewhat Comfortable → (5) Very Comfortable

Provide rationale/supporting evidence:

31. In every situation in which I find myself, I take the high moral ground, that is, I choose to do what is best for all those involved both in the short and long term.

Characteristics: When we are in Phase 3, we have become holistic beings who operate from the physical, mental and emotional planes. Because our thoughts and feelings fully integrate into our perceptions of reality and our actions, all of us needs to be focused on achieving the best actions. This is the quality of Nobility, representing the highest virtue of the human, that is, doing the best that can be done at a particular point in time. [See Chapter 22/Part IV.]

Choose: (1) Closed → (2) Somewhat Closed → (3) Neutral → (4) Somewhat Open → (5) Very Open

Choose: (1) Very Uncomfortable → (2) Some Discomfort → (3) Neutral → (4) Somewhat Comfortable → (5) Very Comfortable

Provide rationale/supporting evidence:

32. I am able to expand my empathetic capabilities into conscious compassionate actions.

Characteristics: Conscious compassion is taking action on your feelings of empathy. [See Chapter 22/Part IV and Chapter 31/Part V.]

Choose: (1) Closed → (2) Somewhat Closed → (3) Neutral → (4) Somewhat Open → (5) Very Open

Choose: (1) Very Uncomfortable → (2) Some Discomfort → (3) Neutral → (4) Somewhat Comfortable → (5) Very Comfortable

Provide rationale/supporting evidence:

33. I recognize that I co-create my reality, and I honor the role of others in co-creating their reality.

Characteristics: We are each unique and, collectively and individually, create our own version of the world through thinking, learning, growing and social exchange. Our freedom to think and create offers the opportunity for amazing diversity and infinite possibilities. [See Chapter 23/Part IV.]

Choose: (1) Closed → (2) Somewhat Closed → (3) Neutral → (4) Somewhat Open → (5) Very Open

Choose: (1) Very Uncomfortable → (2) Some Discomfort → (3) Neutral → (4) Somewhat Comfortable → (5) Very Comfortable

Provide rationale/supporting evidence:

34. Discovering truth is more important than being right.

Characteristics: Truth is relative to the amount of information that has been garnered and, like knowledge, is situation dependent and context sensitive. High order conceptual thinking has a higher level of truth. [See Chapter 24/Part IV.] "Being right" is very much related to the ego. In many situations, there is no right or wrong, just choice. By asserting that one is right, it assumes that other approaches are wrong, thus setting up forces. [See Chapters 3 and 4/Part I.]

Choose: (1) Closed → (2) Somewhat Closed → (3) Neutral → (4) Somewhat Open → (5) Very Open

Choose: (1) Very Uncomfortable → (2) Some Discomfort → (3) Neutral → (4) Somewhat Comfortable → (5) Very Comfortable

Provide rationale/supporting evidence:

35. I purposefully focus my attention on thought that will move me toward my personal and professional goals.

Characteristics: What we choose to focus on, what comes into our attention, is what we use to make decisions and take actions. When this focus is consistent with our goals, we are providing energy towards achieving those goals. [See Chapter 25/Part IV.]

Choose: (1) Closed → (2) Somewhat Closed → (3) Neutral → (4) Somewhat Open → (5) Very Open

Choose: (1) Very Uncomfortable → (2) Some Discomfort → (3) Neutral → (4) Somewhat Comfortable → (5) Very Comfortable

Provide rationale/supporting evidence:

36. Expectations and setting intent empower my thinking and set the course for the future.

Characteristics: Intention is the source with which we are doing something, the act or instance of mentally and emotionally setting a specific course of action or result, a determination to act in some specific way. Expectation indicates the juncture between where you are and your desire, where you want to be. The creation process of intention and expectation is continuous. [See Chapter 25/Part IV.]

Choose: (1) Closed → (2) Somewhat Closed → (3) Neutral → (4) Somewhat Open → (5) Very Open

Choose: (1) Very Uncomfortable → (2) Some Discomfort → (3) Neutral → (4) Somewhat Comfortable → (5) Very Comfortable

Provide rationale/supporting evidence:

37. Conceptual thinking and understanding the theory behind actions supports the discovery of truth.

Characteristics: Through conceptual thinking our higher mental senses tell us when truth is not truth by recognizing forces moving in a different direction. along with the ability to determine the level of truth of an example, conceptual thinking brings with it an understanding of the relationships among concepts and examples. [See Chapter 24.] Theories reflect high-order patterns, that is, not the facts themselves but rather the basic source of recognition and meaning of the broader patterns, another way of expressing concepts. [See Chapter 26/Part IV.]

Choose: (1) Closed → (2) Somewhat Closed → (3) Neutral → (4) Somewhat Open → (5) Very Open

Choose: (1) Very Uncomfortable → (2) Some Discomfort → (3) Neutral → (4) Somewhat Comfortable → (5) Very Comfortable

Provide rationale/supporting evidence:

38. It is necessary to prepare yourself mentally in order to successfully tap into and act on the intuitional.

Characteristics: A high level of mental maturity is necessary to effectively achieve your Intelligent Social Change Journey. This needs to include a balance of critical thinking, thought, connecting theory to practice, and understanding relativism and heuristics. By developing our mental faculties, we have the capacity to receive and apply new thoughts and ideas that generate superior outcomes for ourselves and others. [See Chapter 26 and Chapter 28/Part IV.]

Choose: (1) Closed → (2) Somewhat Closed → (3) Neutral → (4) Somewhat Open → (5) Very Open

Choose: (1) Very Uncomfortable → (2) Some Discomfort → (3) Neutral → (4) Somewhat Comfortable → (5) Very Comfortable

Provide rationale/supporting evidence:

39. Intelligent activities are continuously being created by people as, from one thought to the next, there is mental integrity, a consistency in the truth of thought.

Characteristics: Recall that intelligent activity is described as *a perfect state of interaction where intent, purpose, direction, values and expected outcomes are clearly understood and communicated among all parties, reflecting wisdom and achieving a higher truth.* [See Chapter 27/Part IV.]

Choose: (1) Closed → (2) Somewhat Closed → (3) Neutral → (4) Somewhat Open → (5) Very Open

Choose: (1) Very Uncomfortable → (2) Some Discomfort → (3) Neutral → (4) Somewhat Comfortable → (5) Very Comfortable

Provide rationale/supporting evidence:

40. Wisdom occurs when activity matches the choices that are made and structured concepts are intelligently acted upon for the greater good.

Characteristics: Wisdom involves a sense of balance derived from a strong, pervasive moral conviction. It provides guidance and obligations that flow from a profound sense of interdependence. [See Chapter 27/Part IV.]

Choose: (1) Closed → (2) Somewhat Closed → (3) Neutral → (4) Somewhat Open → (5) Very Open

Choose: (1) Very Uncomfortable → (2) Some Discomfort → (3) Neutral → (4) Somewhat Comfortable → (5) Very Comfortable

Provide rationale/supporting evidence:

41. Earned intuition is the result of all of my experiences and the learning from those experiences.

Characteristics: Earned intuition is that part of intuition emerging from the unconscious that is connected to our conscious experiences and discoveries. When we are focused at the conscious mental level, we are always exploring cause and effect and working backwards. This is not the case with the intuition. Something learned many years ago can emerge, when needed, in the blink of an eye. [See Chapter 28/Part IV.]

Choose: (1) Closed → (2) Somewhat Closed → (3) Neutral → (4) Somewhat Open → (5) Very Open

Choose: (1) Very Uncomfortable → (2) Some Discomfort → (3) Neutral → (4) Somewhat Comfortable → (5) Very Comfortable

Provide rationale/supporting evidence:

42. There is a multiplier effect when ideas are shared.

Characteristics: When knowledge is focused inward, *not* shared, it has diminishing value as others continue to connect with the ever-changing and expanding reservoir of knowledge. As we interact with others, we develop a deeper understanding of others and ourselves and an appreciation for diversity. This understanding helps us create without force, embracing a collaborative advantage, that is, gaining the advantage of other's thinking at or above our personal level of thinking, while simultaneously creating in a way that is uniquely ours. [See Chapter 29/Part IV.]

Choose: (1) Closed → (2) Somewhat Closed → (3) Neutral → (4) Somewhat Open → (5) Very Open

Choose: (1) Very Uncomfortable → (2) Some Discomfort → (3) Neutral → (4) Somewhat Comfortable → (5) Very Comfortable

Provide rationale/supporting evidence:

43. We are in the process of preparing to make a creative leap and understand the direction of change this will bring.

Characteristics: The moment of truth has come in which we have consciously decided to change direction and shift our mind sets to a new level fueled by creativity. We know it will change the frequency of our energy flows, but remain unaware of the exact forms this will take. The creative leap is a leap of faith and trust. We are comfortable with this uncertainty, although confident the shift will be enhancement. Sometime around the fourth grade, the ego pokes its head out, and, through social interactions, the process of individuation begins with a focus on the NOW. By the time the mid-teens come around, the world has imposed a level of order and limits, with a focus on cause-and-effect. As adults, we begin the development of our mental faculties that begins the Intelligent Social Change Journey that takes us back to where we started. (See Chapter 30/Part IV.)

Choose: (1) Closed → (2) Somewhat Closed → (3) Neutral → (4) Somewhat Open → (5) Very Open

Choose: (1) Very Uncomfortable → (2) Some Discomfort → (3) Neutral → (4) Somewhat Comfortable → (5) Very Comfortable

Provide rationale/supporting evidence:

PART V: Living the Future

44. I recognize that tapping into the intuitional plane is a natural state and that I'm on a return journey to this place of high creativity.

Characteristics: Babies are born connected, to their mothers and families, and to the larger energies surrounding them and within them. This represents Phase 3. [See Introduction to Part V.]

Choose: (1) Closed → (2) Somewhat Closed → (3) Neutral → (4) Somewhat Open → (5) Very Open

Choose: (1) Very Uncomfortable → (2) Some Discomfort → (3) Neutral → (4) Somewhat Comfortable → (5) Very Comfortable

Provide rationale/supporting evidence:

45. As we move into Phase 3, we continue to mature our creativity to become masters of this higher level of co-creating.

Characteristics: Our thinking and behavior remains at the highest level of maturity. The freedom of creativity is the foundation of everything that we do. The Alchemy of our environment is such that science, spirit and consciousness are fully integrated. [See Chapter 31/Part V.]

Choose: (1) Closed → (2) Somewhat Closed → (3) Neutral → (4) Somewhat Open → (5) Very Open

Choose: (1) Very Uncomfortable → (2) Some Discomfort → (3) Neutral → (4) Somewhat Comfortable → (5) Very Comfortable

Provide rationale/supporting evidence:

46. When I achieve inner balance, I am able to cope with a range of external situations that are unbalanced.

Characteristics: Balance provides an inner confidence enabling high function in unpredictable environments. [See Chapter 32/Part V.]

Choose: (1) Closed → (2) Somewhat Closed → (3) Neutral → (4) Somewhat Open → (5) Very Open

Choose: (1) Very Uncomfortable → (2) Some Discomfort → (3) Neutral → (4) Somewhat Comfortable → (5) Very Comfortable

Provide rationale/supporting evidence:

47. As a humanity we are bringing our consciousness back into balance as we engage in the Intelligent Social Change Journey.

Characteristics: In our acceleration of development of the mental faculties, we have focused on the material world and suppressed our inner spiritual senses. Humanity is maturing, and it is time for us to bring all that we are to the table, to reach the full potential of who we are—physical, mental, emotional and spiritual—and bring ourselves into balance. [See Chapter 32/Part V.]

Choose: (1) Closed → (2) Somewhat Closed → (3) Neutral → (4) Somewhat Open → (5) Very Open

Choose: (1) Very Uncomfortable → (2) Some Discomfort → (3) Neutral → (4) Somewhat Comfortable → (5) Very Comfortable

Provide rationale/supporting evidence:

48. I have the ability to engage my senses to perceive beauty in myself and others.

Characteristics: Beauty serves as an accelerator to the expansion of consciousness. Beauty enhances the senses in our body and in others. Simultaneously, when our senses are balanced, we are able to perceive greater beauty. [See Chapter 33/Part V.]

Choose: (1) Closed → (2) Somewhat Closed → (3) Neutral → (4) Somewhat Open → (5) Very Open

Choose: (1) Very Uncomfortable → (2) Some Discomfort → (3) Neutral → (4) Somewhat Comfortable → (5) Very Comfortable

Provide rationale/supporting evidence:

49. I recognize the power of beauty and its implications for me and my environment.

Characteristics: Beauty is a short circuit to thinking, enabling us to circumvent the tedium of everyday life in an instant, and inject feelings of appreciation, love and joy into the essence of our lives. Beauty creates a Oneness within, a balancing of our senses, and, when shared, a Oneness without. Much like the potential effects of a butterfly flapping its wings on the other side of the world, beauty shared can multiply exponentially with wide-spread impact. [See Chapter 33/Part V.]

Choose: (1) Closed → (2) Somewhat Closed → (3) Neutral → (4) Somewhat Open → (5) Very Open

Choose: (1) Very Uncomfortable → (2) Some Discomfort → (3) Neutral → (4) Somewhat Comfortable → (5) Very Comfortable

Provide rationale/supporting evidence:

50. As we move fully into Phase 3 of our creative journey, good character becomes an essential element of our expanded self.

   Characteristics: The concept of character represents a quality of goodness and is directly related to growth of the self—individuals and their choices and actions. [See Chapter 34/Part V.]

Choose: (1) Closed → (2) Somewhat Closed → (3) Neutral → (4) Somewhat Open → (5) Very Open

Choose: (1) Very Uncomfortable → (2) Some Discomfort → (3) Neutral → (4) Somewhat Comfortable → (5) Very Comfortable

Provide rationale/supporting evidence:

51. I honor the diversity of others and their potential contributions to the networks of which I am a part.

   Characteristics: I am part of a conscious compassionate community that recognizes our connections to each other and that conveys a sense of belonging and Oneness. [See Chapter 34/Part V.]

Choose: (1) Closed → (2) Somewhat Closed → (3) Neutral → (4) Somewhat Open → (5) Very Open

Choose: (1) Very Uncomfortable → (2) Some Discomfort → (3) Neutral → (4) Somewhat Comfortable → (5) Very Comfortable

Provide rationale/supporting evidence:

52. Moving through the Intelligent Social Change Journey has evolved our social maturity to the highest levels of conscious compassion and co-creation.

   Characteristics: When we were focused in the Phase 1 relationships of cause and effect, it was important to have sympathy in order to keep people in our formula of change. When we moved into the co-evolving of Phase 2, sympathy was not enough; co-evolving requires empathy, the capacity to put oneself in the shoes of another [see Chapter 14]. Phase 3 requires more, that is, the conscious development of compassion. [See Chapter 35/Part V.]

Choose: (1) Closed → (2) Somewhat Closed → (3) Neutral → (4) Somewhat Open → (5) Very Open

Choose: (1) Very Uncomfortable → (2) Some Discomfort → (3) Neutral → (4) Somewhat Comfortable → (5) Very Comfortable

Provide rationale/supporting evidence:

53. Recognizing the Oneness of all people, I employ empathy and compassion to help me understand diverse viewpoints and how to be of service to humanity.

Characteristics: Our identity as social creatures is hardwired into the structure of our brain. [See Chapter 4.] Empathy, objectively experiencing the inner life of another, is inherent in the functioning of our brain, suggesting that through feelings there is an active link between our own minds and bodies, and the minds and bodies of those around us. [See Chapter 36/Part V.]

Choose: (1) Closed → (2) Somewhat Closed → (3) Neutral → (4) Somewhat Open → (5) Very Open

Choose: (1) Very Uncomfortable → (2) Some Discomfort → (3) Neutral → (4) Somewhat Comfortable → (5) Very Comfortable

Provide rationale/supporting evidence:

54. I realize I am a never-ending fountain of creativity and that there are infinite levels of consciousness awaiting my exploration.

Characteristics: Consciousness is a process. As the self grows and makes good choices, developing virtues and cooperating and collaborating with others through knowledge sharing, so, too, does consciousness expand. As co-creators of our reality engaged in intelligent activity, the only limits are those we set on our selves. [See Chapter 37/Part V.]

Choose: (1) Closed → (2) Somewhat Closed → (3) Neutral → (4) Somewhat Open → (5) Very Open

Choose: (1) Very Uncomfortable → (2) Some Discomfort → (3) Neutral → (4) Somewhat Comfortable → (5) Very Comfortable

Provide rationale/supporting evidence:

55. I am conscious of where I am on the simplexity scale (Figure 38-3) and what the implications are for my Phase 1II activities.

Characteristics: In expanded levels of consciousness, out of complexity emerges simplicity, providing a new starting point for our continuing journey, approaching the point of singularity. We are starting to engage in creative co-creation in an environment of punctuated equilibrium. [See Chapter 38/Part V.]

Choose: (1) Closed → (2) Somewhat Closed → (3) Neutral → (4) Somewhat Open → (5) Very Open

Choose: (1) Very Uncomfortable → (2) Some Discomfort → (3) Neutral → (4) Somewhat Comfortable → (5) Very Comfortable

Provide rationale/supporting evidence:

Scoring

Recognizing that average scores are only indicators, nonetheless this learning exercise offers the opportunity to assess your openness to new ways of thinking, your comfort level with new ideas, and your personal level of readiness to expand through the three phases of the Intelligent Social Change Journey. If you average in the neutral zone (level 3) or below, stick with the Phase 1 model, enjoying and applying the kaleidoscope of models that have emerged in support of change, each with a differentiated flavor. If you are beyond the half-way mark moving toward level 4, dig deeper into the co-evolving model and make it your own. Once you pass level 4 you are in a field of choice, and have the opportunity to match your change strategy to your desired approach and outcome.

Take a few minutes to go back and carefully consider your responses. For those responses lower than 3, reflect on what it is about that concept that closes you off or causes some level of discomfort. Quite often, this will be the result of some experience in your history, or a belief or mental model which warrants revisiting. For those responses higher than 3, reflect on how you might use this knowledge on your personal or professional change journey. Can you recall any examples of where this knowledge was used in decision-making or taking action? The more examples you can come up with, the higher the level of truth. (See Chapter 24/Part IV.)

Remember, there is no right and wrong associated with this journey; rather, it is a journey of Becoming. Everyone is a part of this journey at some time, at some level. As we will continue to reiterate throughout this book, *you have choice*. And then, regardless of what you choose, move into the flow and have fun! Learning is experiential.

Chapter 12
The Change Agent's Strategy

*An Example of a Change Strategy
expanding from Phase 1 to Phase 2*

SUBTOPICS: THE GROWTH PATH OF KNOWLEDGE SHARING ... CREATE A SHARED VISION ... BUILD THE BUSINESS CASE ... DEMONSTRATE LEADERSHIP COMMITMENT ... FACILITATE A COMMON UNDERSTANDING ... SET LIMITS ... SHARE NEW IDEAS, WORDS AND BEHAVIORS ... IDENTIFY THE STRATEGIC APPROACH ... DEVELOP THE INFRASTRUCTURE ... MEASURE AND INCENTIVIZE ... PROVIDE TOOLS ... PROMOTE LEARNING ... ENVISION AN EVENT GREATER FUTURE

FIGURES: 12-1. THE GROWTH PATH OF KNOWLEDGE SHARING ... 12-2. A FIRST CUT AT THINGS TO CONSIDER WHEN BUILDING A BUSINESS CASE ... 12-3. KNOWLEDGE MANAGEMENT LEADERS FROM INSIDE THE ORGANIZATION AND OUTSIDE THE ORGANIZATION PASSIONATELY SHARED THEIR COMMITMENT AND KNOWLEDGE ... 12-4. KNOWLEDGE LIFE CYCLE MODEL ... 12-5. TOWARD A COMMON UNDERSTANDING OF KNOWLEDGE ... 12-6. STARTING THE CONVERSATION TO EXPLORE THE TECHNOLOGY EXPLOSION. (CONVERSATIONS THAT MATTER) ... 12-7. A SYSTEMS LOOK IDENTIFYING THE STRATEGIC APPROACH OF IMPLEMENTING KM ... 12-8. A COLLAGE OF TOOLS SUPPORT DON IMPLEMENTATION OF KM.

In any change strategy, the challenge of management and leadership becomes that of communicating and collaborating with the organization's knowledge workers to create an environment, and an understanding on the part of their workforce, that all twelve of these change factors are worthy of their consideration, acceptance and personal attention and actions. When this happens, change will come from a knowledgeable, motivated and supportive workforce.

Unfortunately, leadership and management often use the outdated approach of *telling* workers what they are expected to do and how they are expected to change. In these times of global access to information and informed knowledge workers, this simply does not work. An approach that *can* work, and work well, is to bring knowledge workers into the process, fully participating in selecting, creating and determining the changes needed throughout the organization. This empowerment and trust unleash the energy, knowledge and creativity of the workforce and, above all, brings with it ownership. Through this approach, knowledge workers create their own personal acceptance of each of the six change factors in the individual change model introduced in Chapter 6/Part I. These are: awareness-understanding-believing-feeling good-ownership-empowerment in terms of knowledge and courage to apply that knowledge.

Surviving and thriving in a multifaceted world requires a multifaceted change strategy. Paraphrasing Ashby's (1964) law of requisite variety, there must be more variety in the change strategy than in the system you are trying to change. So how do we change a complex organization to meet the challenges of this new world of exploding information, increasing uncertainty, and ever-increasing complexity? While there is certainly no simple answer—since change is situation and time-dependent—the change process for an organization moving toward becoming an intelligent complex adaptive system[11-1] must engage every individual in the firm as well as external partners. Since organizational networks of people and knowledge become more interconnected and complex as the world becomes more global, the larger an organization the more a self-organizing strategy must come into play.

This change strategy sets out to achieve what we call a *connectedness of choices*. This means that decisions made at all levels of the organization, while different, are clearly based not only on a clear direction for the future, but made in a cohesive fashion with both an understanding of *why* that direction is desirable *and* the role that individual decisions play with respect to immediate objectives and in support of the shared vision. At the top level, a continuous increase of knowledge and sharing based on a common direction of the organization, and a common set of beliefs and values, is the theoretical force behind the change strategy.

The Growth Path of Knowledge Sharing

Implementing change at every level of the organization follows the growth path of knowledge and sharing. For example, when exploring a new idea—whether within an individual or as an organization—closed structured concepts are first created. As these concepts germinate, some focused but limited sharing of these concepts occurs. Over time, particularly if positive feedback happens during the limited sharing, there is increased sharing and a deeper awareness and connectedness through sharing occurs, that is, a common understanding of the concept is shared across a larger number of people. From this framework, individuals and organizations participating in this process *create new concepts*, and from those concepts new innovations emerge and are purposefully shared across and beyond the framework, leading to application of these ideas in everyday work. As connectedness increases, there is also heightened awareness, or consciousness, of the potential value of these ideas to a larger audience, leading motivated individuals and organizations to advance these concepts even further, engendering the rise of social responsibility.

<<<<<<◇>>>>>>

INSIGHT: **As connectedness through sharing increases, there is rising awareness of the value of these ideas to a larger audience, engendering the rise of social responsibility.**

<<<<<<◇>>>>>>

Figure 12-1, based on the seven levels of consciousness (MacFlouer, 1999), represents this path of knowledge sharing. The following progression facilitates increased connectedness and heightened consciousness: (1) closed structured concepts, (2) focused but limited sharing, (3) awareness and connectedness through sharing, (4) creating concepts and sharing these concepts with others, (5) advancement of new knowledge shared with humanity at large, (6) creating wisdom, teaching, and leading, and (7) creating (and sharing) new thought in a fully aware and conscious process. Prior to reaching wisdom at level 6, there is the insertion of value (formed in the context of the greater good). Value was absent in the discussion of knowledge in support of the earlier levels of the model since the positive or negative value of knowledge is situation-dependent and context sensitive, that is, how the knowledge is used. The implication is that as knowledge sharing increases and conscious awareness expands around the value of this focus on, and application of, knowledge theories and frameworks, there is recognition that these theories and models (higher order patterns) and what is learned from their application in a specific context may prove useful for other organizations, communities and/or cities. This is the concept of the "greater good" that moves knowledge toward wisdom.

Wisdom occurs when knowledge is integrated with a strong value set and acted upon with courage. Through leading and teaching (leadership and education), this wisdom facilitates the growth of new concepts, and an expanded connectedness with like individuals and organizations around the world. (See the discussion of wisdom in Chapter 27/Part IV.) It is at this level in the growth of knowledge and sharing where we have built enough wisdom and knowledge to create and share new thoughts in a fully aware and conscious process, i.e., purposefully strategizing what concepts to share and how to share them, consciously contributing to world growth.

The underlying realization in this pattern is that a single individual in an organization (or a single organization in an enterprise, or a single enterprise in a global market) cannot effectively function at a level so far above others that there is a lack of recognition and understanding of the level of that functioning. [Note: This is the threshold introduced in more detail in Chapter 5/Part I.] Historically, there are occurrences where innovators and forward-thinking ideas failed during one period of time only to emerge again during a later period as a leading market product or practice. The old adage *everything in its own time* has helped explain the earlier failure. In the fast-paced and interconnected world of today, we have the ability to create *its own time*, inverting the adage and placing success of forward-thinking ideas squarely in the ability of an organization to create a shared understanding across the global environment. In other words, while ideally the organization will stay ahead of market demand, it may want to encourage sharing and the growth of knowledge across its market sector to ensure a wider and deeper understanding by customers of the value of its contribution to the marketplace.

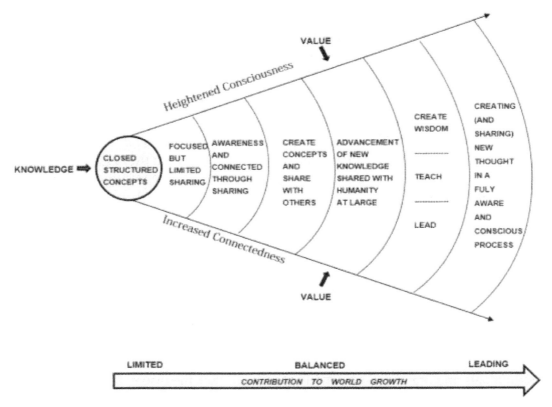

Figure 12-1. *The growth path of Knowledge Sharing.*

For example, in an organization *not* built on flow and sharing, a brilliant idea developed before its time, which is so far beyond current organizational thinking that no one recognizes its value, will have little chance of funding and support. An example is development of the digital watch, which was a product of Swiss watchmakers but was rejected as a ridiculous idea by management. Thus, Seiko picked up the idea and ran with it, becoming the leading watch manufacturer in the world. In an industry where there is little cross-organizational sharing (other than piracy out of context), similarly, when a forward-thinking firm produces a product before its time, the product will have little opportunity for success without the recognition of value, the industry's ability to support and sustain it, and people's awareness of, and desire for, it. The sharing of ideas within and across organizations can plow the ground for receptivity and demand, with initial market advantage going to the first product in the field and the long-term market advantage going to the best and most continuously improved product.

Using Figure 12-1 as a model, the change agent's strategy suggested here is holistic, and not bounded by the organization. Indeed, it encourages interactions across large relationship networks, and sharing and learning across organizational boundaries. As discussed above, while this may at first appear contrary to organizational advantage in a world where many organizations still cling to competition, having the best information and knowledge is only a first step toward being competitive. The greater value for an organization is how this knowledge is used, and the ability of those who are using this knowledge to discern value in it, integrate it, recognize patterns, and *adapt it to changing requirements in a turbulent environment*. This knowledge can rarely be given away because no other organization would know how to discern value, interpret it, recognize patterns, or adapt it, but other organizations can build on it and, from their different perspectives, create new ideas that, in turn, can be built upon by other organizations. Staying at the front of change offers the greatest advantage for sustainability.

<<<<<<<◇>>>>>>>

INSIGHT: **The highest value for an organization is how knowledge is used, and the ability of those who are using it to discern value in it, integrate it, recognize patterns, and adapt it to changing requirements in a turbulent environment.**

<<<<<<<◇>>>>>>>

Since change itself is an emergent characteristic, it is a product of combining, integrating, and correlating elements of the change strategy with the organization's direction, objectives, structure, culture, and leadership. The change strategy must be consistent with the desires of the organization. The means do not justify the end; they serve as an example of the richness and effectiveness of the end state, of the desired approach for how future work gets done. There is a visible consistency in theory and actions throughout the strategy suggested below.

The change strategy model can be viewed in terms of orchestrating and implementing twelve specific elements. These elements are: (1) creating a shared direction; (2) building the business case; (3) demonstrating leadership commitment; (4) facilitating a common understanding; (5) setting limits; (6) sharing new ideas, words, and behaviors; (7) identifying the strategic approach; (8) developing the infrastructure; (9) measuring and incentivizing; (10) providing tools; (11) promoting learning; and (12) envisioning an even greater future. These are detailed below.

(1) Create a Shared Vision

In *The Fifth Discipline*, Peter Senge (1990) emphasizes the importance of a shared vision where employees participate in the development of a corporate vision, and can then make decisions and take actions consistent with the directions set by senior leadership through the shared visioning process. For an example of the visioning process, see the discussion on "Conversations that Count" in Chapter 11. In an unknowable future, the vision must be more of a direction than an end state. In their research on consciousness, Edelman and Tononi (2000) identify the mechanism that provides unity to consciousness, thereby creating a continuous history of thought and a consistency of identity and action. This ability to maintain different parts of the brain in harmony and to pull them together in an organization is facilitated by constant and widespread communication.

The journey toward intelligent activity starts with a shared direction of what the organization will accomplish and *how it will be accomplished*, that is, *how the work gets done*. Learning from history, we realize that it is advantageous for an organization to have a strategic plan. What may be different about this approach is that the plan is a product of the whole organization, with inputs and reviews at every level of, and from every functional area in, the organization. In the development process, goals are worked and reworked to assure the right set of goals addressed at a low enough level to make them real and viable, and a high enough level to provide flexibility and tailoring at the point of action where implementation decisions are made. The plan has the potential to bring the organization's collective vision of its future into clear focus, and communicates leadership's commitment to this vision.

The process of developing the strategic plan is part of the change strategy. The strategic plan as a collective process brings with it a sense of ownership across the organization, and responsibility for the outcome, both laying the groundwork for successful implementation. A way to get even more people involved is to make success stories a part of the plan. Early in the planning cycle, leadership publicizes the desire to locate early successes to serve as examples for each top-level goal or objective of the plan. As the top-level goals/objectives emerge over the course of the planning process, with them emerge examples of innovative thinking that is jumpstarting the organization toward achieving these goals/objectives. Not only does this process identify innovations underway, but it facilitates further ownership of the plan, and encourages organizational units to understand and begin implementation of the plan prior to its publication and distribution, and prior to the plan becoming a dust collector on the shelf. By the time the plan is staffed through the various stakeholders of the organization, the organization is aligned, senior leadership is committed, and implementation has already begun. NOTE: This process can be even more effective if the plan is going to be used as the basis for funding programs, thus providing the opportunity for visibility of success stories.

(2) Build the Business Case

From a corporate view it is essential to have a strong business case for any anticipated change strategy. This business case lays out the current organizational effectiveness level, identifies needed changes and, most importantly, describes the anticipated changes and expected results in terms that make sense from a business perspective. However, the business perspective is not the only perspective to be considered. It is equally important to have the anticipated changes make sense to the employees and other organizational stakeholders such as customers, and the environment and local community as they apply.

While most likely a need or opportunity is driving development of a business case, the actual process of building a business case works best backwards, first carefully considering the result of anticipated changes, that is, what you want the organization to look like and the anticipated performance and market advantage of the organization assuming those changes are complete. This certainly makes sense, and hopefully was developed in (1) above. Then, understanding where the organization currently stands, identify the strategic and tactical actions necessary to achieve those changes. See Figure 12-1.

Figure 12-1, using the same structure as the Phase 1 change model of the Intelligent Social Change Journey (current state-change-future state), offers a first cut at things to consider when building a business case. As we build the business case, we are reminded to consider change from the business perspective, the stakeholder and customer perspective (including a focus on employees) and an environmental and local community perspective. The left box focused on the current level of organizational effectiveness, the current state of the organization. Here we look at the reasons for suggested or needed change, considering these reasons from the viewpoint of every level of the organization and the viewpoints of vendors, partners and customers. We also take the time to look at the current environment in terms of the market, customers, and risk.

The middles circle is the identified needed change to either response to a threat or opportunity, to improve performance or expand a market. Here we examine the basic beliefs and assumptions underlying the recommended change. Are they based on antiquated assumptions or belief system? We identify quantitative parameters, with backup information relative to the reasonableness of the change, including investment requirements and return on investment. We consider the feasibility and fundamental approach for change management, asking: Are the changes consistent with the current structure and culture of the organization or will these have to be significantly revamped to achieve the desired end state? And it is here that we identify the strategic and tactical actions necessary to make this change and explore the risks associated with these actions as well as the risk associated with taking no action.

Finally, we look at the anticipated results, identifying the future market within which the organization is going to move from the viewpoints of the market, customer and risk. Here we identify the anticipated performance and market

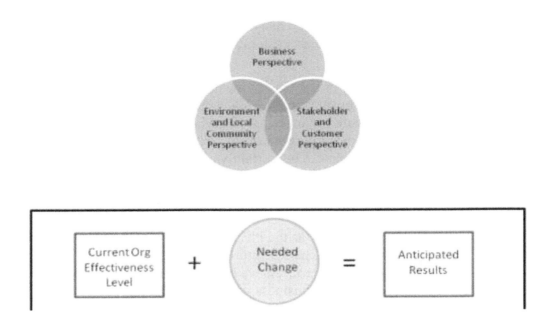

• Identify and thoroughly examine the reasons for suggested or needed change. (Consider every level of the org. and explore from viewpoints of vendors, partners and customers.) • Look at the current environment from the viewpoints of the market, customer and risk (in terms of government regulations, technology breakthroughs, etc.	• Examine the basic beliefs and assumptions underlying the recommended changes. (Are they based on antiquated assumptions or belief systems? • Identify quantitative parameters with backup info relative to reasonableness (investment requirements, return on investment). • Consider the feasibility of and fundamental approach for change management. (Are the changes consistent with the current structure and culture of the organization or will these have to be significantly revamped to achieve the desired end state? • Identify the strategic and tactical actions necessary. (What are the risks associated with these actions?)	• Identify the future market within which the organization is going to move from the viewpoints of the market, customer and risk (in terms of government regulations, technology breakthroughs, etc.) • Identify the anticipated performance and market advantage (long-term org. health; short-term payoffs). • Consider: What are the financial, managerial, sociological, technological and political consequences of the recommended changes as seen by both outsiders and insiders? • Consider the impact on employees, infrastructure and culture. Ask and answer the silent questions from employees: WIFM (what's in it for me?) How will it affect my local work and my local organization? How will it affect the organization as a whole?

Figure 12-2. *A first cut at things to consider when building a business case.*

advantage in terms of both long-term organizational health and short-term payoffs. From a systems viewpoint, we look at the financial, managerial, sociological, technological and political consequences of the recommended changes as seen by both outsiders and insiders. And a critical element related to anticipated results is the impact on employees, infrastructure and culture. Ask and answer the silent questions from employees: WIFM (What's in it for me?), How will it affect my local work and my local and future organization? How will it affect the organization as a whole?

The strength and thoroughness of the business case will depend heavily on the size and history of the organization, the nature of its leadership, and the expectations of its customers and other stakeholders. These balances may be large-scale research balances all the way down to individual knowledge worker competencies, attitudes, and decisions on priorities or work or how to approach problems. As always, since everyone is potentially subjected to internal biases, erroneous assumptions, and misplaced beliefs, it is wise to get a second, or perhaps group, opinion to reevaluate how individuals or teams perceive the situation, their most effective aspects of work, or their balance points.

From another perspective, all changes in organizations create/demand a change in a number of balance points. Balance points are the points of equilibrium for dynamic tensions arising in an organization, or in implementation of change! A balance is necessary to ensure that one facet of implementation doesn't dominate another facet. For example, in a KM program, the processes and technology must work in concert; technology alone is not sufficient. In a KM program, dynamic tensions might include: How much risk are we willing to take to achieve leverage and, conversely, how much leveraging are we willing to do despite the risk? How much data and information should be left at the local level, and how much should be available globally? How much data and information and what data and information should be made explicit? How much data and information and what data and information should be captured in a formal system? In this world of access and excess, the answer is not automatically "more" (Bennet & Bennet, 2004). While often knowledge workers and leaders do not recognize that they are simply changing balance points, it is exactly these changes that can be so threatening to individuals if they do not recognize them as balance points and important aspects of the work.

(3) Demonstrate Leadership Commitment

When a respected senior leader clearly demonstrates commitment to a vision through words and actions, members of the senior leader's relationship network, which includes subordinates, quickly follow. In short, there are champions waiting to emerge throughout the organization: champions of theory and action, and champions of specific processes or projects who are, in fact, *already implementing these processes or projects at some level.* In every organization there are forward-thinking individuals who push the edge of change, no matter what name that change is called. It is the change agent's responsibility to find these individuals and spread the word of their successes, tying them to the vision of the organization. As leader after leader begins to demonstrate and communicate successes, large or small, other leaders recognize potential value to their focus areas with the organization. Interconnected successes quickly spread across the enterprise. As we know, success begets success.

Figure 12-3 is a collage of public photographs published widely on the Internet that reflected DoN leadership commitment to the implementation of Knowledge Management. Many leaders not only came on board, but became advocates. For example, the four-star Admiral of the Pacific Fleet became a Knowledge Management Champion and thought leader.

Figure 12-3. *Knowledge Management leader from inside the organization and outside the organization passionately shared their commitment and knowledge. (Collage shared on the Internet and in presentations around the world.)*

It is appropriate here to discuss the change agent's role in the organization. While the most effective change agent is recognized as organizationally connected to the highest levels of the organization, having free access to senior leadership, a true agent of change cannot be considered a competitive part of the infrastructure, nor can a successful change agent *own* the change they lead. Change agents act as a funnel for nurturing and building change across the organization, identifying successes, picking up the ideas behind those successes and then spreading them throughout the organization. The change agent connects people, integrates ideas and actions, and builds visibility of leadership commitment to those ideas and actions. Simple but consistent actions can facilitate this change. Here are some ideas about how to capture and communicate leadership commitment in a large, widely dispersed, global organization:

* Develop a *short* video, beginning with a two-minute opening by the senior leader of the organization, and featuring project leaders talking about their early successes. Have the senior leader hand-write notes to accompany copies of the video to leaders throughout the organization, asking them to ensure that every employee has the opportunity to see the video.

* Develop pass-it-down training, beginning at the very top of the organization. The concept of pass-it-down training is that leaders at all levels have the opportunity to impress on their teams the importance and significance of the planned change. This process has the added benefit of ensuring that organizational leadership understands the change and how it will affect their part of the organization. Teaching and facilitation are forms of learning.

* Hold a "town hall," featuring senior leadership, virtually supported (television, video, Internet, iPhone) to facilitate geographically dispersed organizations, with live connectivity. Much like a telethon, this event will offer the opportunity for workers at all levels to interact with senior leadership, voicing their concerns and ideas and receiving an immediate response, albeit "we need to think more about that." This process of *event intermediation* ensures a point in time where all senior leaders understand the importance of the change, and have an awareness of what their areas of responsibility are to help move toward that change.

* Capture quotes from early leaders and champions and embed these in presentations, both internal and external, at every level of the organization.

* Hold a *knowledge fair*, where every functional and organizational area is featured showing how they are contributing to achieving the vision, with real, related products already owned by the organization to share with other parts of the organization. Engage your creative imagination. Have senior leadership open the fair, and include enjoyable, memorable events that are centered around the way the organization needs to work, with members of the organization participating in the presentations. Create a groundswell of sharing and understanding by opening the fair to employees, stakeholders, and partners.

* Develop a virtual Internet-based reference tool about the knowledge fair, capturing people talking about their projects and leaders talking about their organizations, all focused on their contribution to achieving the desired change. Circulate this throughout the organization and the organization's stakeholders.

(4) Facilitate a Common Understanding

So often we as human beings leap forward with little thought for the consequences. While a shared vision certainly helps define the direction we are leaping, the larger and more complex an organization the more the imperative to develop a shared understanding of the *reasons behind* the movement toward that vision to ensure a connectedness of choices.

Representations in terms of words and visuals are the tools of trade for facilitating common understanding. Early models should address those areas needing the greatest clarity. Since every organization is at a different stage of development, has a different culture, and may or may not already understand the importance of knowledge and learning to the success of the organization, it is critical to ensure a solid recognition of the power of sharing knowledge, moving the organization from the bureaucratically embedded concept of "knowledge is power" to the emerging concept of "knowledge shared is power squared."

For example, the knowledge life cycle model used throughout the U.S. government (Figure 12-2) was intended to generate "Conversations that Count" on the relationship among data, information, and knowledge; the reality of information decay (information has the potential to become less important over time); and the effects as knowledge spreads across collaborative and competitive bases. Each employee has a story to tell. The intent of this model was to engage response and bring out both positive and negative feelings regarding past experiences, clearing the air to move toward a new way of thinking and building focused thought. Facilitating a common understanding of the knowledge life cycle is so critical that an early designer of KM certification courses spent several years developing a knowledge life cycle model (Firestone and McElroy, 2003).

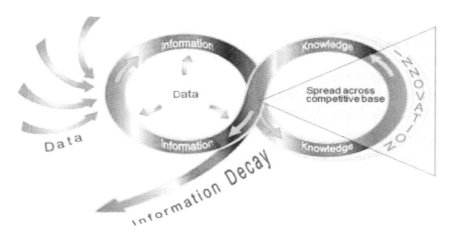

Figure 12-4. *Knowledge Life Cycle Model.*

When Figure 12-4 was used in the Department of the Navy (DoN) journey toward becoming a knowledge-centric organization, there were common stories that emerged. For example, one explication might go like this: "As knowledge is shared across organizations, it becomes more widely used. On the negative side, this means that other organizations now have the same opportunities; on the positive side, since ideas generate ideas, everyone has a greater opportunity to build new knowledge. What becomes of paramount importance is *how those ideas are used*." Another common explication that emerged from looking at this model focused on creativity and went something like this: "Since all people are creative, and everyone in today's world has access to an almost exponentially increasing amount of information, it is likely that any given creative idea will emerge in more than one place. The idea's time has come! As we can see, what is important in terms of market contribution is *continuous learning* (creation of new ideas) and the ability to effectively (and quickly) *act on those ideas*."

Today, of course, we recognize that the competition focus of yesterday is no longer valid. Rather, the question becomes: How do we build collaborative advantage? Perhaps this model has been useful in helping some individuals and organizations move to this new way of thinking.

To build a common understanding of "knowledge," a simple visual of a red apple with a bite taken out of it can be used (see Figure 12-5). Within the apple are listed many of the IT advances important to success, which can be updated as time moves us forward and as appropriate for a specific organization. The word "knowledge" streams out of the empty space where the bite was taken. The message delivered with this visual is simple and straightforward: while all that we are doing in information technology and information management is critically important, it is not until the bite (of information) is taken, chewed, digested, and acted upon that it becomes knowledge. Knowledge is created within the individual, and it is actionable. While organizational knowledge could certainly be considered an emergent phenomenon, the creation of knowledge and recognition of patterns at the organizational level is through people.

Once again, the process and thinking that goes into developing the pictures and models an organization uses to convey the way work gets done are just as important, if not more important, than the outcome. We will discuss this further in the next change element on setting limits.

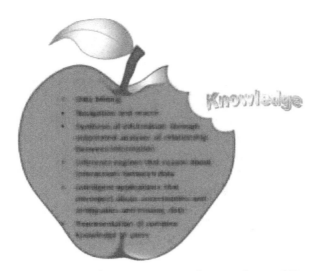

Figure 12-5. *Toward a common understanding of Knowledge.*

(5) Set Limits

All of the models discussed above limit the field of the possible in order to focus on a concept, facilitate a deeper understanding of that concept, and provide a mechanism for communicating that concept. We also set limits (provide focus) through developing and refining descriptions and definitions. Focusing on a concept in this manner provides the opportunity for developing new ideas and new thinking. For example, the U.S. Federal Chief Information Officer Council invited cross-agency participation, and representatives from the private sector and academia, to focus on what Knowledge Management meant to the Federal government. The results of this partnering were a clearer understanding of the role of Chief Knowledge Officers in the U.S. government, and definition of the fourteen learning objectives for a government certification course. In essence, these learning objectives defined the scope of Knowledge Management for the Federal sector and its large contract base as seen at that point in time. Limiting the scope of what was considered part of KM provided the opportunity to focus in these areas in order to add value to the bottom line of the organization.

Several graphics were developed to represent the technology explosion and the relationship of knowledge and change in this explosion. These are to encourage "Conversations that Matter." Figure 12-6 is one of those graphics, which started the conversation to define the field of KM.

A second example is one that might sound familiar; it has occurred in many government and private sector organizations. It is also analogous to any new change effort that the environment dictates—and management agrees—will add value to

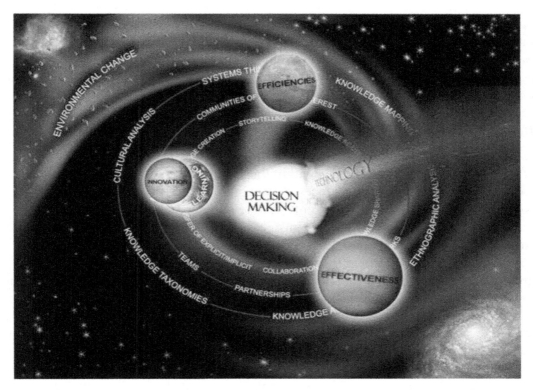

Figure 12-6. *Starting the conversation to explore the technology explosion.
(Conversations that Matter)*

organizational effectiveness. When eBusiness became the leading concept of the day, money was pulled from current change efforts to fund the new idea on the block. When a new concept emerges and is either supported by senior leadership, or should be, it is the change agent's task to clearly build the relationship between the new idea and efforts currently underway to harness any possible synergy. Too often, ongoing change efforts are tossed aside for new ideas before they have a chance to add value to the organization, and, eventually, as this pattern repeats itself, it is difficult for employees to take management change efforts seriously. This results in an organizational culture encouraging a wait-and-see attitude regarding all change strategies. By building on current efforts—and then fading out or merging these efforts with the new as is determined favorable to the organization over time (with employee input)—it is possible to take full advantage of new concepts, approaches, and perceptions.

A potential first step toward achieving this strategy is for the leaders of each change effort to coauthor and publish articles on the focus of each of these efforts, and how they fit together to work toward achieving the organization's mission. This process helps develop agreed-upon definitions, brings about focus, and builds working relationships that will help both efforts succeed. Returning to our specific example, how would we provide focus and create synergy between eBusiness (eB) and Knowledge Management (KM)? The focus of KM is on intellectual capital, and that means people; while eB is the interchange and processing of information via electronic techniques. These definitions reflect a common focus viewed through different lenses.

Both eB and KM bring with them a focus on processes. KM provides a methodology for creating processes within the organization to promote knowledge creation, haring and application processes that build on early total quality and business process reengineering concepts. In like manner, an integral part of implementing eB is the application of business process improvement or reengineering to streamline business processes to facilitate the electronic exchange of business information. KM, implemented by and at the organizational level while supporting empowerment and responsibility at the individual level, focuses on understanding the knowledge needs of an organization and the sharing and creation of knowledge through communities and Web-enabled collaboration, *connecting people*. The knowledge systems supporting these communities, based on interoperability concepts to ensure enterprise-wide sharing, build on information management, taking into account the human factor. While both KM and eB are in the business of information exchange, the KM focus is specifically on the *knowledge sharing aspect of this exchange*. This focusing of KM and eB—including clear definitions and the setting of limits—provides a rich fabric for the two strategic efforts to complement each other and for the organization to recognize that together these efforts offer synergistic opportunities for long-term success.

(6) Share New Ideas, Words and Behaviors

Thinking in new ways demands new words, or putting old words together in new ways, to communicate new thinking; and those new words (or combinations of old words) drive new behaviors. In like manner, new behaviors drive new thinking and new words. As early as 1784, Hugh Blair identified a clear, close alliance between thought and language, "Thought and Language act and re-act upon each other mutually" (Erlbaum, 1982). Later theorists such as Brown, Black, Bloomfield, Skinner, Quine, Popper, Wittgenstein and Whorf regarded language as a major form of behavior, a significant entity in its own right. Emig (1983) contended that language is a powerful, if not unique, way of constructing reality and acting on the world. (See the discussion on co-creating reality in Chapter 23/Part IV.) More recently, as we have come to realize that we are patterns of energy in an energetically connected world, the *sounds* of words can be a vibrational match to the knowing gained by experience. This, of course, is also the allure of music, storytelling and poetry.

Our movies have so much to say about our culture, and offer the opportunity of experience without direct activity. The 2016 movie titled *Arrival*, directed by Denis Villeneuve and distributed by Paramount, stars Amy Adams as linguist Louise Banks. When 12 extraterrestrial spacecraft appear around the Earth, she is asked to join the team exploring the reasons for their visit. Along with theoretical physicist Ian Donnelly (Jeremy Renner), Louise is given a language of symbols, which triggers visions in her head which are flash-forwards. The symbol translated as "weapon" winds up to represent the concept of "tool", and they are given a gift—the concept of time—which is one of 12 gifts to be provided to humanity. This fascinating treatment offers *new symbols to represent new concepts*. All written language is based on symbols and patterns of those symbols, although we are so familiar with our native language that we no longer think of them as such. Symbolic Representation is a Knowledge Capacity introduced in Chapter 21/Part III. An example of Symbolic Representation is an emogi, a small icon used to express a concept or emotion in electronic communication.

Think back to a time when you came up with a new descriptive word or perhaps used an older word in a new way. This was an expression of something more than what the sound or word previously represented. When those around you hear you repeat this, they begin to understand the meaning behind the word, albeit possibly somewhat different than you intended, and may even add it to their active vocabulary. Whether purposefully or accidentally, this is how words and their relationships to concepts come into being.

While the theoretical tapestry that builds relationships among thinking, language, and actions is varied and inconclusive, it is clear that there is a relationship, and that effective use of words and understanding the concepts these words represent has the potential to affect thoughts and behaviors. As an example, take the concepts of clustering and clumping. While these words have long been a part of Webster's collection, the way they are used in forward-thinking organizations today drives a necessary change in behavior. *Clustering* and *clumping* define different ways of organizing (and accessing) data and information. Clustering is how data and information are usually organized, bringing together those things that are similar or related. This way of organizing is driven by the content of the data and information itself.

Clumping is organizing data and information driven by the decisions that need to be made. At the enterprise level, those authoritative data fields that are needed for decision-making are identified and connected (or clumped together) to provide real-time input to emerging decision-making requirements. In a system, that means linking secondary data and information needed by the individual who will use the primary information for decision-making. For example, if a decision-maker has repeated failure of an engine part that is only periodically used, not only is it important to know how to fix it and have spare parts available for this recurring problem, but it might save considerable time, effort, and dollars if the decision-maker had known that the engine was scheduled for replacement six months down the road. There are often pieces of information that, if known, would change the decisions we make on a daily basis. When a segment of the organization creates a database or information system for the organization or enterprise, it is responsible for thinking through how that information will be used and by whom, and what additional known or potentially available information may be required to ensure the best decisions. We don't know what we don't know. *With knowledge comes the responsibility to use and share it wisely, and to help others use and share it wisely.*

<<<<<<<◇>>>>>>>

INSIGHT: **With knowledge comes the responsibility to use and share it wisely, and to help others use and share it wisely.**

<<<<<<<◇>>>>>>>

A second example is the increasing use of the word *verication*. Verication, not yet discovered by dictionary updaters, is the process of consulting a trusted ally. We as humans do it regularly. When we do not have explicit evidence to verify or validate the correctness of a decision, or question the explicit evidence we do have because of our "gut" feeling, we can vericate the decision. This means going to a recognized expert with whom you have a relationship (a trusted ally, often also a colleague or friend) to get their opinion, that is, grounding your decision through an expert's experience and learning. We do this when we hire a consultant team to advise on a planned initiative. Having a word for this behavior helps leaders and workers to recognize it as an acceptable practice in decision-making, increasing the value of intellectual capital in the organization.

To share new ideas, words, and behaviors consistent with the vision of the organization, an aggressive, comprehensive communications strategy, both internal and external, is essential to ensure the connectedness of choices discussed above. Internal successes and external validation provide strong explicit evidence in support of the business case. The use of teams and communities—an important part of the ICAS[12-1] implementation strategy—helps facilitate the flow of information and knowledge across the organization. Here are a few ideas on how to do that:

* Create a *meme* (an idea that catches on, and becomes embedded in the culture). An example of a meme is "change through ex-change" or the famous army slogan, "be all you can be." These are expressions that take on a life of their own. "Knowledge shared is knowledge squared" is also a meme.

* Build a story on the vision of your organization and circulate it widely, using it as a basis for discussions.

*Promote "Conversations that Matter" where graphics and images are used to stimulate the imagination around a specific focus area such as visioning the future. See Chapter 11.

* Participate in external studies and research projects with respected, high-name-recognition organizations such as APQC (American Productivity Quality Center). When participating in a study, rotate representatives and create forums for these representatives to share what they are learning with the larger organization.

(7) Identify the Strategic Approach

There is no substitute for strategic thinking at all levels of the organization. Knowledge workers need to think strategically as well as locally, and conceptually as well as logically. The first key to any kind of "thinking" is an understanding of what needs to be thought about. For example, develop a draft concept of operations for the new organization and spread it across the current organization for response. Put it up on a server and open it up for virtual comment (with ownership of comments). This can be important. If a knowledge worker has a point to make, it should be a point they will claim, and one the organization will seriously consider.

Systems thinking can be used to explore the various levels of a strategy. For example, a primary reason for implementing Knowledge Management was because the information explosion was increasing decision-making complexity, driving additional investment in IT and forming a reinforcing loop. See Figure 12-7. Three balancing loops were put in place, one at the individual level, a second focused at the organizational level, and the third at the enterprise-wide level.

A key part of the change strategy is creation of a community of practice to help facilitate change, engaging integrators throughout the organization. One person, or one part of the organization, cannot accomplish change; it must come from within at every level of the organization, yet with a consistent focus and direction. Integrators are knowledge workers who are respected, trusted, and who regularly exchange information and knowledge with others. The integrator role is highly dependent on personality and values, and is a role that emerges over time in relationship networks. (See the discussion of Relationship Network Management in Chapter 10.) These individuals, key to both formal and informal networks, are usually obvious in an organization, but can be identified through social network analysis. Develop these integrators into leaders and champions. Implement their good ideas; and, above all, engage them in multiple teams and communities.

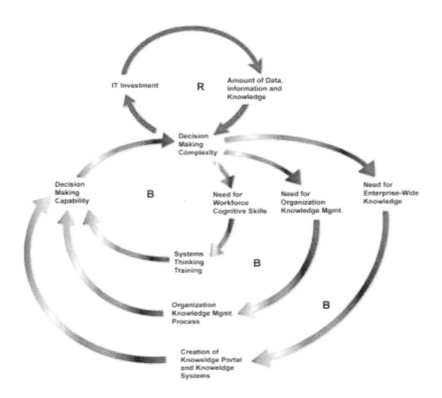

Figure 12-7. *A systems look identifying the strategic approach of implementing KM.*

(8) Develop the Infrastructure

As technology advances, a seamless infrastructure is essential to facilitate the collaboration and free flow of information that enables effective decision-making. While short-term change can occur through mandates, it is often short-term in effectiveness as well. Long-term change requires embedding the change in the culture of the organization, the way work is done. At the same time, the infrastructure must be put in place to support the vision of *how* work will be done.

We live in a technology-enabled world with global implications. More and more work is done at a distance, driving the need for collaboration and knowledge systems that support interoperability. Development and support of, and rewards to, teams and communities ensure *use* of the technology and information infrastructures; education and training of the workforce, whether virtual or face-to-face, ensure the *ability to successfully use it*.

The organization's career center, in conjunction with or as part of the human resources department, can benefit long-term change in a number of areas. Here are some ideas:

* Conduct a gap analysis of the skill sets of the current organization and the desired organization, addressing the competencies necessary to achieve projected missions, strategies and initiatives to help the organization attract new personnel and sustain the capabilities to accomplish its mission.

* Identify the work that will be done within the organization, and that work which will be outsourced in support of the organization. For the government, this includes identifying the work that is inherently governmental.

* Create a Workforce Strategic Plan to develop strategies and specific plans for hiring, training, and professional development, with the goal to promote integrative competencies throughout the workforce. A thoughtful, visionary, and forward-thinking plan can lay the foundation for positive organizational transformation. Integrative competencies provide connective tissue, creating the knowledge, skills, abilities, and behaviors that support and enhance other competencies. They have a multiplier effect through their capacity to enrich the individual's cognitive capabilities while enabling integration of other competencies, leading to improved understanding, performance and decisions. Examples are information literacy, systems thinking, and pattern thinking.

* Develop a career path guide to provide individual guidance to employees in meeting the continuing challenges of technological change. The guide should include an explication of roles in the new organization with related learning objectives and job requirements.

* Create a virtual tool for individuals to use in developing their personal career paths. The tool could help the workforce assess their current and required competencies, as well as helping them generate a career progression plan to attain competencies needed for future job assignments based on individual, long-term goals. While the individual becomes responsible for their own career advancement in a knowledge organization, the organization must consistently encourage, nurture and support career development.

* Embed change elements and future skills needed into all ongoing short and long-term education and training initiatives.

(9) Measure and Incentivize

In a survey conducted a few years ago in a government organization implementing a KM system pilot, responders identified the most important factors in successful KM implementation in this relative order: culture (29%), processes (21%), metrics (19%), content (17%), leadership (10%) and technology (4%). What is fascinating, and a product of the organization's culture as well as that of many industry organizations, is that metrics (how success is measured and communicated) appeared more important than content (that which is in the system itself). Metrics are critical to most organizations, and have become part of the culture of the organization as well as the managing system. Recognizing this aspect of your organization from the very beginning of a change approach can mean the difference between success and failure of your change efforts.

Metrics drive behavior, and can be a powerful force of behavioral change. One change approach is to ensure metrics are used that measure the organization's intent for the future, not just measuring past actions. Senior leadership can sponsor a working team focused on developing metrics *guidance* for the organization that includes participation from across functional and organizational units. While metrics must be specifically tailored to the organization, there are three types of specific measures to monitor and guide change initiatives from different perspectives: outcome metrics (concerning the overall organization and measuring large-scale characteristics such as increased productivity or revenue for the organization); output metrics (measuring project level characteristics such as the effectiveness of lessons learned to new business captured); and system metrics (monitoring the usefulness and responsiveness of the supporting technology tools). Have your team develop an overall process for developing metrics, including sample metrics and case studies. Again, recall that what you measure identifies what management feels is important, and drives the way work is done. Measure for the future. (See Bennet and Bennet (2007) for an in-depth treatment on metrics in a knowledge organization.)

An active and highly visible awards program that rewards both individual and team behaviors draws out successes and involves a larger number of employees in change efforts. Once again, behaviors that are rewarded will become behaviors that are embedded into the infrastructure of the organization and its culture. Here are some ideas:

    * Develop an awards program rewarding teams who are early implementers, with senior leaders presenting the awards. Create events to publicize these awards.

    * Sponsor spin-off communities of practice and interest that recognize and reward both individual and group contributions. Examples of awards programs would include a monetary award for the individual who is voted (by members of the community) as the most knowledgeable, most accessible, and with the best response rate; and a group award to all members of the community who participate in a specific solution.

    * Give promotions in terms of leadership and monetary remuneration to those individuals (and teams!) who best emulate the desired behavior for the *future* organization.

(10) Provide Tools

Buckminster Fuller once said that if you want to change a culture, provide tools. Any change approach can benefit when we recognize the truth of this observation. Writing this change strategy out is intended as a tool for the interested reader.

As guidance and policy is issued, tools that provide approaches to, and resources for, accomplishing that guidance and policy are distributed. The tools themselves are a product of subject matter experts across the organization who come together for a period of time to develop these resources. Note that the process of development, as well as the product, is part of the change strategy. Virtual toolkits are then made freely available in various formats to ensure access by all employees, stakeholders, and organizational partners, with the understanding that change in a complex organization must be validated externally while driven internally. Change cannot occur in isolation, and with the permeable and porous boundaries necessary for successful organizations in a global world, it is difficult for a single organization, or part of an organization, to move forward when those surrounding them are operating at a stale level of thinking. Share the tools widely.

In the DoN strategy, areas of initial focus for tools included Information Literacy and other integrative competencies such as Systems Thinking, Complexity Thinking and Pattern Thinking. Include any additional tools specifically required for your organization to survive and grow such as team and community care and feeding, metrics guidance, and security and privacy issues in an open information environment. Figure 12-8 is a collage of some of the tools supporting DoN implementation of Knowledge Management.

Figure 12-8. *A collage of tools supporting DoN implementation of KM.*

(11) Promote Learning

No organization or individual can change without learning, nor once change is made can any organization or individual continue to function and be of value in a changing environment without continuous learning. Though this important concept emerged over a decade ago in the Total Quality environment, and Senge (1990) pushed the learning organization into higher-level executive thinking, we need to keep our awareness on, followed by appropriate actions, the need to have systems in place to help facilitate learning in a virtual world.

A first step is to embed learning into the everyday life of the organization, with the organization and its leaders encouraging and providing opportunities for learning, and every knowledge worker taking responsibility for—and being accountable for—their own learning. (See Bennet et al., 2015b.) Here are several ideas to begin this approach:

* Issue continuous learning guidance for the entire workforce, placing increased responsibility on employees to remain current and expand their knowledge by taking advantage of new ways of learning. Distributed learning technologies, experiential learning, and other nontraditional approaches to education and training have overtaken the traditional classroom student/instructor approach. With these new approaches, knowledge workers have the ability to take responsibility for and direct their own learning and development in a variety of ways, and on a continual basis, throughout their careers. For example, the guidance sets the expectation that all knowledge workers participate in 120 hours of continuous learning activities (using organizational toolkits, participating in community exchanges, attending conferences, etc.) each year in addition to the minimum competencies established in their career fields and required for specific workforce assignments.

* Make continuous learning a bullet in every individual's performance appraisal. Each employee would develop a continuous learning plan in concert with their manager and team leaders, self-certifying completion of this plan during performance appraisals.

* Set the organizational expectation—and validate that expectation by example at the highest levels of the organization—that every leader will be a mentor, and that every employee has the responsibility for sharing what they are learning with their peers.

* Ensure rotational assignments, allowing individuals to build viable networks based on relationships (and, when possible, across organizational boundaries in their fields of expertise).

Following the growth path of knowledge sharing show in Figure 12-1, reaching out to external colleagues and partners is critical to continued expansion. By sharing with peers—for example, through participation in conferences and cross-organizational communities—there is the opportunity to advance the whole career field, which causes a multiplier effect. (See Chapter 30/Part IV).

(12) Envision an Even Greater Future

The place from which we currently act and respond, our point of reference, is reflective of the model upon which our organizational structures are grounded. As a groundswell of change is created through this strategy, in conjunction with the creative change ideas that will emerge from within, the organization's point of reference will also change. To ensure this process of continuous improvement, new ideas and new thoughts need to come into focus and enlarge the future vision, and be embedded in all of the documentation and educational resources supporting that vision. An example is creating a knowledge-centric organization. What is critical for future success is an organization's ability to take the best of each new management movement or initiative and discern the value, determine the fit, and integrate the best of each into the organization in a way that makes sense.

In the complex world in which we live, there is no lack of new management approaches, and assuredly each approach offers potential value. What is difficult to achieve is the balance between recognizing and sustaining that which is good in an organization, embedding that which has been determined valuable and is currently being implemented, and embracing the value offered by new ideas and management approaches. What is that balance? What are the potential gains and losses from this approach? How do we facilitate the gains and mitigate the losses? Finally, since a complex organization cannot be controlled in the classical meaning of the term—nor should it be—how do we ensure that value, as it emerges, is shared across the organization?

This dilemma of balance extends through every aspect of an organization. A visible example is the insertion of new technology. At what point does the organization wishing to succeed in the future global world embrace this new technology? How fast should this transition move? What mindsets and strategies (such as moving the security focus from technology to information) need to be changed?

In this new world, many organizations are moving forward at a fast pace, with a vision and strategy, but without a predetermined path. Yet planning is a gift of the human mind! (Planning is discussed in depth in Chapter 16/Part III.) The path has been and will continue to be forged by dedicated professionals in each organization, working individually and collectively, but always aware of the organization's mission. The vision is to increase the number of dedicated professionals, and to ensure that every single individual in the organization has awareness of—and is committed to achieving—the vision of the organization. As this vision turns and changes in response to the turbulent environment, the understanding of individuals within the organization must turn and change in concert with it.

This focus on people is holistic, ranging from the creation of theory and the building of shared understanding to the development of infrastructure to support individual and organizational learning and development of knowledge centricity. Enterprise-level leadership ranges from promulgating guidance and policy, to providing tools, to rewarding success. Effectively, this complex change strategy cannot help but encourage a natural progression toward intelligent activity, contributing to the cultural change essential to take full advantage of the opportunities offered by a changing and uncertain environment, and facilitating a connectedness of choices through the sharing of new thought in a fully aware and conscious process.

In 2001 the U.S. Department of the Navy (DoN) became the first government organization to be designated among the top ten "Most Admired Knowledge Enterprises (MAKE)" in the United States. The Navy was specifically noted for the leadership of its knowledge-based programs and initiatives, and for its emphasis on organizational learning. In May 2005 a case study of the DoN was performed by researchers from *InsideKnowledge* as part of a three-organization series on the decline in the effectiveness of KM when there was no longer an Enterprise Chief Knowledge Officer as part of the structure. Quite to their surprise, they discovered that KM was alive and well in the DoN, integrated heavily into the system at all levels. As the Editor Simon Lelic (2005) wrote:

> This month's cover story details what can confidently be described as the most comprehensive and far-reaching knowledge-management initiative ever attempted anywhere in the world ... KM has ... become a fundamental aspect of the way the U.S. Department of the Navy operates ... From the highest to the lowest ranks, from the corridors of Washington, D.C., to the front line of military engagement, there is a prevailing understanding that knowledge, and by extension Knowledge Management, is everyone's business.

[The strategy presented in this chapter is that used by the U.S. Department of the Navy (DoN) in implementing Knowledge Management (KM).]

Questions for Reflection:

Comparing the way that you implement change with this strategy, what are the impacts of any steps that you do not include?

Why might this strategy be effective to move from Phase 1 to 2 of the Intelligent Social Change Journey, and what limitations might apply if you are moving from Phase 2 to 3?

Are you asking the right questions to engage stakeholders in the co-creation of solutions?

A Preview of Part III: Learning in the Present
[Excerpt from Chapter 16/Part III]

Time is the glue that holds space together. Time and space are interwoven. The higher the amount of intelligent activity, the closer together they become. The lower the amount of activity that leads to intelligent activity—which leads to unintelligent activity—the more forces are created and the more time and space are separated (MacFlouer, 2004-16). Thus, delays of time are inevitable in the presence of certain space conditions. As is described in *Urantia* (1952):

> Time is a succession of instants that is perceived by analysis, while space is a system of associated points that is perceived by synthesis. These two dissimilar concepts are coordinated and associated by the integrating insight of each individual personality... only man possesses this time-space perceptibility.

A difficulty we have in understanding space in the physical plane is due to the fact that while our material bodies exist in space, space also exists in these same bodies. It may help our understanding of space relationships, from a relative point of view, if we think of space as a property of all material bodies. As a body moves through space, it takes with it all of its properties, even the space which is within it. Thus, at the material level all patterns of reality occupy space. This, of course, begs the question of whether the pattern of an idea, a thought form, occupies space, that is, is the immaterial non-spatial? This is explored in Chapter 26/Part IV.

The advent of Quantum mechanics and relativity theory brought with it a new understanding of time, space and objects as in some way continuous. As Wilber (1993) describes, space is not blank but serves a surrounding function to objects. On the other hand, the boundaries of objects are defined by the space around them. Space cannot exist separate from objects, and objects must be enclosed by space, so in this sense space and objects are one. Wilber (1993, p. 82) goes on to say,

> Furthermore, objects, in order to exist, must endure; that is, duration or time is necessary for the existence of objects … Conversely, the existence of duration depends upon objects, for without objects to endure, there could be no duration; and in this sense, time and objects are one. It follows that space and time are also one. Hence space, time, and objects are mutually dependent and inseparable.

# # #

Appendix A: The Overarching ISCJ Model

The Intelligent Social Change Journey (ISCJ)

NOTE: Each model builds on the understanding gained from experiencing the previous phase

Phase 1: LEARNING FROM THE PAST

CHARACTERISTICS: Linear and Sequential, Repeatable, Engaging past learning, Starting from current state., Cause and effect relationships.

Phase 2: LEARNING IN THE PRESENT

CHARACTERISTICS: Recognition of patterns; Social interaction; Co-evolving with environment through continuous learning, quick response, robustness, flexibility, adaptability, alignment.

Phase 3: CO-CREATING OUR FUTURE

CHARACTERISTICS: Creative imagination; Recognition of global Oneness; Mental in service to the intuitive; Balancing senses; Bringing together past, present and future; Knowing; Beauty; Wisdom.

SOCIAL STATE (Depth of Connection)

SYMPATHY → EMPATHY → COMPASSION

MOVEMENT

EXPANDED CONSCIOUSNESS → (Open to the Spiritual)

CONSCIOUSNESS is considered a state of awareness and a private, selective and continuously changing process, a sequential set of ideas, thoughts, images, feelings and perceptions and an understanding of the connections and relationships among them and our self.

FORCES occur when one type of energy affects another type of energy in a way where they are moving in different directions. Bounded (inward focused) and/or limited knowledge creates forces.

REDUCTION OF FORCES → (Engage forces by choice)

INCREASED INTELLIGENT ACTIVITY → (Growth of wisdom)

INTELLIGENT ACTIVITY represents a perfect state of interaction where intent, purpose, direction, values and expected outcomes are clearly understood and communicated among all parties, reflecting wisdom and achieving a higher truth.

KNOWLEDGE (The capacity (potential or actual) to take effective action)

	Phase 1	Phase 2	Phase 3
NATURE:	•Product of the past •Context sensitive, situation dependent •Partial, incomplete	•Expanded knowledge sharing, social learning, cooperation, collaboration •Questioning of why? •Pursuit of truth	•Recognition that with knowledge comes responsibility. •Conscious pursuit of larger truth •Knowledge selectively used as a measure of effectiveness
REFLECTION:	•Review of interactions, feedback •Determination of cause and effect (logic) •(Inward focus) Questioning decisions and actions: Why What did I intend? What really happened? Why were there differences? What would I do same? What would I do differently?	•Deeper development of conceptual thinking (higher mental thought) •Connecting power of diversity and individuation to whole •(Moving toward outward focus) •Recognition of different world views; the exploration of information from different perspectives •Expanded knowledge capacities.	•Valuing of creative ideas. Asking larger questions: How does this idea serve humanity? Are there any negative consequences? •(Outward focus). Openness to other's ideas with humility: What if this idea is right? Are my beliefs or other mental models limiting my thought? Are hidden assumptions or feelings interfering with intelligent activity?
COGNITIVE SHIFTS:	•Recognition of importance of feedback •Ability to recognize systems; impact of external forces •Recognition and location of "me" in the larger picture (conscious awareness) •Early pattern recognition and concept development	•Ability to recognize and apply patterns at all levels within a domain of knowledge to predict outcomes •Growing understanding of complexity. •Increased connectedness of choices; recognition of direction you are heading; expanded meaning-making •Expanded ability to bisociate ideas; increased creativity	•Sense and knowing of Oneness •Development of both lower (logic) and upper (conceptual) mental faculties, which work in concert with the emotional guidance system •Application of patterns across knowledge domains for greater good •Recognition of self as a co-creator of reality •Ability to engage in intelligent activity. •Developing the ability to tap into the intuitional plane at will

Developed by Mountain Quest Institute. Contact alex@mountainquestinstitute.com for permissions

Taken from Bennet, et al. (2017). *The Profundity and Bifurcation of Change. Parts I through V.* Frost, WV: MQIPress.

Appendix B: Five-Book Table of Contents

The Profundity and Bifurcation of Change
The Intelligent Social Change Journey

For Each:
Cover
Title Page
Quote from *The Kybalion*
Table of Contents
Tables and Figures
Appreciation

Preface

Introduction to the Intelligent Social Change Journey

Part I: LAYING THE GROUNDWORK

Part I Introduction

Part V: LIVING THE FUTURE

ADDENDUM: Manifesting Our Choice *by David and Alex Bennet*

APPENDICES:
Appendix A: The Overarching ISCJ Model
Appendix B: The Table of Contents for All Parts
Appendix C: *An Infinite Story*
Appendix D: Engaging Tacit Knowledge
Appendix E: Knowing
Appendix F: Values for Creativity

ENDNOTES

REFERENCES

About Mountain Quest
About the Authors

TOOLS

Part I: Introduction
3-1. Force Field Analysis
4-1. Self Belief Assessment
4-2. Humility
5-1. Engaging Tacit Knowledge (See Appendix D.)

Part II: Learning From the Past
7-1. Personal Plane-ing Process
7-2. The Five Whys
9-1. Engaging Outside Worldviews
9-2. Practicing Mental Imagining
10-1. Grounding through Nature
10-2. Relationship Network Management
11-1. Co-Creating Conversations that Matter

Part III: Learning in the Present
13-1. Trust Mapping
14-1. Building Mental Sustainability
16-1. Integrating Time into the Self Experience
16-2. Scenario Building
17-1. Thinking Patterns
17-2. Storying: Capture (see Appendix G)
17-3. Storying: Sculpt (see Appendix G)
17-4. Storying: Tell (see Appendix G)
18-1. Connecting through the Heart

Appendix F
Values for Creativity
[Supports discussion of values in Chapter 9 and Chapter 29/Part IV.]

$\mathbf{A}$ creative environment is fueled by the values of integrity, empathy, transparency, collaboration, learning, and contribution that foster trust and a spirit of collaborative success (Avedisian & Bennet, 2010).

Integrity is defined as "steadfast adherence to a strict moral or ethical code" (American Heritage Dictionary, 2006). A person or organization with integrity is "whole," aligning words and actions, keeping commitments, doing the right thing, and engaging in fair dealing. Empathy, discussed in Chapter 35/Part V is the act of identifying with another's struggle as if it were one's own, and is the ultimate expression of a sense of equality. "Empathy requires a porous boundary between I and thou that allows the identity of two beings to mingle in a shared mental space" (Rifkin, 2009, p. 160). Empathy asserts the unconditional value of the human person and the meaning of his growth and the growth of his fellow man. When coupled with integrity, empathy builds the foundation not for just collaboration and participation, but for true fraternity, reciprocity, and integration.

Integrity and empathy provide the pre-conditions for the effectiveness of other more operational values by creating trust and mutual respect, and providing a non-judgmental environment, all of which form the basis of communication through shared understanding. Empathy and integrity are not mutually independent. First, empathy needs to be understood, confirmed and practiced in the light of integrity. Without integrity, empathy may degenerate into sentimentality. Second, integrity is softened by empathy. Without empathy, integrity may become judgmental, and even harsh and unforgiving. Together, empathy and integrity serve as a foundation for effective teamwork and facilitating knowledge creation, sharing and leveraging, and enabling new, quick, flexible, and effective responses.

The concept of **transparency** is defined as: easily seen through or detected and free from guile; candid or open (The American Heritage Dictionary, 2000). Again, we see a level of interdependency emerging. Empathy and integrity facilitate transparency by fostering trust, while transparency, in turn, reinforces trust. Unless transparency is balanced by empathy and integrity, it could foster misunderstanding and breakdown trust and relationships rather than support them.

Transparency supports connecting with others, and when you are connecting with someone else, you are connecting with yourself. Walsch (2009) says that when you are communicating with a mind outside of your mind—moving from an internal dialogue into an external dialogue—it puts you in touch with a part of your self that is bigger than your own mind. As Walsch (2009, p. 32) explains,

> In an external dialogue, another person can bring you fresh energy, provide a different perspective. They can come to the subject with a clear head, free of the self-judgment through which you are looking at everything. They see you as you really are, proving the irony that sometimes you have to get out of yourself to get into yourself. Sometimes you have to stop looking at yourself to see yourself.

Beyond sharing documents on websites, transparency extends to openly sharing ideas, feelings, personal view points, and different levels of knowledge (Bennet and Bennet, 2008a). Applying the levels of knowledge model, transparency moves beyond surface knowledge to a focus on shallow knowledge, with the responsibility to ensure some level of understanding and meaning that makes information actionable in a changing, uncertain and complex environment. Further, by building on surface and shallow knowledge, and developing deep knowledge, decision-makers at all levels understand underlying relationships and patterns which enable them to shift their frame of reference as the context and situation shift. In this way, transparency contributes not only to better problem-solving and decision-making, but also to fostering creativity and innovation, and the sharing of expertise.

Walsch (2009) says that we are living on the edge of what he called *The Time of Instaparency*. This is a time when everything is known instantly, transparently. As he adds, "Such moment-to-moment awareness of all that's going on everywhere produces alterations in perspective that start dominoes falling all over the place" (p. 53).

Participation is a keystone for the Net Generation, who reach out and creatively engage ideas and people around the world. This participation extends to political engagement and community service. **Collaboration** means, "to work together, especially in a joint intellectual effort" (American Heritage Dictionary, 2000). In the current environment, the meaning of collaboration has extended from relatively intact internal groups at the team, unit, or company level to a fluid, changing interdependent network of diverse contributors across the internal and external environment. A knowledge worker has a new type of peer network, one that moves from autonomy to interdependence, from deference to dialogue, and from a primary focus on doing a job well to a focus on contribution to collective purposes (Heckscher, 2007, p.108-109). In this peer network, alignment around such values as collaboration, transparency, and contribution make it possible for knowledge workers to work together in environments that are open, changing, and diverse. Collaboration is a core value embraced by the Net Geners, involving engagement and participation. "Collaboration as Net Geners know it, is achieving something *with* other people, experiencing power through other people, not by ordering a gaggle of followers to do your bidding." (Tapscott, 2009, p. 163).

Closely linked to participation and collaboration, **contribution** measures success and performance in the context of helping peers and the organization move toward a common mission and strategy. Participation is the act of engagement, collaboration is how to engage, and contribution is the result of that engagement. The purpose-driven orientation of contribution is a motivating force in the lives of Net Generation knowledge workers. Through global connectivity, Net Geners share openly, engaging others ideas and contributing their ideas freely. As an operational value **learning** is integrally related to the ability to contribute. Learning in the CUCA environment means receiving, understanding, thinking critically, and learning how to adapt and apply knowledge quickly in new and unfamiliar situations.

Learning affects every other value, offering a way of practicing and applying each of the values in every aspect of work life including interactions with peers, customers, vendors, how work gets done, and how success is measured. This learning is collaborative. For example, demonstrating the interdependence between learning, empathy and collaboration, Tapscott says,

> It goes without saying that collaborative learning, with its emphasis on mindfulness, attunement to others, nonjudgmental interactions, acknowledgement of each person's unique contributions, and recognition of the importance of deep participation and a shared sense of meaning coming out of embedded relationships, can't help but foster greater empathic engagement. (Tapscott, 2009, p. 607)

Bringing this conversation full circle, creativity itself could be considered an operational value in terms of the ability to perceive new relationships and new possibilities, see things form a different frame of reference, or realize new ways of understanding/having insight or portraying something. Since innovation represents the creation of new ideas and the transformation of those ideas into useful applications, the combination of creativity and contribution as operational values bring about innovation.

[Excerpted from Avedisian and Bennet, 2010]

Endnotes

8-1. Part of the University of Mannheim, the Mannheim School of Social Sciences, located in Mannheim, Baden-Württemberg, Germany, is recognized for its strength in empirical and analytical research, and for using innovative quantitative techniques in its research design.

9-1. The term philistinism is descriptive of anti-intellectualism, a social attitude that undervalues and despises art, beauty, spirituality and intellect. A philistine person is an individual who is smugly narrow of mind and of conventional morality whose materialistic views and tastes indicate a lack of and indifference to cultural and aesthetic values (Webster, 1962, p. 1099). In *Culture and Anarchy: An Essay in Political and Social Criticism* (1869, pp. 28-29), Matthew Arnold said:

Now, the use of culture is that it helps us, by means of its spiritual standard of perfection, to regard wealth as but machinery, and not only to say as a matter of words that we regard wealth as but machinery, but really to perceive and feel that it is so. If it were not for this purging effect wrought upon our minds by culture, the whole world, the future, as well as the present, would inevitably belong to the Philistines. The people who believe most that our greatness and welfare are proved by our being very rich, and who most give their lives and thoughts to becoming rich, are just the people whom we call the Philistines. Culture say: "Consider these people, then, their way of life, their habits, their manners, the very tones of their voices; look at them attentively; observe the literature they read, the things which give them pleasure, the words which come forth out of their mouths, the thoughts which make the furniture of their minds; would any amount of wealth be worth having with the condition that one was to become just like these people by having it?"

12-1. The term ICAS refers to the Intelligent Complex Adaptive System model of organizations. It is briefly introduced in Chapter 8 and used as an example of a co-evolving organization in Chapter 14/Part III. (Bennet & Bennet, 2004)

References

Abrahamson, E. (2004). *Change Without Pain: How Managers Can Overcome Initiative Overload, Organizational Chaos, and Employee Burnout*. Boston, MA: Harvard Business School Press.

American Heritage Dictionary of the English Language (4th ed.) (2006). Boston: Houghton Mifflin Company.

Argyris, Chris (2000). "The Relevance of Actionable Knowledge for Breaking the Code" in Beer, M. and Nohria, N. (Eds.) (2000). *Breaking the Code of Change*. Boston, MA: Harvard Business School Press, 394-415.

Argyris, C. (1993). *Knowledge for Action*. San Francisco, CA: Jossey Bass.

Argyris, C. and Schon, D. (1978). *Organizational Learning: A Theory of Action Perspective*. Reading, MA: Addison-Wesley.

Arnold, M. (1869 in 1960-1977). "Culture and Anarchy: An Essay in Political and Social Criticism" in Super, R.H. (ed.), *The Complete Prose Works of Matthew Arnold*, Vol. V: *Culture and Anarchy with Friendship's Garland and Some Literary Essays* (1965): 28-29. Ann Arbor: The University of Michigan Press.

Ashby, W. R. (1964). *An Introduction to Cybernetics*. London: Methuen.

Avedisian, J. and Bennet, A. (2010). "Values as Knowledge: A New Frame of Reference for a New Generation of Knowledge Workers" in *On the Horizon*, Vol. 18, No. 3, 255-265.

Bainbridge, C. (1996). *Designing for Change: A Practical Guide to Business Transformation*. New York: John Wiley & Sons.

Bakker, A.B. and Schaufeli, W.B. (2008). "Positive Organizational Behavior: Engaged Employees in Flourishing Organizations" in *Journal of Organizational Behavior*, Vol. 29 No. 2, 147-154.

Bateson, G. (1972). *Steps to an Ecology of the Mind*. New York: Ballantine.

Begley, S., (2007). *Train Your Mind Change Your Brain: How a New Science Reveals Our Extraordinary Potential to Transform Ourselves*. New York: Ballantine Books.

Beer, Michael and Nohria, Nitin (Eds.) (2000). *Breaking the Code of Change*. Boston, MA: Harvard Business School Press.

Bennet, A. and Bennet, D. (2013). *Decision-Making in The New Reality*. Frost, WV: MQIPress.

Bennet, A. and Bennet, D. (2010a). "Multidimensionality: Building the Mind/Brain Infrastructure for the Next Generation Knowledge Worker" in *On the Horizon*, Vol. 18, No. 3, 240-254.

Bennet, A. and Bennet, D. (2010b). "Leaders, Decisions and the Neuro-Knowledge System" in Wallis, S., *Cybernetics and Systems Theory in Management: Tools, Views and Advancements*. Hershey, PA: IGI Global.

Bennet, A. and Bennet, D. (2008a). "The Depth of Knowledge: Surface, Shallow, or Deep?" in *VINE: The Journal of Information and Knowledge Management Systems,* Vol. 38, No. 4, 405-420.

Bennet, D. and Bennet, A. (2008e). "Engaging Tacit Knowledge in Support of Organizational Learning" in *VINE: Journal of Information and Knowledge Systems,* 38(1), 72-94.

Bennet, A. and Bennet, D. (2006a). "Learning as Associative Patterning" in *VINE: Journal of Information and Knowledge Systems*, Vol. 36, No. 4, 371-376.

Bennet, A. and Bennet, D. (2004). *Organizational Survival in the New World: The Intelligent Complex Adaptive System.* Boston, MA: Elsevier.

Bennet, A., Bennet, D. and Avedisian, J. (2015a). *The Course of Knowledge: A 21st Century Theory.* Frost, WV: MQIPress.

Bennet, A., Bennet, D. and Lewis, J. (2015c). *Leading with the Future in Mind: Knowledge and Emergent Leadership.* Frost, WV: MQIPress.

Bennet, D., Bennet, A. and Turner, R. (2015b). *Expanding the Self: The Intelligent Complex Adaptive Learning System.* Frost, WV: MQI Press.

Bennis, W. and Nanus, B. (1985). *Leaders: Strategies for Taking Charge.* New York: Harper & Row.

Berger, P.L. and Luckmann, T. (1967). *The Social Construction of Reality: A Treatise in the Sociology of Knowledge.* Garden City, NJ: Anchor.

Berman, M. (1981). *The Reenchantment of the World.* Ithaca, NY: Cornell University Press.

Berzonsky, M.D. (1994). ''Kohlberg'' in *Encyclopedia of Psychology*, 2nd ed., Vol. 2. New York: Wiley and Sons.

Blakemore, S., and Frith, Y. (2005). *The Learning Brain: Lessons for Education.* Malden, MA: Blackwell.

Bohm, D. (1980). *Wholeness and the Implicate Order.* London: Routledge & Kegal.

Boud, D., Keogh, R., and Walker, D. (Eds.) (1994). *Reflection: Turning Experience into Learning.* New York: Routledge Falmer.

Bownds, M. D. (1999). *The Biology of Mind: Origins and Structures of Mind, Brain, and Consciousness.* Bethesda, MD: Fitzgerald Science Press.

Carr, C. (1996). *Choice, Chance & Organizational Change*: *Practical Insights from Evolution for Business Leaders & Thinkers*. New York: American Management Association.

Carpenter, H. (2009). "Designing for Innovation through Competitive Collaboration". Retrieved on 11/02/14 from http://www.cloudave.com/1036/designing-for-innovation-through-competitive-collaboration/

Carrasco, M., Ling, S., and Read, S. (2004). "Attention Alters Appearance" in *Nature Neuroscience* 7, 308-313.

Carroll, S. (2016). *The Big Picture: On the Origins of Life, Meaning, and the Universe Itself.* New York: Dutton.

Cherryholmes, , C.H. (1992). "Notes on Pragmatism and Scientific Realism" in *Educational Researcher*, 13-1 (August-September).

Collins, D. (1998). *Organizational Change: Sociological Perspective*. London: Routledge.

Conner, D.R. (1998). *Leading at the Edge of Chaos: How to Create the Nimble Organization*. New York: John Wiley & Sons, Inc.

Conrad, R.M. and Donaldson, J.A. (2011). *Engaging the Online Learner: Activities and resources for Creative Instruction*. San Francisco: Jossey-Bass.

Cozolino, L. J. (2006). *The Neuroscience of Human Relationships: Attachment and the Developing Social Brain*. New York: W.W. Norton.

Cozolino, L. J. (2002). *The Neuroscience of Psychotherapy: Building and Rebuilding the Human Brain*. New York: Norton.

Cozolino, L., and Sprokay, S. (2006). "Neuroscience and Adult Learning" in Johnson, S. and Taylor, T. (Eds.), *The Neuroscience of Adult Learning*. San Francisco: Jossey-Bass, 11-19.

Creswell, J.W. (2014). *Research Design: Qualitative, Quantitative & Mixed Methods approaches*. Thousand Oaks, CA: SAE.

Crotty, M. (1998). *The Foundations of Social Research: Meaning and Perspective in the Research Process*. Thousand Oaks, CA: Sage.

Csikszentmihalyi, M. (1993). *The Evolving Self: A Psychology for the Third Millennium*. New York: HarperCollins Publishing.

Csikszentmihalyi, M. (1990). *Flow: The Psychology of Optimal Experience*. New York: Harper Perennial.

Davis, S. and Meyer, C. (1998). Blur: The Speed of change in the Connected Economy. Reading, MA: Addison-Wesley.

Delavigne, K.T. and Robertson, J.D. (1994). *Deming's Profound Changes: When Will the Sleeping Giant Awaken?* Englewood Cliffs, NJ: PTR Prentice Hall.

Dewey, J. (1938/1997). *Experience and Education*. New York: Simon & Schuster.

Dilts, R. (2003). *From Coach to Awakener*. Capitola, CA: Meta Publications.

Dobbs, D. (2007). "Turning Off Depression" in F. E. Bloom (Ed.), *Best of the Brain from Scientific American: Mind, Matter, and Tomorrow's Brain*. New York: Dana Press, 169-178.

Dunning, J. (2014). Discussion of consciousness via the Internet on December 13.

Dweck, C. (2012). *Mindset. How You Can Fulfill Your Potential*. London: Robinson.

Edelman, G., and Tononi, G. (2000). *A Universe of Consciousness: How Matter Becomes Imagination*. New York: Basic Books.

Emig, J. (1983). *The Web of Meaning: Essays on Writing, Teaching, Learning and Thinking*. New Jersey: Boynton/Cook Publishers.

Encarta World English Dictionary (1999). New York: St Martin's Press.

Erlbaum, L. (1992). *Writing: The Nature, Development and Teaching of Written Communication*, Vol. II. Lawrence Erlbaum Associates.

Dyer, W.G. (1984). *Strategies for Management Change*. Reading, MA: Addison-Wesley Publishing Company, Inc.

Fay, B. (1987). *Critical Social Science*. Ithaca, NY: Cornell University Press.

Fowler, J.W. (1995). *Stages of Faith: The Psychology of Human Development and the Quest for Meaning*. New York: HarperCollins.

Frost, P.G.H. (1996). "The Ecology of Miombo Woodlands" in *Woodland and Welfare in Africa*. CIFOR, Bogorpp, 11-55.

Gazzaniga, M.S. (2008). *Human: The Science Behind What Makes Us Unique*. New York: HarperCollins.

Gell-Mann, M. (1994). *The Quark and the Jaguar: Adventures in the Simple and the Complex*. NY: W.H. Freeman and Company.

Goodman, E. (1979). *Turning Points: How and Why Do We Change*. New York: Fawcett Columbine.

Guba, E.G. (1990). "The Alternative Paradigm Dialog" in Guba, E.G. (Ed.), *The Paradigm Dialogue*. Newbury Park, CA: Sage, 17-30.

Hambrick, D.C., Nadler, D.A., and Tushman, M.L. (1998). *Navigating Change: How CEOs, Top Teams and Boards Steer Transformation*. Boston, MA: Harvard Business School Press.

Hammond, S. A. and J. Hall (1996). Retrieved 09/10/16 from www.thinbook.com

Hawkins, D.R. (2002). *Power VS Force: The Hidden Determinants of Human Behavior*. Carlsbad, CA: Hay House.

Heckscher, C. (2007). *The Collaborative Enterprise*. New Haven, CT: Yale University Press.

Heron, J. and Reason, P. (1997). "A Participatory Inquiry Paradigm" in *Qualitative Inquiry, 3*, 274-294.

Hetherington, M. (2014). *Getting Grounded: Connecting with the Earth for Greater Health, Patience, Serenity and Insight*. Australia: Mind Heart Publishing.

Hey, K.R. and Moore, P.D. (1998). *The Caterpillar Doesn't Know: How Personal Change is Creating Organizational Change*. New York: Free Press.

The Hindu (2001). "Mastering Materialism". Online edition of India's National Newspaper, Sunday, July 15, 2001. Retrieved 06/22/2016 from http://www.thehindu.com/2001/07/15/stories/13150611.htm

Hodgkin, R. (1991). "Michael Polanyi—Profit of Life, the Universe, and Everything" in *Times Higher Educational Supplement*, September 27, 15.

Hurst, D.K. (1995). *Crisis & Renewal: Meeting the Challenge of Organizational Change*. Boston, MA: Harvard Business School Press.

Irvine, W.B. (2006). *On Desire: Why We Want What We Want*. New York: Oxford University Press.

Jacobs, R.W. (1994). *Real Time Strategic Change: How to Involve an Entire Organization in Fast and Far-Reaching Change*. San Francisco: Berrett-Koehler Publishers.

Jacobs, D. (1981). *Change: How to Live with, Manage, Create and Enjoy It*. New York: Programs on Change.

Jarvis, P. (2004). *Adult Education and Lifelong Learning: Theory and Practice*. New York: RoutledgeFalmer.

Johnson, S. (2006). "The Neuroscience of the Mentor-Learner Relationship" in S. Johnson and Taylor, K. (Eds.), *The Neuroscience of Adult Learning: New Directions for Adult and Continuing Education*. San Francisco: Jossey-Bass, 63-70

Jones, D. (nd). *Celebrate What's Right with the World* (Training Video). Star Thrower Distribution.

Kanter, R.M. (1983). *The Change Masters: Innovation for Productivity in the American Corporation*. New York: Simon & Schuster.

Katsafanas, P. (2016). "Nietzsche's Account of Self-Conscious Agency." Draft of a paper to be published in Sandis, C. (Ed.), *Philosophy of Action from 1500 to the Present Day*. Oxford: Oxford University Press.

Keidel, R.W. (1995). *Seeing Organizational Patterns: A New Theory and Language of Organizational Design*. San Francisco: Berrett-Koehler Publishers.

Kemmis, S. and McTaggart, R. (2000). "Participatory Action Research" in Denzin, K. and Lincoln, K. S. (Eds.), *Handbook of Qualitative Research* (2nd Ed). Thousand Oaks, CA: Sage, 567-605.

Kemmis, S. and Wilkinson, M. (1998). "Participatory Action Research and the Study of Practice" in. Atweh, B., Kemmis, S. and Weeks, P. (Eds.). *Action Research in Practice: Partnerships for Social Justice in Education*. New York Routledge, 21-36.

Kirkpatrick, D.L. (1985). *How to Manage Change Effectively*. San Francisco: Jossey-Bass Publishers.

Koestler, A. (1967). *The Ghost in the Machine* (1990 reprinted.) London: Hutchinson (Penguin Group).

Kohlberg, L. (1981). *Philosophy of Moral Development: Moral Stages and the Idea of Justice*, Harper, San Francisco, CA.

Kolb, D. A. (1984). *Experiential Learning: Experience as the Source of Learning and Development*. New Jersey: Prentice-Hall.

Kopmeyer, M.R. (1970). *Thoughts to Build Upon*. Louisville, KY: Kopmeyer Publisher.

Kotter, J.P. (2008). *A Sense of Urgency*. Boston, MA: Harvard Business Press.

Kotter, J.P. (1996). *Leading Change*. Boston, MA: Harvard Business School Press.

Kuntz, P G. (1968). *The Concept of Order*. Seattle, WA: University of Washington Press.

The Kybalion (1940/1912). *The Kybalion: A Study of Hermetic Philosophy of ancient Egypt and Greece*. Yogi Pub. Society.

Lakoff, G. and Johnson, M. (1999). *Philosophy in the Flesh: The Embodied Mind and Its Challenge to Western Thought*. New York: Basic Books.

Lebow, R. and Simon, W.L. (1997). *Lasting Change: The Shared Values Process that Makes Companies Great*. New York: Van Nostrand Reinhold.

LeDoux, J. (2002). *Synaptic Self: How Our Brains Become Who We Are*. New York: Viking.

LeDoux, J. (1996). *The Emotional Brain: The Mysterious Underpinnings of Emotional Life.* New York: Touchstone.

Lelic, S. (2005). "The Art of War: Empowering Front-Line Decision Making" in *InsideKnowledge* (May). England.

Lewin, K. (1946). "Force Field Analysis" in *The 1973 Annual Handbook for Group Facilitators*, 111-13.

Lewis, J. (2014). "ADIIEA: An Organizational Learning Model for Business Management and Innovation" in *The Electronic Journal of Knowledge Management*, v12-2, 98-107.

Lincoln, Y.S. and Guba, E.G. (1985). *Naturalistic Inquiry*. Beverly Hills, CA: Sage.

Lincoln, Y.S., Lynham, S.A. and Guba, E.G. (2011). "Paradigmaic controversies, contradictions, and Emerging Confluences Revisited" in Denzin, N.K. and Lincoln, Y.S., *The SAGE Handbook of Qualitative Research* (4th ed.). Thousand Oaks, CA: Sage, 97-128.

Linstone, H.A. (1977). "Confessions of a Forecaster" in Linstone, H.A. and Simmonds, W.H.C., *Futures Research: New Directions*. Reading, MA: Addison-Wesley Publishing Company, Inc.

Lippitt, G.L., Langseth, P. and Mossop, J. (1985). *Implementing Organizational Change*. San Francisco: Jossey-Bass Publishers.

Lipton, B. (2005). *The Biology of Belief: Unleashing the Power of Consciousness*. Carlsbad, CA: Hay House.

Luthans, F. (2002). "The Need for and Meaning of Positive Organizational Behavior" in *Journal of Organizational Behavior*, Vol. 23 No. 6, 695-706.

Luthans, F. and Avolio, BJ. (2009). "The 'Point' of Positive Organizational Behavior" in *Journal of Organizational Behavior,* Vol. 30 No. 2, 291-307.

Luthans, F. and Youssef, C.M. (2004). "Human, Social, and Now Positive Psychological Capital Management: Investing in People for Competitive Advantage" in *Organizational Dynamics*, 33(2), 143-160.

MacFlouer, Niles (2004-16). *Why Life Is...* Weekly radio shows: BBSRadio.com (#1-#480) and KXAM (#1-#143). Retrieved from http://www.agelesswisdom.com/archives_of_radio_shows.htm

MacFlouer, N. (1999). *Life's Hidden Meaning*. Tempe, AZ: Ageless Wisdom Publishers.

Mahoney, D. and Restak, R. (1998). *The Longevity Strategy: How to Live to 100 Using the Brain-Body Connection*. New York: John Wiley & Sons, Inc.

Maira, A. and Scott-Morgan, P. (1997). *Accelerating Organization: Embracing the Human Face of Change*. New York: McGraw-Hill.

Makridakis, S., Hogarth, R. and Gaba, A. (2009). *Dance with Chance: Making Luck Work for You*. Oxford: One World.

Malafsky, G.P. and Newman, B.D. (2010). "Organizing Knowledge with Ontologies and Taxonomies" in *U.S. Forest Service Knowledge Sharing & Conservation Toolkit*. Frost, WV: Mountain Quest Institute.

Martel, L. (1986). *Mastering Change: The Key to Business Success*. New York: Simon and Schuster.

May, Rollo (1975). *The Courage to Create*. New York: Bantam.

Mayer-Schönberger, V. and Cukier, K. (2013). *Big data: A revolution that will transform how we live, work, and think*. New York: Houghton Mifflin Harcourt.

McHale, J. (1977). "Futures Problems or Problems in Futures Studies" in Linstone, H.A. and Simmonds, W.H.C. (Eds.), *Futures Research: New Directions*. Reading, MA: Addison-Wesley Publishing Company, Inc.

McWhinney, W. (1997). *Paths of Change: Strategic Choices for Organizations and Society*. Thousand Oaks, CA: SAGE Publications, Inc.

Merriam, S. B., Caffarella, A. S. and Baumgartner, L. M. (2007). *Learning in Adulthood: A Comprehensive Guide*. San Francisco, CA: Jossey-Bass and Sons, Inc.

Merriam Webster (2016). Retrieved 06/22/2016 from www.merriam-wester.com/dictionary/faith; Retrieved 07/04/16 from http://www.merriam-webster.com/dictionary/propaganda ; Retrieved 07/06/16 from http://www.merriam-webster.com/dictionary/equal ; Retrieved 07/06/16 http://www.merriam-webster.com/dictionary/personality ; Retrieved 07/07/16 http://www.merriam-webster.com/dictionary/instinct ; Retrieved 08/26/16 http://learnersdictionary.com/definition/desire ; Retrieved 08/27/16 http://www.webster-dictionary.org/definition/Agape ; Retrieved 08/28/16 http://www.merriam-webster.com/dictionary/Quantum%20leap ; Retrieved 09/30/16 http://www.merriam-webster.com/dictionary/virtue ; Retrieved 10/01/16 http://www.merriam-webster.com/dictionary/sympathy ; Retrieved 10/01/16 http://www.merriam-webster.com/dictionary/serendipity ; Retrieved 11/07/16 http://www.merriam-webster.com/dictionary/karma

Mertens, D.M. (2010). *Research and Evaluation in Education and Psychology: Integrating Diversity with Quantitative Qualitative, and Mixed Methods* (3rd ed.). Thousand Oaks, CA: Sage.

Mertens, D.M. (2009). *Transformative Research and Evaluation*. New York: Guilford.

Milgram, S. (1977-2010). *The Individual in a Social World: Essays and Experiments* (3rd expanded ed.). London: Pinter and Martin.

Miller, J. G. (1978). *Living Systems*. New York: McGraw-Hill Book Company.

Mink, O.G., Esterhuysen, P.W., Mink, B.P., and Owen, K.Q. (1993). *Change at Work: A Comprehensive Management Process for Transforming Organizations*. San Francisco: Jossey-Bass Publishers.

Morgan, D. (2007). "Paradigms Lost and Pragmatism Regained: Methodological Implications of Combining Qualitative and Quantitative Methods" in *Journal of Mixed Methods Research 1*(1), 48—76.

Morgan, G. (1988). *Riding the Waves of Change: Developing Managerial Competencies for a Turbulent World*. San Francisco: Jossey-Bass Publishers.

Morrisson I. (1996). *The Second Curve: Managing the Velocity of Change*. New York: Ballantine Books.

Mulford, P. (2007). *Thoughts Are Things*. New York: Barnes & Noble.

Nadler, D.A. (1998). *Champions of Change: How CEOs and Their Companies Are Mastering the Skills of Radical Change*. San Francisco: Jossey-Bass.

Naidu, A.S. (2013). *Redox LIFE*. Pomona, CA: Bio-Rep Network.

Netday and Blackboard (2006). "Learning in the 21st Century: A National Report of Online Learning". Retrieved 02/20/08 from http://www.blackboard.com/inpractice/K12/onlinelearningreport

Neuman, W.L. (2009). *Social Research Methods: Qualitative and Quantitative Approaches* (7th ed.). Boston: Allyn & Bacon.

Nevis, E., Lancourt, J. and Vassalo, H.G. (1996). *Intentional revolutions: A Seven Pint Strategy for Transforming Organizations*. San Francisco, CA: Jossey-Bass.

Nickles, L. (2001). *The Change Agents: Decoding the New Workforce and the New Workplace*. New York: St. Martin's Press.

Nolan, R.L. and Croson, D.C. (1995). *Creative Destruction: A Six-Stage Process for Transforming the Organization*. Boston, MA: Harvard Business School Press.

Oakshott, M. (1933). *Experience and Its Modes*. Cambridge, UK: Cambridge University Press.

Ober, C., Sinatra, S.T., and Zucker, M. (2014). *Earthing: The Most Important Health Discovery Ever!* Laguna Beach, CA: Basic Health Publications, Inc.

Ozbekhan, H. (1973-4). "The Emerging Methodology of Planning" in *Fields Within Fields*, No. 10, Winter, 63-80.

Pasmore, W.A. (1994). *Creating Strategic Change: Designing the flexible, High-Performing Organization*. New York: John Wiley & Sons, Inc.

Patton, M.Q. (1990). *Qualitative Evaluation and Research Methods* (2nd ed.). Newbury Park, CA: Sage.

Peale, N.V. (1952). *The Power of Positive Thinking*. New York: Prentice-Hall.

Phillips, D.C. and Burbules, N.C. (2000). *Postpositivism and Educational Research*. Lanham, MD: Rowman & Littlefield.

Piaget, J. (1968). *Structuralism*. New York: Harper Torchbooks.

Profozich, D. (1997). *Managing Change with Business Process Simulation*. Upper Saddle River, NJ: Prentice-Hall, Inc.

Quinn, R.E. (1996). *Deep Change: Discovering the Leader Within*. San Francisco: Jossey-Bass Publishing.

Ranadive, V. (1999). *The Power of Now: How Winning Companies Sense & Respond to Change Using Real-Time Technology*. New York: McGraw-Hill.

Rifkin, J. (2009). The *Empathic Civilization: The Race to Global Consciousness in a World in Crisis*. New York: Penguin Group.

Rose, Steven (2005). *The Future of the Brain: The Promise and Perils of Tomorrow's Neuroscience*. New York: Oxford University Press.

Russell, B. (1950). "The Desires Driving Human Behavior" (Nobel Prize Acceptance Speech).

Salk, J. (1973). *The Survival of the Wisest*. New York: Harper & Row.

Scharmer, C. O. (2009). *Theory U: Leading from the Future as It Emerges*. San Francisco: Berrett-Koehler.

Schwartz, S. A. (2017). "The 8 Laws of Change." Keynote address presented at the Alliance for Global Consciousness Open House. Downloaded from www.glidewing.com/workshops/course/view.php?id=26

Schwartz, S. A. (2015). *The 8 Laws of Change: How to Be an Agent of Personal and Social Transformation*. Rochester, VT: Park Street Press.

Scott, C. (2016a). *Life Bites*. Frost, WV: MQIPress.

Scott-Morgan, P., Hoving, E., Sit, H. and van der Slot, A. (2001). *The End of Change: How Your Company Can Sustain Growth and Innovation While Avoiding Change Fatigue*. New York: McGraw Hill.

Senge, Peter (1990). *The Fifth Discipline*. New York: Doubleday.

Sentell, G. (1998). *Creating Change-Capable Cultures*. Alcoa, TN: Pressmark International.

Schore, A. N. (1994). *Affect Regulation and the Origin of the Self: The Neurobiology of Emotional Development*. Hillsdale, NJ: Erlbaum.

Shelley, A. (2007). *Organizational Zoo: A Survival Guide to Work Place Behavior*. Fairfield, CT: Aslan Publishing.

Siegel, D. J. (2007). *The Mindful Brain: Reflection and Attunement in the Cultivation of Well-Being*. New York: W. W. Norton & Company.

Simon, H. (1947). *Administrative Behavior*. New York: Macmillan.

Slater, Philip (1974). *Earthwalk*. Garden City, NY: Doubleday.

Smith, M.K. (2003). "Michael Polanyi and Tacit Knowledge" in *The Encyclopedia of Informal Education*, 2, www.infed.org/thinkers/Polanyi.htm

Smith, R. (1997). *The 7 Levels of Change: Create, Innovate and Motivate with the Secrets of the World's Largest Corporations*. Arlington, TX: The Summit Publishing Group.

Srivastva, S. and D.L. Cooperrider (Eds.). (1990). *Appreciative Management and Leadership*. San Francisco: Jossey-Bass.

Stewart, J. (2000). *The Unity of Hegel's Phenomenology of Spirit: A Systematic Interpretation*. Evanston, IL: Northwestern University Press.

Strebel, P. (1998). *The Change Pact: Building Commitment to Ongoing Change*. London: Financial Times Pittman Publishing.

Tapscott, D. (2009). *Grown up Digital*. McGraw Hill, New York.

Tashakkori, A. and Teddlie, C. (1998). *Mixed Methodology: Combining Qualitative and Quantitative Approaches*. Thousand Oaks, CA: Sage.

Theobald, R. (1982). "The Roots of Change" in *The Phenomenon of CHANGE*. New York: Rizzoli for Cooper-Hewitt Museum, The Smithsonian Institution's National Museum of Design.

Thompson, L. (1994). *Mastering the Challenges of Change: Strategies for Each Stage in Your Organization's Life Cycle*. New York: American Management Association.

Tomasko, R.M. (1993). *Rethinking the Corporation: The Architecture of Change*. New York: American Management Association.

The Urantia Book (1955). Chicago: URANTIA Foundation.

Van de Ven, A.H. (2000). "Professional Science for a Professional School: Action Science and Normal Science" in Beer, M. and Nohria, N. (Eds.) (2000). *Breaking the Code of Change*. Boston, MA: Harvard Business School Press, 394-415.

Vickers, G. (1977). "The Future of Culture" in Linstone, H.A. and Simmonds, W.H.C., *Futures Research: New Directions*. Reading, MA: Addison-Wesley Publishing Company, Inc.

Vollmann, T.E. (1996). *The Transformation Imperative: Achieving Market Dominance through Radical Change*. Boston, MA: Harvard Business School Press.

Walsch, N.D. (2009). *When Everything Changes Change Everything: In a Time of Turmoil, a Pathway to Peace*. Ashland, OR: EmNin Books.

Warner Brothers (2011). *Green Lantern*. Movie.

Watzlawick, P. (1974). *How Real is Real?* New York: Random House.

Watzlawick, P., Weakland, J. and Fisch, R. (1974). *Change: Principles of Problem Formation and Problem Resolution*. New York: W.W. Norton & Company.

Weber, M. (1905). *The Protestant Ethic and the Spirit of Capitalism*. Retrieved 06/22/2016 from https://www.marxists.org/reference/archive/weber/protestant-ethic/ch05.htm (Chapter V)

Webster's New World Dictionary of the American Language (1962). (College Edition).

Wilber, K. (1996). *A Brief History of Everything*. Boston: Shambhala.

Wilber, K. (1993). *The Spectrum of Consciousness*. Wheaten, IL: Quest Books.

Wind, J.Y. and Main, J. (1998*). Driving Change: How the Best Companies Are Preparing for the 21st Century*. New York: The Free Press.

Wright, T.A. and Quick, J.C. (2009). "The Emerging Positive Agenda in Organizations: Greater than a Trickle, But Not Yet a Deluge" in *Journal of Organizational Behavior*, Vol. 30 No. 2, 147-159.

Youngblood, M.D. (1994). *Eating the Chocolate Elephant: Take Charge of Change through Total Process Management*. Richardson, TX: Micrografx, Inc.

Zull, J. E. (2002). *The Art of Changing the Brain: Enriching the Practice of Teaching by Exploring the Biology of Learning*. Sterling, VA: Stylus.

Index

About the Mountain Quest Institute

MQI is a research, retreat and learning center dedicated to helping individuals achieve personal and professional growth and organizations create and sustain high performance in a rapidly changing, uncertain, and increasingly complex world. Drs. David and Alex Bennet are co-founders of MQI. They may be contacted at alex@mountainquestinstitute.com

Current research is focused on Human and Organizational Systems, Change, Complexity, Sustainability, Knowledge, Learning, Consciousness, and the nexus of Science and Spirituality. MQI has three questions: The Quest for Knowledge, The Quest for Consciousness, and The Quest for Meaning. **MQI is scientific, humanistic and spiritual and finds no contradiction in this combination**. See www.mountainquestinstitute.com

MQI is the birthplace of Organizational Survival in the New World: The Intelligent Complex Adaptive System (Elsevier, 2004), a new theory of the firm that turns the living system metaphor into a reality for organizations. Based on research in complexity and neuroscience—and incorporating networking theory and knowledge management—this book is filled with new ideas married to practical advice, all embedded within a thorough description of the new organization in terms of structure, culture, strategy, leadership, knowledge workers and integrative competencies.

Mountain Quest Institute, situated four hours from Washington, D.C. in the Monongahela Forest of the Allegheny Mountains, is part of the Mountain Quest complex which includes a Retreat Center, Inn, and the old Farm House, Outbuildings and mountain trails and farmland. See www.mountainquestinn.com The Retreat Center is designed to provide full learning experiences, including hosting training, workshops, retreats and business meetings for professional and executive groups of 25 people or less. The Center includes a 26,000 volume research library, a conference room, community center, computer room, 12 themed bedrooms, a workout and hot tub area, and a four-story tower with a glass ceiling for enjoying the magnificent view of the valley during the day and the stars at night. Situated on a 430 acres farm, there is a labyrinth, creeks, four miles of mountain trails, and horses, Longhorn cattle, Llamas and a myriad of wild neighbors. Other neighbors include the Snowshoe Ski Resort, the National Radio Astronomy Observatory and the CASS Railroad.

About the Organizational Zoo Ambassadors Network

The Organizational Zoo Ambassadors Network (OZAN) is an international group of professionals interested in using The Organizational Zoo concepts as part of their capability development programs. Zoo Ambassadors have been trained in the application of OZAN Tools and approaches. They freely share their experiences through an international network which interacts primarily through a wiki supplemented by occasional face to face events and some on-line learning modules. See http://www.organizationalzoo.com/ambassadors/

About Quantra Leadership Academy

Quantra Leadership Academy (aka QLA Consulting) is a **transformational leadership and personal development training company run by** Dr. Theresa Bullard**. QLA is dedicated to helping individuals and organizations innovate their way of thinking to achieve breakthrough results.** There is one question that lies at the foundation of QLA: *What is your potential?* When you tap into your potential, greatness happens, you experience breakthroughs, "Ah-ha" moments occur, and you get into "The Zone" of peak performance. It is our passion to help you access your full potential, sustain what you achieve, and be able to refuel whenever you want. When you get to the point where you can do this on demand that is when you become a self-transforming agent of change. QLA shows you how to get there and gives you tools to accelerate your progress. By blending science, consciousness studies, and mental alchemy, or the art and science of transforming your mindset, we help you **reach your potential** and become more successful in essential areas of your work and life. *To help you* **access more of your potential,** *we offer a progression of transformative tools and trainings that integrate quantum principles, cutting-edge methods, and ancient wisdom for using your mind more creatively and effectively.* For more info: www.QLAconsulting.com

About the Authors

Dr. Alex Bennet, a Professor at the Bangkok University Institute for Knowledge and Innovation Management, is internationally recognized as an expert in knowledge management and an agent for organizational change. Prior to founding the Mountain Quest Institute, she served as the Chief Knowledge Officer and Deputy Chief Information Officer for Enterprise Integration for the U.S. Department of the Navy, and was co-chair of the Federal Knowledge Management Working Group. Dr. Bennet is the recipient of the Distinguished and Superior Public Service Awards from the U.S. government for her work in the Federal Sector. She is a Delta Epsilon Sigma and Golden Key National Honor Society graduate with a Ph.D. in Human and Organizational Systems; degrees in Management for Organizational Effectiveness, Human Development, English and Marketing; and certificates in Total Quality Management, System Dynamics and Defense Acquisition Management. Alex believes in the multidimensionality of humanity as we move out of infancy into full consciousness.

Dr. David Bennet's experience spans many years of service in the Military, Civil Service and Private Industry, including fundamental research in underwater acoustics and nuclear physics, frequent design and facilitation of organizational interventions, and serving as technical director of two major DoD Acquisition programs. Prior to founding the Mountain Quest Institute, Dr. Bennet was CEO, then Chairman of the Board and Chief Knowledge Officer of a professional services firm located in Alexandria, Virginia. He is a Phi Beta Kappa, Sigma Pi Sigma, and Suma Cum Laude graduate of the University of Texas, and holds degrees in Mathematics, Physics, Nuclear Physics, Liberal Arts, Human and Organizational Development, and a Ph.D. in Human Development focused on Neuroscience and adult learning. He is currently researching the nexus of Science, the Humanities and Spirituality.

Dr. Arthur Shelley is a capability development and knowledge strategy consultant with over 30 years professional experience. He has held a variety of professional roles including managing international projects in Australia, Europe, Asia and USA and has facilitated professional development program with organizations as diverse as NASA, Cirque du Soleil, World Bank, government agencies and corporates. He has facilitated courses in Masters programs on Executive Consulting, Leadership, Knowledge Management, Applied Research Practice and Entrepreneurship in face to face, blended and on-line modes. Arthur is the author of three books: *KNOWledge SUCCESSion (2017) Being a Successful Knowledge Leader (2009)*; *The Organizational Zoo, A Survival Guide to Workplace Behavior (2007).* In 2014 he was awarded with an Australian Office of Learning and Teaching citation for "Outstanding contributions to student learning outcomes". Arthur is a regular invited speaker and workshop facilitator at international conferences to discuss his writing or to share experiences as the former Global Knowledge Director for Cadbury Schweppes. He is founder of The Organizational Zoo Ambassadors Network (a professional peer mentoring group), creator of the RMIT University MBA mentoring program and co-facilitator of the Melbourne KM Leadership Forum. Arthur has a PhD in Project Management, a Master of Science in Microbiology/Biochemistry, a Graduate Certificate in Tertiary Learning and Teaching and a Bachelor of Science. Arthur may be reached at arthur.shelley@rmit.edu.au

Dr. Theresa Bullard combines a Ph.D. in Physics with a life-long path of embracing the new paradigm of Science and Consciousness. Her passion and ability to bridge these worlds are her strengths and distinguish her as an exceptional teacher, speaker, leader and change-agent. Theresa is the founder of QLA Consulting Inc., President of the Board of Directors of Mysterium Center, an International Instructor with the Modern Mystery School, and co-founder of the Universal Kabbalah Network. She has over 15 years of experience in science research, international speaking, and transformational training. Author of *The Game Changers: Social Alchemists in the 21ˢᵗ Century*, along with several guided meditation albums and audio tools for accessing Quantum conscious states, her mission is to help individuals and organizations thrive in a changing world. Theresa may be contacted at Theresa@quantumleapalchemy.com

Dr. John Lewis is a speaker, business consultant, and part-time professor on the topics of organizational learning, thought leadership, and knowledge & innovation management. John is a proven leader with business results, and was acknowledged by Gartner with an industry "Best Practice" paper for an innovative knowledge management implementation. He is a co-founder at The CoHero Institute, creating collaborative leadership in learning organizations. John holds a Doctoral degree in Educational Psychology from the University of Southern California, with a dissertation focus on mental models and decision making, and is the author of *The Explanation Age*, which Kirkus Reviews described as "An iconoclast's blueprint for a new era of innovation." John may be contacted at John@ExplanationAge.com

Other Books by These Authors

Possibilities that are YOU! by Alex Bennet

This series of short books, which are published under *Conscious Look Books*, are conversational in nature, taking full advantage of your lived experience to share what can sometimes be difficult concepts to grab onto. But, **YOU ARE READY!** We live in a world that is tearing itself apart, where people are out of control, rebelling from years of real and perceived abuse and suppression of thought. Yet, this chaos offers us as a humanity the opportunity to make a giant leap forward. *By opening ourselves to ourselves, we are able to fully explore who we are and who we can become.* With that exploration comes a glimmer of hope as we begin to reclaim the power of each and every mind developed by the lived human experience!

These books share 22 large concepts from *The Profundity and Bifurcation of Change*. Each book includes seven ideas offered for the student of life experience to help you become the co-creator you are. Available in soft cover from Amazon.

Titles:

All Things in Balance
The Art of Thought Adjusting
Associative Patterning and Attracting
Beyond Action
The Bifurcation
Connections as Patterns
Conscious Compassion
The Creative Leap
The Emerging Self
The Emoting Guidance System
Engaging Forces
The ERC's of Intuition
Grounding
The Humanness of Humility
Intention and Attention
Knowing
Living Virtues for Today
ME as Co-Creator
Seeking Wisdom
Staying on the Path
Transcendent Beauty
Truth in Context

A 23rd little book titled **The Intelligent Social Change Journey** provides the theoretical foundation for the **Possibilities that are YOU! series.** Also available in soft cover from Amazon

Other Books by MQI Press (www.MQIPress.net)

MQIPress is a wholly-owned subsidiary of Mountain Quest Institute, LLC, located at 303 Mountain Quest Lane, Marlinton, West Virginia 24954, USA. (304) 799-7267

Other Bennet eBooks available from in PDF format from MQIPress (US 304-799-7267 or alex@mountainquestinstitute.com) and Kindle format from Amazon.

The Course of Knowledge: A 21st Century Theory
by Alex Bennet and David Bennet with Joyce Avedisian (2015)

Knowledge is at the core of what it is to be human, the substance which informs our thoughts and determines the course of our actions. Our growing focus on, and understanding of, knowledge and its consequent actions is changing our relationship with the world. Because **knowledge determines the quality of every single decision we make**, it is critical to learn about and understand what knowledge is. **From a 21st century viewpoint,** we explore a theory of knowledge that is both pragmatic and biological. Pragmatic in that it is based on taking effective action, and biological because it is created by humans via patterns of neuronal connections in the mind/brain.

In this book we explore *the course of knowledge.* Just as a winding stream in the bowls of the mountains curves and dips through ravines and high valleys, so, too, with knowledge. In a continuous journey towards intelligent activity, context-sensitive and situation-dependent knowledge, imperfect and incomplete, experientially engages a changing landscape in a continuous cycle of learning and expanding. *We are in a continuous cycle of knowledge creation such that every moment offers the opportunity for the emergence of new and exciting ideas, all waiting to be put in service to an interconnected world.* Learn more about this **exciting human capacity**! AVAILABLE FROM AMAZON in Kindle Format. AVAILABLE FROM MQIPress in PDF.

Expanding the Self: The Intelligent Complex Adaptive Learning System
by David Bennet, Alex Bennet and Robert Turner (2015)

We live in unprecedented times; indeed, turbulent times that can arguably be defined as ushering humanity into a new Golden Age, offering the opportunity to embrace new ways of learning and living in a globally and collaboratively entangled connectedness (Bennet & Bennet, 2007). In this shifting and dynamic environment, life demands accelerated cycles of learning experiences. Fortunately, we as a humanity have begun to look within ourselves to better understand the way our mind/brain operates, the amazing qualities of the body that power our thoughts and feelings, and the reciprocal loops as those thoughts and feelings change our physical structure. This emerging knowledge begs us to relook and rethink what we know about learning, providing a new starting point to expand toward the future.

This book is a treasure for those interested in how recent findings in neuroscience impact learning. The result of this work is an expanding experiential learning model called the Intelligent Complex

Adaptive Learning System, adding the fifth mode of social engagement to Kolb's concrete experience, reflective observation, abstract conceptualization and active experimentation, with the five modes undergirded by the power of Self. A significant conclusion is that should they desire, adults have much more control over their learning than they may realize. AVAILABLE FROM AMAZON in Kindle Format. AVAILALBE FROM MQIPress in PDF.

Decision-Making in The New Reality: Complexity, Knowledge and Knowing
by Alex Bennet and David Bennet (2013)

We live in a world that offers many possible futures. The ever-expanding complexity of information and knowledge provide many choices for decision-makers, and we are all making decisions every single day! As the problems and messes of the world become more complex, our decision consequences are more and more difficult to anticipate, and our decision-making processes must change to keep up with this world complexification. This book takes a consilience approach to explore decision-making in The New Reality, fully engaging systems and complexity theory, knowledge research, and recent neuroscience findings. It also presents methodologies for decision-makers to tap into their unconscious, accessing tacit knowledge resources and increasingly relying on the sense of knowing that is available to each of us.

Almost every day new energies are erupting around the world: new thoughts, new feelings, new knowing, all contributing to new situations that require new decisions and actions from each and every one of us. Indeed, with the rise of the Net Generation and social media, a global consciousness may well be emerging. As individuals and organizations, we are realizing that there are larger resources available to us, and that, as complex adaptive systems linked to a flowing fount of knowing, we can bring these resources to bear to achieve our ever-expanding vision of the future. Are we up to the challenge? AVAILABLE FROM AMAZON in Kindle Format. AVAILABLE FROM MQIPress in PDF.

Leading with the Future in Mind: Knowledge and Emergent Leadership
by Alex Bennet and David Bennet with John Lewis (2015)

We exist in a new reality, a global world where the individuated power of the mind/brain offers possibilities beyond our imagination. It is within this framework that thought leading emerges, and when married to our collaborative nature, makes the impossible an everyday occurrence. *Leading with the Future in Mind*, building on profound insights unleashed by recent findings in neuroscience, provides a new view that converges leadership, knowledge and learning for individual and organizational advancement.

This book provides a research-based *tour de force* for the future of leadership. Moving from the leadership of the past, for the few at the top, using authority as the explanation, we now find leadership emerging from all levels of the organization, with knowledge as the explanation. The future will be owned by the organizations that can master the relationships between knowledge and leadership. Being familiar with the role of a knowledge worker is not the same as understanding the role of a knowledge leader. As the key ingredient, collaboration is much more than "getting along"; it embraces and engages. Wrapped in the mantle of collaboration and engaging our full resources—physical, mental, emotional and spiritual—we open the door to possibilities. We are dreaming the future together. AVAILABLE FROM AMAZON in Kindle Format. AVAILABLE FROM MQIPress in PDF.

Other books available from the authors and on Amazon..

The Game Changers: Social Alchemists in the 21st Century

by Theresa Bullard, Ph.D. (2013), available in hard and soft formats from Amazon.
Just about everywhere we look right now change is afoot. What is all this change about? Why now? And how do we best adapt? Many have called this time a "quickening", where the speed with which we must think, respond, and take action is accelerating. Systems are breaking down, people are rising up, and there is uncertainty of what tomorrow will bring. This book is dedicated to times such as these, times of great transformation. It can be seen as a companion guide on how to navigate the tumultuous tides of change. It aims to put such current events into a possible context within the evolutionary and alchemical process that humanity is going through. In it, author, physicist, and change-agent, Theresa Bullard, Ph.D., discusses emerging new paradigms, world events, future trends, and ancient wisdom that help reveal a bigger picture of what is happening. She offers insights and solutions to empower you, the reader, to become a more conscious participant in these exciting times of change. With this knowledge you will be more equipped to harness the *opportunities* that such times present you with.
AVAILABLE FROM AMAZON in Kindle Format ... Paperback

The Organizational Zoo: A Survival Guide to Work Place Behavior

by Arthur Shelley (2006), available in hard and soft formats from Amazon.
Organizational Zoo is a fresh approach to organizational culture development, a witty and thought-provoking book that makes ideal reading for students and management. When you think of your organization as containing ants, bees, chameleons, and other creatures on through the alphabet, your work world becomes more manageable. Discover the secret strengths and weaknesses of each distinct animal so that you can communicate more productively—or manipulate more cunningly. Your choice!
AVAILABLE FROM AMAZON in Paperback

The Explanation Age

by John Lewis (2013) (3rd Ed.), available in hard and soft formats from Amazon.
The technological quest of the last several decades has been to create the information age, with ubiquitous and immediate access to information. With this goal arguably accomplished, even from our mobile phones, this thought-provoking book describes the next quest and provides a blueprint for how to get there. When all organizational knowledge is framed as answers to our fundamental questions, we find ubiquitous and visual access to knowledge related to who, where, how, etc., yet the explanations are still buried within the prose. The question of "why" is arguably the most important question, yet it is currently the least supported. This is why business process methodologies feel like "box-checking" instead of "sense-making." This is why lessons learned are not actually learned. And this is why the consequential options and choices are captured better within a chess game than within the important decisions faced by organizations and society. With implications for business, education, policy

making, and artificial intelligence, Dr. Lewis provides a visualization of explanations which promotes organizational sense-making and collaboration. AVAILABLE FROM AMAZON in Paperback

KNOWledge SUCCESSion: Sustained Capability Growth Through Strategic Projects
by Arthur Shelley (2016), available in hard and soft formats from Amazon.
KNOWledge SUCCESSion is intended for executives and developing professionals who face the challenges of delivering business benefits for today, whilst building the capabilities required for an increasingly changing future. The book is structured to build from foundational requirements towards connecting the highly interdependent aspects of success in an emerging complex world. A wide range of concepts are brought together in a logical framework to enable readers of different disciplines to understand how they either create barriers or can be harvested to generate synergistic opportunities. The framework builds a way to make sense of the connections and provides novel paths to take advantage of the potential synergies that arise through aligning the concepts into a portfolio of strategic projects. AVAILABLE FROM AMAZON. Kindle Format ... Paperback

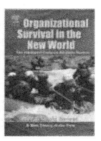

Knowledge Mobilization in the Social Sciences and Humanities: Moving from Research to Action
by Alex Bennet and David Bennet (2007), available in hard and soft formats from Amazon.
This book takes the reader from the University lab to the playgrounds of communities. It shows how to integrate, move and use knowledge, an action journey within an identified action space that is called knowledge mobilization. Whether knowledge is mobilized through an individual, organization, community or nation, it becomes a powerful asset creating a synergy and focus that brings forth the best of action and values. Individuals and teams who can envision, feel, create and apply this power are the true leaders of tomorrow. When we can mobilize knowledge for the greater good humanity will have left the information age and entered the age of knowledge, ultimately leading to compassion and—hopefully—wisdom. AVAILABLE FROM AMAZON. Kindle Format ... Paperback
AVAILABLE FROM MQIPress in PDF and Softback.

Being a Successful Knowledge Leader: What Knowledge Practitioners Need to Know to Make a Difference.
by Arthur Shelley (2009). AVAILABLE FROM AMAZON. Paperback
Being a Successful Knowledge Leader explores the challenges of leading a program of knowledge-informed change initiatives to generate sustained performance improvement. The book explores how to embed knowledge flows into strategic development cycles to align organizational development with changing environmental conditions. The high rate of change interferes with the growth of organizational knowledge because what is relevant only generates a competitive advantage for a short time. Also, the people who possess this knowledge are more mobile than previously. Combined, these factors can have a detrimental impact on performance and need to be mitigated against to ensure capabilities are built rather than diluted overtime. The characteristics for success that a knowledge

leader needs to possess are explored from a unique perspective to stimulate creative thinking around how to develop and maintain these in emergent times.

Organizational Survival in the New World: The Intelligent Complex Adaptive System
by Alex Bennet and David Bennet (Elsevier, 2004), available in hard and soft formats from Amazon. In this book David and Alex Bennet propose a new model for organizations that enables them to react more quickly and fluidly to today's fast-changing, dynamic business environment: The Intelligent Complex Adaptive System (ICAS). ICAS is a new organic model of the firm based on recent research in complexity and neuroscience, and incorporating networking theory and knowledge management, and turns the living system metaphor into a reality for organizations. This book synthesizes new thinking about organizational structure from the fields listed above into ICAS, a new systems model for the successful organization of the future designed to help leaders and managers of knowledge organizations succeed in a non-linear, complex, fast-changing and turbulent environment. Technology enables connectivity, and the ICAS model takes advantage of that connectivity by fostering the development of dynamic, effective and trusting relationships in a new organizational structure. AVAILABLE FROM AMAZON in Kindle Format ... Hardback ... Paperback

Other MQIPress books available in PDF format at www.MQIPress.net (US 304-799-7267 or alex@mountainquestinstitute.com) and Kindle format from Amazon.

REMEMBRANCE: Pathways to Expanded Learning with Music and Metamusic®
by Barbara Bullard and Alex Bennet (2013)
Take a journey of discovery into the last great frontier—the human mind/brain, an instrument of amazing flexibility and plasticity. This eBook is written for brain users who are intent on mining more of the golden possibilities that lie inherent in each of our unique brains. Begin by discovering the role positive attitudes play in learning, and the power of self affirmations and visualizations. Then explore the use of brain wave entrainment mixed with designer music called Metamusic® to achieve enhanced learning states. Join students of all ages who are creating magical learning outcomes using music and Metamusic.® AVAILABLE FROM AMAZON in Kindle Format.

The Journey into the Myst (Vol. 1 of The Myst Series)
by Alex Bennet and David Bennet (2012)
What we are about to tell you would have been quite unbelievable to me before this journey began. It is not a story of the reality either of us has known for well over our 60 and 70 years of age, but rather, the reality of dreams and fairytales." This is the true story of a sequence of events that happened at Mountain Quest Institute, situated in a high valley of the Allegheny Mountains of West Virginia. The story begins with a miracle, expanding into the capture and cataloging of thousands of pictures of

electromagnetic spheres widely known as "orbs." This joyous experience became an exploration into the unknown with the emergence of what the author's fondly call the Myst, the forming and shaping of non-random patterns such as human faces, angels and animals. As this phenomenon unfolds, you will discover how the Drs. Alex and David Bennet began to observe and interact with the Myst. This book shares the beginning of an extraordinary *Journey into the Myst*. AVAILABLE FROM AMAZON in Kindle Format. AVAILABLE FROM MQIPress in PDF.

Patterns in the Myst (Vol. 2 of The Myst Series)
by Alex Bennet and David Bennet (2013)

The Journey into the Myst was just the beginning for Drs. Alex and David Bennet. Volume II of the Myst Series brings Science into the Spiritual experience, bringing to bear what the Bennets have learned through their research and educational experiences in physics, neuroscience, human systems, knowledge management and human development. Embracing the paralogical, patterns in the Myst are observed, felt, interpreted, analyzed and compared in terms of their physical make-up, non-randomness, intelligent sources and potential implications. Along the way, the Bennets were provided amazing pictures reflecting the forming of the Myst. The Bennets shift to introspection in the third volume of the series to explore the continuing impact of the Myst experience on the human psyche. AVAILABLE FROM AMAZON in Kindle Format. AVAILABLE FROM MQIPress in PDF.

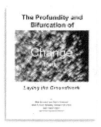

The Profundity and Bifurcation of Change *Part I: Laying the Groundwork* by Alex Bennet and David Bennet with Arthur Shelley, Theresa Bullard and John Lewis

This book lays the groundwork for the **Intelligent Social Change Journey** (ISCJ), a developmental journey of the body, mind and heart, moving from the heaviness of cause-and-effect linear extrapolations, to the fluidity of co-evolving with our environment, to the lightness of breathing our thought and feelings into reality. Grounded in development of our mental faculties, these are phase changes, each building on and expanding previous learning in our movement toward intelligent activity. As we lay the groundwork, we move through the concepts of change, knowledge, forces, self and consciousness. Then, recognizing that we are holistic beings, we provide a baseline model for individual change from within.

The Profundity and Bifurcation of Change *Part II: Learning from the Past* by Alex Bennet and David Bennet with Arthur Shelley, Theresa Bullard and John Lewis

Phase 1 of the Intelligent Social Change Journey (ISCJ) is focused on the linear cause-and-effect relationships of logical thinking. Knowledge, situation dependent and context sensitive, is a product of the past. **Phase 1 assumes that for every effect there is an originating cause.** This is where we as a humanity, and as individuals, begin to develop our mental faculties. In this book we explore cause and effect, scan a kaleidoscope of change models, and review the modalities of change. Since change is easier and more fluid when we are grounded, we explore three interpretations of grounding. In preparation for expanding our consciousness, a readiness assessment and sample change agent's strategy are included. (Release 01/15/17)

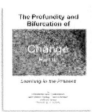

The Profundity and Bifurcation of Change *Part III: Learning in the Present* by Alex Bennet and David Bennet with Arthur Shelley, Theresa Bullard and John Lewis

As the world becomes increasingly complex, Phase 2 of the Intelligent Social Change Journey (ISCJ) is focused on **co-evolving with the environment**. This requires a deepening connection to others, moving into empathy. While the NOW is the focus, there is an increasing ability to put together patterns from the past and think conceptually, as well as extrapolate future behaviors. Thus, we look closely at the relationship of time and space, and pattern thinking. We look at the human body as a complex energetic system, exploring the role of emotions as a guidance system, and what happens when we have stuck energy. This book also introduces Knowledge Capacities, different ways of thinking that build capacity for sustainability.

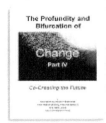

The Profundity and Bifurcation of Change Part IV: Co-Creating the Future by Alex Bennet and David Bennet with Arthur Shelley, Theresa Bullard and John Lewis

As we move into Phase 3 of the Intelligent Social Change Journey (ISCJ), **we fully embrace our role as co-creator**. We recognize the power of thought and the role of attention and intention in our ever-expanding search for a higher level of truth. Whether we choose to engage it or not, we explore mental discipline as a tool toward expanded consciousness. In preparing ourselves for the creative leap, there are ever-deepening connections with others. We now understand that the mental faculties are in service to the intuitional, preparing us to, and expanding our ability to, act in and on the world, living with conscious compassion and tapping into the intuitional at will.

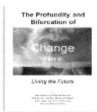

The Profundity and Bifurcation of Change Part V: Living the Future by Alex Bennet and David Bennet with Arthur Shelley, Theresa Bullard, John Lewis and Donna Panucci

We embrace the ancient art and science of Alchemy to **explore the larger shift underway for humanity** and how we can consciously and intentionally speed up evolution to enhance outcomes. In this conversation, we look at balancing and sensing, the harmony of beauty, and virtues for living the future. Conscious compassion, a virtue, is introduced as a state of being connected to morality and good character, inclusive of giving selfless service. We are now ready to refocus our attention on knowledge and consciousness, exploring the new roles these play in our advancement. And all of this—all of our expanding and growth as we move through the Intelligent Social Change journey—is giving a wide freedom of choice as we approach the bifurcation. What will we manifest?

Available in Softback from www.amazon.com

Available in Kindle format from www.amazon.com

Available in PDF format from www.MQIPress.net

Made in the USA
Monee, IL
25 October 2020